the Crime and Mystery Book

CLUES

15c

February, 1933

ALL STAR
DETECTIVE STORIES

A CLAYTON MAGAZINE

A STEVE RANEY STO
By ERLE
STANLE
GARDN

Beginning

The Man from San Quentin

the Crime and Mystery Book

A Reader's Companion

Ian Ousby

195 illustrations, 31 in colour

Thames and Hudson

'Are you—who make your living snooping—sneering at my curiosity about people and my attempts to satisfy it?'

'We're different,' I said. 'I do mine with the object of putting people in jail, and I get paid for it, though not as much as I should.'

'That's not different,' he said. 'I do mine with the object of putting people in books, and I get paid for it, though not as much as I should.'

'Yeah, but what good does that do?'

'God knows. What good does putting them in jail do?'

The Continental Op talking with the novelist Fitzstephan in Dashiell Hammett's *The Dain Curse*

Design by Avril Broadley

British Library Cataloguing-in-Publication Data

A catalogue record for this book is available from the British Library

ISBN 0-500-27978-0

Printed in Hong Kong

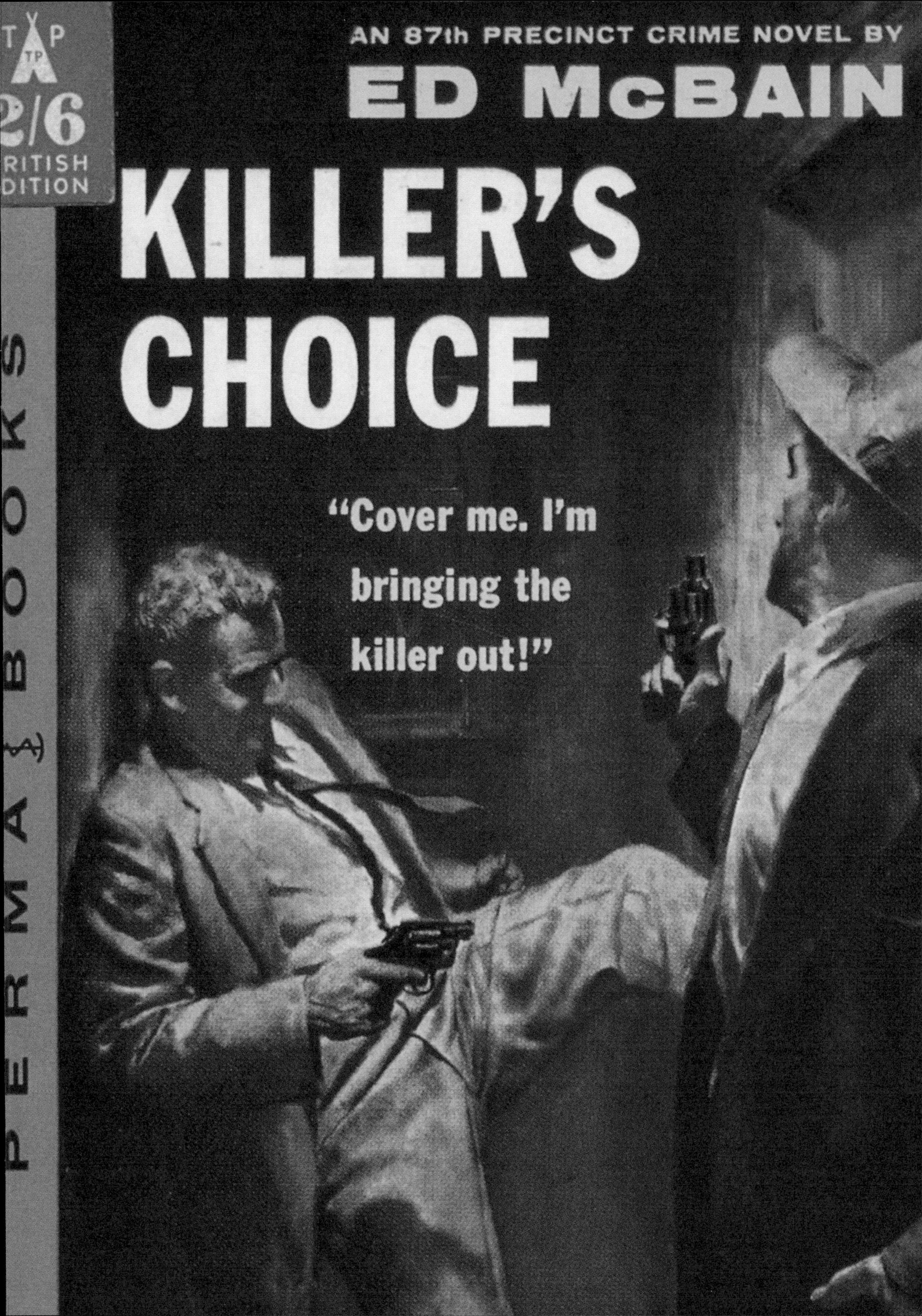
T P
2/6
RITISH
DITION
AN 87th PRECINCT CRIME NOVEL BY
ED McBAIN
KILLER'S
CHOICE
"Cover me. I'm
bringing the
killer out!"
PERMA BOOKS

contents

Le Mystère de la Chambre Jaune

par
GASTON LEROUX

THE NAMING OF PARTS

Murder, and any other crime, is not a part of entertainment, but an integral part of life. We are all murderers, we are all spies, we are all criminals, and to choose a crime as the mainspring of a book's action is only to find one of the simplest ways of focusing eyes on our life and our world.
Nicolas Freeling

Literature is whatever people read.
Mickey Spillane

You only have to go into a bookshop or a public library to be reminded that not all novels are just novels. Bookshops divide them into different categories: some are shelved simply under 'Fiction' but the rest come under separate headings, as 'Crime and Mystery', 'Horror', 'Science Fiction' and so forth. The number of headings varies according to the size of the bookshop, and the headings themselves vary according to the preference of its owners. But 'Crime and Mystery' is always there and always generously represented, even if some bookshops like to call it 'Crime', or 'Mystery', or just 'Thrillers'. It is prominent in libraries too, and even those which put all their fiction holdings on the same shelves often distinguish it with an emblem stuck to the spine: sometimes the silhouette of a revolver, sometimes a pair of handcuffs.

This variety of terms betrays a faint uncertainty, if only about how exactly to define the form. And these labels, of course, fall a long way short of exhausting

the repertoire. Some older readers still like to speak of 'detective stories' and 'murder mysteries'; a few remember the colloquial label of 'whodunnit'. Even a brief talk with a real fan will open a Pandora's box of further distinctions, most bewildering to the uninitiated yet each attracting fierce brand loyalty from admirers in the know. There are 'cosies' and 'hard-boiled novels'. There are 'police procedurals' and 'crime stories' (for even this innocent phrase can take on specialized nuances). Then there are 'timetable mysteries' and 'locked-room mysteries' and 'inverted tales'…

A brief look at what other languages do by way of description and definition serves only to compound bewilderment. The French speak of the *roman policier* or police novel (which they colloquially call the *polar*) even for books which do not have policemen in them, and they are joined in this habit by the Italians, with the *racconto poliziesco*, and the Spanish, with the *novela policíaca*. The Germans firmly put the emphasis on the opposite side of the law, referring to the *Kriminalroman* (not the 'crime novel' but the 'criminal novel'), which these days is more usually shortened to the expressive *Krimi*.

Most of these languages have, like English, an additional battery of terms, suggesting either greater looseness or greater precision. Where the English might talk of a 'thriller', the Spanish talk of a *cuento espeluznante* or (roughly) 'frightening story', and the Italians of a *libro giallo* or *giallo*, a 'yellow novel' or

Gaston Leroux's *The Mystery of the Yellow Room*, first published in French in 1907, pioneered the 'locked-room mystery', which shifts the puzzle from the question of who committed the crime to the question of how the murderer got into (or out of) an apparently sealed setting.

just a 'yellow'. The French, who took especially to heart the form that the Americans and the English usually call 'hard-boiled', chose to borrow the label 'black novel' which the pulp writer Cornell Woolrich used. *Romans noirs*, obviously, deal not just with what is puzzling but also with what is sinister and even morbid.

Sensibly, most readers pay little heed to terminology. They know what they like and have no difficulty finding it. Some prefer stories about olde-worlde villages packed with olde-worlde malice. Others prefer the mean streets of the city and the sort of malice that comes through the door carrying a gun. Some favour intricacy and others atmosphere. Yet even to list these choices in their simplest terms is still to urge the question of what we really do know about the form which

somehow embraces them all. It traffics in crime and the pursuit of criminals, mysteries and the pursuit of solutions: that much is obvious, and it helps to mark a rough and ready line between 'Crime and Mystery' and ghost stories, horror stories, and so forth. Ghost and horror stories may deal with crimes, but show no particular interest in their criminality as such. They certainly deal with mysteries, but like to leave at least some of the mystery unexplained: their interest is in what is inexplicable.

Yet these considerations do not help explain why readers never bother to look under 'Crime and Mystery' for works like *Oedipus Rex* or Dostoevsky's *Crime and Punishment*, even though they apparently contain enough of the relevant ingredients to qualify. The reason lies in a distinction between serious literature and

popular literature which has been ingrained throughout the history of the novel. Some fiction is serious: it educates, informs, enlightens, improves and exalts readers. Other fiction just entertains: it helps readers escape from reality; it merely passes or wastes the time. Each serious novel, it is claimed, creates its own form for itself and so is *sui generis*. Works like *Middlemarch* or *Crime and Punishment* have no genre, or at least have no genre beyond their broad agreement to tell some sort of story in prose – to be novels rather than plays or poems. Popular novels, on the other hand, are 'genre literature': they continually invoke genre and agree to be bounded by it. Formulae are established, then repeated from book to book with just enough variation to guarantee that the reader is entertained by novelty as well as reassured by familiarity.

It would take a long time to unpack all the assumptions on which these claims depend. Modern academic criticism, with its suspicion of cultural hierarchies, has begun the process in a spirit of deliberate challenge, and the present book will need to return at various points to this debate. But what is being offered here is above all a history – a history of a type of popular literature which began in subservience to the traditional assumptions about genre and about popular literature, and then, long before criticism raised its theoretical voice, discovered its own grounds of discontent with those assumptions and sought increasingly to escape from genre and from popular literature, as from the confines of a ghetto.

From Edgar Allan Poe and his stories about Dupin in the 1840s, to Sir Arthur Conan Doyle and his Sherlock Holmes stories at the end of the century and then to Agatha Christie and the other novelists of the Golden Age in the 1920s and

John Dickson Carr, who also used the pseudonym Carter Dickson, was a Golden Age writer who made his reputation by specializing in locked-room mysteries.

Opposite **Basil Rathbone and Nigel Bruce, Hollywood's most famous Sherlock Holmes and Dr Watson, in their first film, *The Hound of the Baskervilles* (1939). In all, they made fourteen films together, ending with *Dressed to Kill* in 1946.**

Penguin Crime 2/6

The case of the constant suicides
John Dickson Carr

1930s: the tradition of crime and mystery writing soon came to rejoice in refining its formulaic shape. It dealt in crime and the detection of crime, which were after all serious subjects. Yet it transformed them into entertainment, chiefly by converting them into puzzles and the solution of puzzles. The discovery of the body – which if, it did not happen in the first chapter was still to be expected from the very start of the story – posed a question for the detective, the other characters and the reader. The detective, sometimes anticipated by the ingenious reader, supplied the answer in the last chapter. Crime and mystery writing as a result enjoyed a particular niche, somewhere contentedly below serious literature because of its limited ambition yet definitely a cut above the cheaper types of popular literature because of its intellectual sophistication.

In the Golden Age between the wars detective novelists were much given to congratulating themselves on this genteel achievement. They had perfected what was at once an ideal recreation and, in its own modest way, a literary form of classical severity. Yet discontent was already present as well. Conan Doyle had tried to kill Sherlock Holmes off as far back as the 1890s, the first of many detective novelists to grow contemptuous of his success because the genre was not serious enough to satisfy him. By 1930 or so, when the Golden Age was apparently still in full bloom, doubt and worry were spreading that the formulae which

The work of James M. Cain – like the hard-boiled novels by his fellow Americans Dashiell Hammett and Raymond Chandler – signalled a reaction against the genteel detective fiction of the Golden Age.

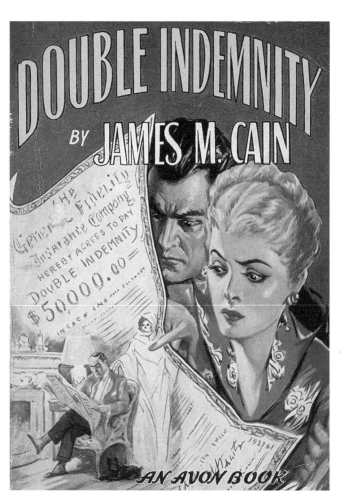

had been so carefully developed were approaching exhaustion. Novelty was getting harder and harder to achieve, and stale repetition was already beginning to set in.

It was certainly time to vary the formulae or devise new ones. Perhaps, since the precise rules of the Golden Age had shown their confining limitations, it was time to break with the whole idea of formulae altogether? Detective fiction had certainly become rarefied by sealing itself off from the preoccupations of serious fiction. Perhaps it could actually start to become serious itself? Such thoughts and possibilities have animated most of what has happened since the 1930s to make the term 'detective fiction' sound dated and redundant. The reaction began with the rise of Dashiell Hammett, Raymond Chandler and the 'hard-boiled school' in America. It continued with the work of Simenon and James M. Cain and the emergence of novels which, while continuing to propound and solve some sort of mystery, were equally interested in putting forward a view of policemen or criminals for which the Golden Age had no room. Though once-fashionable labels like the 'police procedural' and the 'crime novel' have come to sound as dated as the term 'detective fiction', the tendency they announced continues today.

The fruitful, if muddled ambitions which marked the break with detective fiction in the classic mould have brought new achievement, new disappointment, continuing ambivalence. The ambivalence was there from the start, in writers like Hammett and Chandler who, for all the refreshing energy they unleashed in their writing, were still on some level wrestling with unanswered questions. Were they simply introducing new formulae or abandoning formulae altogether? If they did abandon formulae, would that

JÜRGEN ALBERTS
Mediensiff
Kriminalroman

HAFFMANS KRIMINALROMANE

Crime and mystery fiction has many names. Germans call a detective novel or thriller a _Kriminalroman_, usually shortened to _Krimi_.

open their writing to new seriousness or would it cut it off from its vital roots?

Even as Hammett's career was ending in prolonged silence and Chandler's in decline, critics were still inclined to take the simple view of their achievement. The hard-boiled novel was hailed as sweeping away the falsity of what had preceded it, as being realistic and hence serious. The same cries greeted the police procedural and the crime novel in turn, each briefly looking somehow closer to the real thing, somehow truer to life, than what had gone before – until time exposed its mannerisms, its conventions and, eventually, its datedness. This pattern, of course, is not unique to crime

and mystery writing. For a long time now, each new generation in the history of fiction of all sorts and no declared sort at all has marched under the banner of realism, only to be trodden underfoot by the next generation with the next version of the same motto emblazoned on its banner. The cycle of hope and disappointment repeats itself.

But the result is not to leave just a trail of extinct ideas. Literary history does not work like evolution. Although the hopes that originally accompanied the hard-boiled school, or the police procedural, or the crime novel, when they first emerged may now look as faded as the ambitions which created the work of the Golden Age, that does not mean their achievement has been made redundant. Except in a spirit of pastiche, nobody today can sit down to write a classic detective novel or a hard-boiled novel or a police procedural in the original and pure sense of these terms. Yet nobody can neglect the example of any of these schools, since each has contributed to a steadily expanding range of possibilities, indeed, to a quite remarkably wide range for a genre which does not yet have two hundred years of history to its name. Larger questions – about the distinction between popular and serious literature, about formulae as limitation or source of vitality, about the validity of the whole idea of genre – may go unanswered. But one thing is certain. Crime and mystery writers today have more reason to address them, and more material with which to address them, than ever before.

REVELATIONS
OF
A DETECTIVE

Chapter 1 ORIGINS

EDGAR ALLAN POE'S 'TALES OF RATIOCINATION'

'The Murders in the Rue Morgue', a short story Poe wrote in 1841, introduced a character whom he grandly named Monsieur C. Auguste Dupin. Despite being an intellectual of secluded habits, rarefied pursuits and a snobbish disdain for the rest of mankind, Dupin sets out to investigate a particularly baffling as well as grotesque crime he has seen reported in the newspapers. Two women have been brutally murdered in a room apparently sealed so securely that nobody could have left afterwards. Dupin succeeds where the authorities have failed. His investigation shows that the murders were committed by an enraged and agile ourang-outang which had escaped from its owner. Poe obviously took special pride in his creation, for he twice brought Dupin back in his fiction. In 'The Mystery of Marie Rogêt' (first serialized in 1842–43) Dupin solves the murder of a girl which, as the title broadly hints, was based on the real-life case of Mary Rogers in New York. And in 'The Purloined Letter' (originally published in a magazine in 1845) Dupin works out where the cunning Minister D— has hidden the document he plans to exploit to his political advantage.

Poe included these three stories about Dupin in the collection of *Tales* he published later in 1845. But they stand noticeably apart from the Gothic terrors and disasters which occupy the rest of the volume and his stories in general. Poe

himself acknowledged as much when he called them 'tales of ratiocination' to distinguish them from other works which he liked to label 'grotesque' or 'arabesque'. Today we would call them detective stories. Indeed historians of the genre commonly take them to be the first detective stories of any consequence. Of course, they can point to a handful of earlier precedents: in the Bible, when Daniel nails the guilt of the Elders who seek to discredit Susanna, for example, and in Voltaire's *Zadig*, when the hero describes what a particular horse and dog look like just from the traces they leave. But it was Poe who first brought the ingredients of detective fiction together, and brought them together with prescient economy.

In the compass of only three short stories written in four years he managed to establish a pattern which has long since been made familiar, to the point of becoming formulaic. He presented the reader with a brilliant (and also eccentric) detective; a puzzling crime which requires more than ordinary intelligence or common sense to solve; and a dénouement which emerges not through divine revelation or simple accident but through the methodical investigations of the detective. For good measure Poe also gave the detective an admiring friend to chronicle his work and even, in the character of the Minister D— in 'The Purloined Letter', an opponent whose intelligence mirrors and rivals the detective's own. Later writers would develop these touches as eagerly as they

'Yellowbacks' – the railway literature of the Victorians – marked the emergence of the detective as a popular hero in the later decades of the nineteenth century.

adopted the central pattern Poe had so firmly established.

Yet the way in which 'The Murders in the Rue Morgue' begins hardly makes a promising start to a new type of story. It opens with an essay, running to several pages, about the 'analytical faculty' and its delight in solving enigmas and conundrums or deciphering hieroglyphics. Like most of Poe's amateur philosophizing and psychologizing, this essay manages almost to bury some acute insights in appallingly pretentious language. And in any event it hardly sounds like the start to any sort of story at all, much less a story which will turn out to be about an ourang-outang going on the rampage, almost beheading one

Opposite **Edgar Allan Poe in a Gothic setting: a reminder that the creator of the detective story usually wrote about destruction and horror, not the triumph of the intellect.**

The murderous ourang-outang in Edgar Allan Poe's 'The Murders in the Rue Morgue'. Illustration by Harry Clarke (1919).

woman and stuffing her companion halfway up a chimney.

After a fashion, though, Poe does make his point. Detective fiction, while dealing with crime, and often sordid and gory crime, would from the start tackle it in a cerebral fashion. It would stand aloof from the sensationalism of its own material. Poe's essay on the analytical faculty celebrates the power of the human mind (or rather the mind of the extraordinary individual) to triumph over whatever is mysterious, whatever is puzzling. The forces of disorder and unreason, which elsewhere threaten and usually destroy the characters in Poe's stories, can, it seems, be subjugated after all – and by the solitary intellect working from the comfort of an armchair.

The detective story, then, began as a dream of reason and of the triumphs reason can achieve. This, plainly, is what is being celebrated when the ourang-outang is identified as the killer and recaptured at the end of 'The Murders in the Rue Morgue'. The beast has been returned to its cage. This victory for reason has little, if anything, to do with justice or the social order – to which, after all, ourang-outangs do not commonly pose a serious threat. Dupin turns to detection for the excitement and satisfaction it brings him, and for no other motive. He never misses a chance of showing off his superiority to the narrator, whose job is just to tag along behind him without second-guessing the solution. And he is particularly determined to score points over the police, who in Poe's work for the first time assume the role they would play in so much later detective fiction: sceptical, if not downright scornful, of the detective at the start of the case, they are humbly amazed by his brilliance at the dénouement. The reader is invited to join

them in their amazement – to join, indeed, in admiration both for an extraordinary individual and for an ideal of reason practised, as Poe believed art should be practised, for its own sake.

THIEF-TAKERS AND POLICEMEN FROM VIDOCQ TO DICKENS

Poe's stories might have served as a paradigm for detective fiction at its most rigorous and extreme – the puzzle for the pleasure of the puzzle, disentangling for the pleasure of disentangling – but that is only one form an interest in crime and mystery can take. Other writers have found it less easy or less desirable to disassociate their interest from questions of justice and social order, let alone from the simpler excitements of criminal-catching. Certainly the nineteenth century did not encourage such a separation. The age witnessed massive change in the ramshackle machinery of law and law enforcement inherited from previous generations. Questions were being asked

about the nature of crime and the nature of punishment, and, most urgently, about how criminals could best be caught and who best could do the catching.

France led the way among European nations. Its *Gendarmerie*, the fruit of Napoleon's vision of order, was the first police force in the modern sense of the term. Its *Sûreté* was the first proper detective force, larger and more effective than, for example, the Bow Street Runners who had been operating from the London magistrates' court since the middle of the previous century. Even Poe obliquely acknowledged that France was detection's natural home when he chose to make Dupin French (a Chevalier of the Légion d'honneur, no less) and set Dupin's adventures in Paris, even though he knew so little about the city that in 'The Mystery of Marie Rogêt' he had sassafras grass growing on the banks of the Seine. The tribute may have been grudging – Poe certainly allowed Dupin more than his share of malicious glee at the expense of thick-headed gendarmes – but it was unavoidable.

It was unavoidable not just because of the solid bureaucratic achievement embodied in the Gendarmerie and the Sûreté, but because of the popular fame Eugène-François Vidocq, appointed the first head of the Sûreté in 1812, had earned with the four volumes of *Mémoires* published under his name in 1828 and 1829. The fact that Vidocq's *Mémoires* were the largely fictional work of two hack writers was neither here nor there. Even Vidocq's protest, added to later editions, that the *Mémoires* had been written and published without his permission did nothing to prevent the publicity bandwagon rolling exuberantly on its way. His disclaimer may even have been designed to help it, for Vidocq had nothing if not a flair for publicity. Even

Monsieur C. Auguste Dupin, wearing glasses, with the Prefect of Police in 'The Mystery of Marie Rogêt'. Poe anticipated Conan Doyle and countless later writers in making his amateur detective and the police regard each other with contempt.

Ghost-written though they may have been, the *Mémoires* of Eugène-François Vidocq (above), **first head of the French Sûreté, gave him a legendary reputation for endless cunning and unflagging resource.**

confidence and, once he has gathered the evidence he seeks, reveals himself with a cry of 'I am Vidocq, and I arrest you!'

It is like the snarl of a predator at the moment of striking. And while the predator in action may be more exciting to the popular imagination than the intellectual at work, he is no more reassuring. In fact, there is nothing reassuring about Vidocq. Before he became a detective he had been a criminal – as well as the most notorious prison-breaker of his day – and, rather than concealing his past, the memoirs boast about and embroider it. The story of the criminal who repents and undergoes a change of heart may be an old one and a good one, but it is not quite the story which the memoirs choose to tell. Despite his occasional protestations of regret and his occasional nods to accepted values, Vidocq sounds as if he has just changed teams. In his new occupation he remains the rapacious and self-interested trickster.

Dupin is forced to acknowledge him, though in predictably disparaging terms as 'a good guesser, and a persevering man' but 'without educated thought'.

Education certainly plays little part in how the Vidocq of the *Mémoires* goes about detection. Working among dangerous criminals on the streets of Paris, he is the flamboyant adventurer where Dupin is the armchair intellectual. Perseverance contributes a lot to the triumphs he records: in one case he keeps warm while watching a suspect's house by spending the night up to his neck in a dunghill. But he owes most to his flair for the dramatic. Vidocq is among the first, if not the very first, of countless detectives portrayed as masters of the impenetrable disguise and the cunning trap theatrically sprung. Again and again he worms his way into his unsuspecting victim's

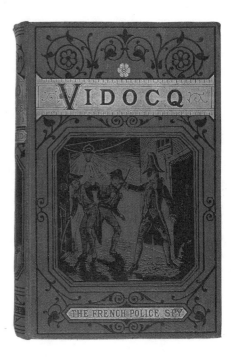

'I Am Vidocq, and I Arrest You!'

Emile Morice and Louis-François L'Héritier, the two hack writers responsible for Vidocq's *Mémoires*, embroidered his life almost beyond recognition. But the reality was colourful enough. Born in Arras in 1775, he started out like the hero of a picaresque novel: fighting duels, running away from home, enlisting as a soldier and then deserting. Held in jail at Lille, he was accused and convicted of forging a document used by fellow-prisoners in their escape. Thereafter he made himself notorious by frequent and often successful attempts to break out – from Bicêtre and La Force, as well as from the galleys of Toulon and Brest.

Vidocq always denied the accusation of forgery which had set him on this path, but he certainly gained a familiarity with criminals and their ways which made him useful to the Paris police as an informer. He was appointed chief of the newly formed Sûreté in 1812, held the job until 1827 and briefly returned to it in 1832. There is no reason to accept the claims made by the *Mémoires* for his talents and achievements: altering his height four or five inches at will, for example, and personally capturing criminals at an average rate of nearly two a day. But, equally, there is no reason to doubt that he served the fledgling organization well. The charges of corruption which prompted his first resignation and made his second stint at the Sûreté a *débâcle* say more about the political intrigues and professional jealousies of the time than about his competence.

In retirement his life was hardly less adventurous. Vidocq ran a paper factory staffed largely by ex-convicts at Saint-Mandé (near Vincennes), wrote books and, long before Allan Pinkerton had the idea in Chicago, set up his own private detective agency, the *Bureau des Renseignements*, or Information Office. He even visited London with an exhibition consisting of paintings, artificial fruit, criminal curios and himself. He died in poverty in 1857.

Newly transformed from convict to policeman, Vidocq struggles with a criminal as he makes his first arrest.

Javert, a figure of sinister power in Victor Hugo's Les Misérables and one of several characters in nineteenth-century fiction directly descended from the Vidocq of the Mémoires.

Contemporaries were perfectly familiar with the maxim that you set a thief to catch a thief. Precisely this principle had dictated the system of law enforcement which the nineteenth century had inherited. It had also reduced that system to a ramshackle mess crying out for reform. Colourful and intriguing though he might have been, the Vidocq of the *Mémoires* also reminded people that the new age of policing had not necessarily broken with the mistakes or dangers of the past: the distinction between law-breaker and law-enforcer was still blurred. And so Vidocq left writers about detection and detectives a disturbing legacy, which Balzac would explore in the character of Vautrin in

Le Père Goriot (1835), *Illusions perdues* (1837–43) and *Splendeurs et misères des courtesans* (1838–47) and Victor Hugo would explore in the character of Javert in *Les Misérables* (1862) – to cite only two of the oblique but unmistakable portraits of Vidocq which followed the *Mémoires*.

Writers addressed the same issues in Britain, where Vidocq's *Mémoires* appeared in translation in 1829, the very year when London got its first coherently organized police force, thanks to the initiative of Sir Robert Peel. Consideration grew more urgent when a Detective Department, or Office, of plainclothes policemen was added to the Metropolitan Police in the early 1840s, albeit modestly and semi-officially. Against such a background, popular literature could hardly be expected to resist the chance of repeating Vidocq's success. Thomas Gaspey's *Richmond: or, Scenes in the Life of a Bow Street Runner*, which had appeared in 1827, anticipated Vidocq's memoirs in a timid and tentative sort of way. In later decades it was joined by *Recollections of a Detective Police-Officer* (1856) and a host of other 'yellowbacks' dealing with police detectives, and by stage melodramas of which Tom Taylor's *The Ticket-of-Leave Man* (1863) was by far the most important.

In putting his detective on the stage Taylor was in a sense returning him to his natural home, since like other English writers he was determined to preserve all of the flamboyant theatricality that Vidocq had displayed. It would still be quite a while before the detective as master of disguise had become a cliché too worn for writers to use. But at the same time Taylor, like Gaspey and the 'yellowback' writers before him, was determined to make the detective acceptable in ways Vidocq had not been.

HAWKSHAW AND THE
TICKET-OF-LEAVE MAN

Tom Taylor – barrister, civil servant, academic and journalist as well as playwright – was one of those formidably hard-working Victorians who has since been almost completely forgotten. Of his plays only the comedy *Our American Cousin* (1858) is sometimes remembered, and then largely because Abraham Lincoln was assassinated during a performance of it in Washington DC. Yet Taylor, who dabbled in virtually every type of play popular with nineteenth-century theatregoers, also contributed to the literature of crime and detection in *The Ticket-of-Leave Man* (1863).

Bob Brierly, the released convict or 'ticket-of-leave man' of the title, is a young lad from Lancashire who gets innocently entangled in James Dalton's scheme for passing forged banknotes. Only May Edwards stands by him when he is arrested and sent to prison. On his release Bob tries hard to go straight but Dalton frustrates his attempts at honest work, hoping that desperation will once more make him a useful tool. Innocence persecuted by the apparently overwhelming power of evil is a stock theme of melodrama, and Taylor exploits all the other fashionable elements of the genre to the hilt. Dalton's crony Moss talks in 'thieves' cant' (or criminal slang) and May Edwards sings sentimental ditties at the drop of a hat. Fights and chases ring down the curtain at the end of each act until the last, when Tom is finally vindicated, the villains are confounded, and an uplifting moral can be offered instead: 'You see, there may be some good left in a TICKET-OF-LEAVE MAN after all.'

Taylor also stirs some novel ingredients into the familiar stew. He lays his scene not in London's East

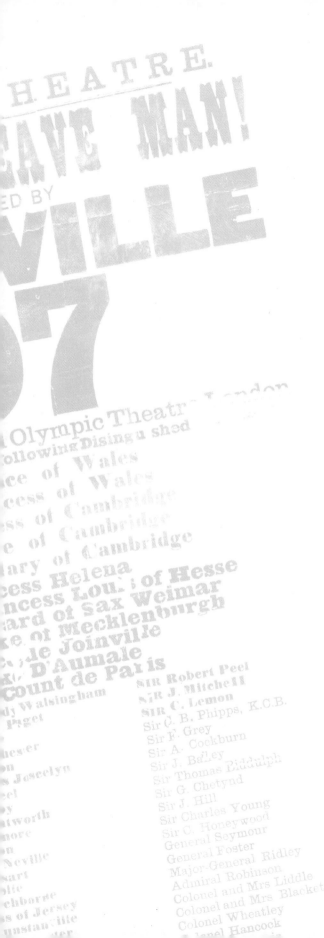

End – the territory of Dickens' *Oliver Twist* and innumerable previous works of criminal low life – but in the City. Corruption in the world of high finance could fascinate audiences in the 1860s as much as in the 1980s and 1990s (and for very similar reasons). This apparently respectable milieu demanded an apparently respectable villain. James 'The Tiger' Dalton, with 'as many outsides as he has aliases', is cool and resourceful in pursuing his deep-laid strategy to ensnare Bob. He has less in common with Fagin or Bill Sikes than he does with Moriarty and the other 'Napoleons of Crime' who would flourish from the turn of the century onwards.

Most remarkable is the way *The Ticket-of-Leave Man* portrays Dalton's opponent, the detective Hawkshaw. Dickens and the pseudonymous hacks who wrote 'yellowback' reminiscences had gone a long way to making the police detective into a contemporary hero, and Taylor completes the apotheosis. It comes as no surprise to hear that Hawkshaw is 'the 'cutest detective in the force' and 'the hero of the gold dust robberies, and the famous Trunk-line-transfer forgeries', or to learn that he is as great a master of disguise as Dalton. After all, what playwright could resist the dramatic opportunities which disguise offered? Yet Hawkshaw is no mere swaggering adventurer out to enhance his own reputation. Building on hints from yellowback writers concerned to render the police detective sympathetic, Taylor makes Hawkshaw dedicated to extricating Bob from Dalton's scheming and determined to exonerate him from false charges. This motive gives Hawkshaw a pivotal role in the play's moral scheme, as the 'good angel' opposing the 'bad angel' for influence over the hero's soul. And it looks forward to the role of protector of the innocent and defender of the falsely accused which detectives from Sherlock Holmes onwards would regularly play.

This may be one reason why, when Taylor and *The Ticket-of-Leave Man* itself had long been forgotten, Hawkshaw was not. 'Hawk' seems already to have been a slang word for a detective before Taylor, as it had long been slang for anyone with predatory powers or designs, including criminals such as card sharpers or confidence tricksters. After Taylor, though, 'hawk' was modified to 'hawkshaw' and in that form survived long enough to join all the other colourful terms for detectives used by American hard-boiled writers of the 1920s and 1930s: see 'A Hard-Boiled Dictionary', p. 106, under *dick*.

Inspector Bucket, the home-loving and deceptively ordinary policeman in Dickens' *Bleak House*. Watercolour drawing by Kyd (Clayton Clark).

Opposite **Moments of high drama from M.G. Lewis' *The Monk* (1796), one of the Gothic novels whose appeal to fear anticipated the sensation novels by Wilkie Collins, Mary Elizabeth Braddon and other writers of the mid-nineteenth century.**

an adventurer, and he only once dons the literal disguise then still mandatory for detectives. Instead he subtly adapts his personality to deal with characters who otherwise live separately from each other, caught and baffled in their private mysteries. By the end he has seen off a gang of minor villains, arrested a murderer and helped the heroine to discover the identity of her long-lost mother. In a society of the powerless he has taken on an aura of convincing power, at once awesome and humane, mysterious and kindly: Vidocq's street knowledge without Vidocq's ruthlessness, Dupin's intellectual prowess without Dupin's self-absorption.

SENSATION NOVELS

Contemporaries had their own name for books like *Bleak House*, whose ample structure was held together by crime and mystery and whose ending was announced by the capture of criminals and the resolution of mysteries. They called them 'sensation novels', a term which meant very much what 'shocker' would later come to mean and 'thriller' means today. Such books set out to play on the reader's sensations, to shock and to thrill. As a generic label, 'sensation novel' does little to indicate the particular stature of Dickens' achievement in *Bleak House* but it at least roughly indicates the distance separating a book like *Bleak House* from Poe's 'tales of ratiocination'.

The sensation novel inherited from the Gothic novel of the late eighteenth and early nineteenth centuries a reliance on the appeal to fear. But where the Gothic novel located its terrors in monasteries and medieval castles, the sensation novel resolutely preferred contemporary settings. It dealt with the world of the telegraph and the railway,

Their detectives became increasingly moral: in their private lives middle-class, family-loving men, in their work model servants of an efficient but humane state.

This is also how Dickens portrayed detectives in the magazine articles he wrote about the Detective Department in 1850 and 1851, when it still seemed something of a novelty. He combined naïve enthusiasm for the men's skill in disguise with equally naïve admiration for their respectability. In fact, these articles would be entirely negligible if they did not present the first crude observations that Dickens went on to refine almost beyond recognition in *Bleak House* (1852–53). Of course, *Bleak House* is not a detective novel in any sense a follower of Poe would recognize. Yet in seeking to embody the society of the day in all its complex fabric, it finds crime and mystery to be recurrent threads. Consequently, the policeman Inspector Bucket pervades the novel. However, Bucket is unassuming, domesticated, too middle-aged ever to seem adventurous, much less

the lunatic asylum and the magistrates' court, seeking wherever possible to be not just up-to-date but controversial in its revelations. The terrors which modern life engenders have little to do with the supernatural – the sensation novel ruled out the clank of ghostly chains in the Gothic cellarage – and spring only incidentally from physical danger. They come instead from family mysteries and guilty secrets in the past, and they involve a whole paraphernalia of lost or missing wills, forged documents and false identities. These in turn generate the dense, labyrinthine plots which give

The villains of sensation novels such as Mary Elizabeth Braddon's *Lady Audley's Secret* are women with the same classic Pre-Raphaelite beauty, brooding and compelling, evoked by Dante Gabriel Rossetti in this 1861 sketch of William Morris' wife Jane.

sensation novels their three-volume bulk and threaten to lead to what Henry James, speaking of Dickens' later work, would contemptuously dismiss as 'the manufacture of fiction'.

In his last novel, *The Mystery of Edwin Drood* (1870), Dickens addressed himself more single-mindedly to writing a sensation novel than he had before, devising a plot focused tightly on the murder – or at least the disappearance – of the title character. Left unfinished at his death, the novel was destined to remain a curiosity, albeit one which has fascinated several generations of critics and scholars. During the 1860s the sensation novel had already produced a steady stream of bestsellers, with Mrs Henry Wood's *East Lynne* (1861), Mary Elizabeth Braddon's *Lady Audley's Secret* (1862) and, above all, the work of Dickens' own close friend, Wilkie Collins. Collins summed up his aesthetic, it is said, in a single phrase: 'Make 'em laugh, make 'em cry, make 'em wait'. That might stand as the motto of all the sensation novelists, though few practised the art of sheer suspense – making 'em wait – with such skill. In *The Woman in White* (1859–60), for example, he managed to give breathless, tantalizing purpose to a narrative still leisurely enough to find room for legal mysteries of quite bewildering ramifications and sub-plots involving political intrigue, as well as two heroines and two villains. One of Collins' villains, Count Fosco, is the most memorable readers would encounter until the appearance of Professor Moriarty in the Sherlock Holmes stories.

In *The Moonstone* (1868) Collins undertook the trickier task of sustaining suspense while concentrating on a single detective puzzle of a sort Poe could have used in one of his Dupin stories.

The Mystery of THE MYSTERY OF EDWIN DROOD

When Dickens died in June 1870 he had written six of the twelve monthly instalments in which he planned to serialize *The Mystery of Edwin Drood*. In them he had plainly decided to challenge his friend Wilkie Collins and other popular writers of the day by writing a sensation novel. He abandoned the broad social concerns and leisurely pace of novels like *Bleak House* and *Our Mutual Friend* for a narrative tightly focused on a single, mysterious event: the disappearance of the title character, a complacent young sprig pampered by the prospect of an arranged marriage to his fellow-ward Rosa Bud and by the solicitude of his uncle John Jasper, the choirmaster of Cloisterham cathedral. Jasper leads the enquiry into his fate and suspicion falls on the quarrelsome Neville Landless, recently arrived in Cloisterham with his twin sister Helena. At the same time, doubts surround Jasper himself, for he leads a double life as an opium addict and is, moreover, in love with Rosa. A detective enters the scene in the form of the mysterious Dick Datchery.

And there the text breaks off. Dickens had left behind exactly the sort of challenge which literary scholars and lovers of detective fiction have never been able to resist. The chief mystery, obviously, is the fate of Edwin Drood. Has he arranged his disappearance or has he been killed? If he is dead, who killed him? But the puzzles do not end here. Who is Dick Datchery? If he is not a new character (and Dickens would surely have hesitated to introduce a major new character with his story so far underway), is he a familiar one in disguise: Rosa's guardian Grewgious, or the legal clerk Bazzard, or the sailor Tartar, or even Helena Landless? Who will Rosa choose to marry from the list of her suitors? Certainly not Drood or Jasper, so perhaps it may prove to be Tartar or Neville? And what role in the dénouement will be played by minor characters such as the Princess Puffer, who runs the opium den Jasper visits, and Durdles, the stonemason who has guided him on a curious expedition round the cathedral graveyard at night?

Speculation started in the immediate aftermath of Dickens' death, when eagerness to cash in on a popular talking point could take disreputable forms. A continuation of *Drood* by Henry Morland, first published in the USA in 1871–72, was reissued with the claim that it had sprung from the pen of Wilkie Collins and Charles Dickens the Younger (who did in fact advise one of the many *Drood* playwrights about the ending his father had contemplated). Another effort, published in Vermont in 1873, was attributed to 'the Spirit Pen of Charles Dickens, through a Medium'. Later and more respectable endings were supplied by the pseudonymous Gillan Vase (1878) and the children's writer Leon Garfield (1980). A growing body of scholarship – to which G.K. Chesterton, the ghost-story writer M.R. James, and Andrew Lang, compiler of fairy books, all made regular contributions – was summed up in Sir William Robertson Nicoll's *The Problem of 'Edwin Drood'* (1912). Postmodernism has brought the scholarly and fictional traditions together: Carlo Fruttero and Franco Lucentini's *La verità sul caso D* (1989; translated as *The D Case*, 1994) intersperses Dickens' text with comments from a convention of fictional detectives who include Dupin, Porfiry Petrovich (from Dostoevsky's *Crime and Punishment*), Father Brown, Poirot and Maigret.

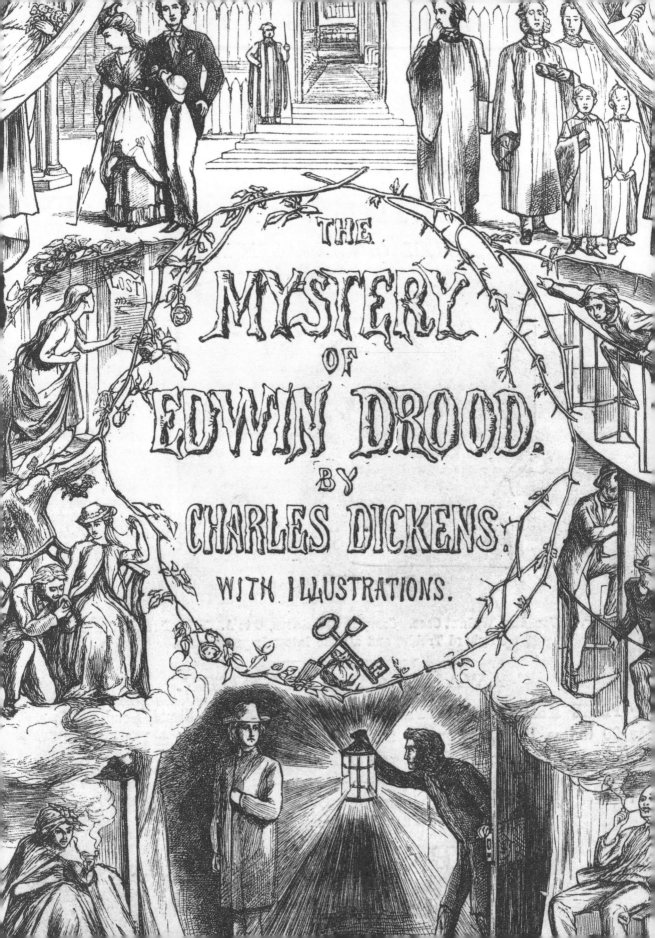

THE MYSTERY OF EDWIN DROOD.

BY

CHARLES DICKENS.

WITH ILLUSTRATIONS.

Fruttero and Lucentini's proposed solution is in tune with the playfully deconstructionist mood of the times. Earlier scholars could not agree on Datchery's identity but usually favoured Jasper as the villain of the piece, though he was vigorously defended by the actor and amateur Dickensian Sir Felix Aylmer in *The Drood Case* (1964). Jasper's guilt would firmly align the novel with the interest in double lives and haunted murderers which runs throughout Dickens' work. Advocates of all the various endings have found clues not just in the completed half of the novel itself but in the working notes Dickens had made, the list of titles he had debated and the remarks he had let slip to his illustrators, friends and family. These, however, are at best scanty and ambiguous, underlining the questions rather than providing the answers. The rejected title that stood next in the list to Dickens' final choice was *Dead? Or Alive?*

Scarcely less tantalizing is the biggest clue of all: the design for the cover of the monthly instalments. Dickens' son-in-law Charles Collins originally drew it but Luke Fildes, the illustrator who took over when Collins fell ill, revised and finished it. The vignette at the top obviously encapsulates the situation when the novel starts: during a cathedral service Jasper, in his choirmaster's robes, looks with gnawing envy at Rosa as she hangs on Edwin's arm. But the other vignettes are less clear in their import. Those on the left seem to concern Rosa, who is looking at a poster announcing Edwin's disappearance and being wooed by a suitor whose moustache prevents him being Drood or Jasper. Tartar perhaps? Neither scene appears in the half of the story Dickens lived to write. Nor does the chase up the spiral staircase on the right-hand side. In Collins' original sketch the two lower figures were policemen; in Fildes' version the clerical garb of the bottom figure identifies him as Crisparkle, the canon of Cloisterham who has befriended the Landlesses, but the middle figure defies identification. Essentially unchanged from Collins' draft, Jasper leads the chase and points unwittingly at himself in the scene above.

A suggestive symmetry also informs the central panel at the bottom. The man on the right must surely be Jasper, his position here corresponding to his position at the top of the page. He stands at the door of a darkened chamber, perhaps one of the cathedral's vaults or catacombs, shining his lantern on the stern figure who confronts him. Comparison with the upper panel invites the viewer to identify the apparition as Edwin. But is it Edwin alive and returned to confront his would-be murderer? Or is it a drug-induced phantom of the victim in Jasper's mind? (After all, the scene is flanked by the Princess Puffer and the Chinaman from the opium den, wreathed in smoke from their pipes.) Or is one of the other characters – Datchery would be the obvious candidate – posing as Edwin to surprise his murderer into confession?

Colonel Herncastle
seizes the diamond
from its rightful
Indian guardians in
the Prologue to
Wilkie Collins' *The
Moonstone*, the
most influential of
the many Victorian
novels whose plots
introduce rare jewels
and exotic settings.

Daringly, it does not even involve murder, which most crime and mystery writers have since agreed in finding essential to their purpose. Instead, the puzzle comes from the theft of a diamond – the moonstone of the title – which is kept under locked guard. The stone disappears in the first volume and the thief is identified at the end of the third.

The difficulty for Collins – and for all detective novelists who followed – is what happens in the middle: how, from the writer's point of view, to delay the answer without boring or irritating the reader with what is manifestly padding. The more the writer insists on making his narrative depend on the puzzle – the more rigorously sub-plots, love interest, incidental touches of characterization and all the other common resources of fiction are excluded – the starker the problem grows.

This problem has defeated enough writers to underline the good sense of Poe's instinct that his 'tales of ratiocination' should simply be short stories, where the gap between question and answer is a matter of pages rather than chapters. Some readers and critics have been driven to conclude that the short story, where compression is all, is the ideal vehicle for the detective puzzle; expansion into the novel merely opens the way to flaws. Yet in *The Moonstone* Collins, without the benefit of all the successes and failures modern writers have at their disposal, managed to write not just an engrossing detective novel but an engrossing long detective novel. He did so by relying on a technique which had already served him well in *The Woman in White*: he parcelled out the story of the diamond's disappearance between the various characters, making each of them describe the scenes of which they had direct knowledge, like a succession of witnesses giving evidence in court. Each of them has a distinctive style of narration and brings a new perspective on the other participants in the story. Ingeniously, the needs of both characterization and mystification are served simultaneously.

Collins made this method so much his own that the success of *The Moonstone* is an unrepeatable trick – or, rather, a trick that could be repeated, as Michael Innes did in *Lament for a Maker* (1938), only in a spirit that openly combines homage with bravura. In other respects, however, later detective novelists owe a great deal to *The Moonstone*, so squarely does it stand in the emergent traditions of the form. This is particularly true of what Collins did with his detective, Sergeant

THE WOMAN IN WHITE
OLYMPIC THEATRE

Cuff, the policeman sent to investigate the loss of the diamond. The periodic shifting in narrative viewpoint prevents Cuff from dominating the novel as Dupin had dominated the stories in which he appeared. And the portrait of Cuff carries a stage further the modifications to the police detective which Dickens and other writers had introduced since the time of Vidocq.

Where Inspector Bucket is an unassuming man whom it is dangerous to underrate, Cuff is almost nondescript. His only striking feature is his eyes, which 'had a very disconcerting trick … of looking as if they expected something more from you than you were aware of yourself'. Disconcerting eyes would soon become a standard attribute of fictional detectives. But otherwise, Cuff 'might have been a parson, or an undertaker, or anything else you like, except what he really was'. This is not just a professional ploy, a form of permanent disguise like Bucket's knack of changing his personality to suit whoever he is dealing with. Cuff certainly knows his job: he can gather clues, make deductions and mislead people about the real drift of his inquiries with the best of them. But to him detection is also simply a job, no longer the exercise of an extraordinary and mysterious power as it had been for Dupin or Vidocq. Cuff can be baffled, he can share the detection with other characters and he can absent himself for long stretches of the story, re-entering it to announce that he has retired and to admit that he got part of the solution to the mystery wrong.

Fictional detectives, then, do not have to be great or infallible. Dupin and Vidocq had already shown in their different ways that greatness and infallibility could make detectives insufferable or sinister; Cuff now showed they could after all be human, their seeming ordinariness at least partly genuine. This reassuring conclusion was also being reached in France, where the popularity of the *roman-feuilleton* paralleled that of the three-decker sensation novel in Britain, and the popularity of Emile Gaboriau paralleled and finally outshone that of Wilkie Collins. Nowadays Gaboriau's name turns up in literary histories but hardly ever on anyone's private reading list, but, beginning with *L'Affaire Lerouge* (a serial in 1865 and a book in 1866), his work carried the detective story to a wider audience than it had previously reached. In doing so, it played a crucial role in moulding the image of the detective.

In France this image was still overshadowed by the memory of Vidocq, as even the name of Inspecteur Lecoq, Gaboriau's most famous detective, bears witness. Their resemblance goes further.

Lecoq is (almost inevitably) a master of disguise. He is also vain and ambitious. Yet Gaboriau stresses that he is honest, making his less admirable characteristics seem more like foibles than sinister blemishes, and making him as sedulously respectable as Bucket and Cuff. Moreover, he brings Lecoq's dedication to his work vividly to life: few writers had so effectively portrayed a detective single-mindedly on the hunt for clues, no longer a predator pouncing on his prey but a bloodhound straining at the leash. This whiff of nervous excitement, along with the attributes Dickens and Collins had introduced, paved the way for later police detectives, from Simenon's Maigret onwards.

Yet there was a big gap in time between Lecoq and Maigret, much of it filled by detectives of a rather different stripe: private detectives, eccentric detectives, colourful detectives, charismatic detectives. Here Gaboriau failed to leave his mark, but only narrowly. He was avowedly a disciple of Poe, and before Lecoq came to engross his attention he had given the spotlight in *L'Affaire Lerouge* to a detective obviously inspired by Dupin. Père Tabaret (nicknamed Tire-au-clair) is a retired pawnbroker turned private consultant, a promising idea which Gaboriau backs up by having Tabaret make some impressively solid deductions. Yet the character of Tabaret himself does not really work. The detective is so overburdened with eccentricities and mannerisms that often he strikes the reader as just a tiresome zany. The task of building constructively on what Poe had done with Dupin would fall to another writer, of subtler temperament than Gaboriau: Sir Arthur Conan Doyle. The result was Sherlock Holmes – and his impact was, quite simply, immeasurable.

Although he is largely forgotten today, Emile Gaboriau widened the international popularity of the detective story in the years between Wilkie Collins' *The Moonstone* of 1868 and Conan Doyle's *A Study in Scarlet*, published in 1887.

PRICE SIXPENCE

THE
MYSTERY
OF
ORCIVAL

EMILE GABORIAU

Yellowbacks

In the age of air travel we have fat novels with glitzy covers which we call 'airport bestsellers'. In the age of railway travel the Victorians had station bookstall literature which they called 'yellowbacks', because they were usually bound in gaudy yellow pictorial boards. This cheap and cheerful reading, published in series such as Routledge's Railway Library, covered the gamut from popular classics to mild (though only mild) pornography. It also included a flood of books presented as the reminiscences of real policemen but actually fiction written by hacks.

William Russell was the pioneer with *Recollections of a Detective Police-Officer*, written under the guise of 'Waters'. Already serialized in a magazine between 1849 and 1853, it first appeared as a yellowback in 1856 and was many times reprinted. Russell went on to write *Experiences of a French Detective Officer* 'adapted from the MSS. of Theodore Duhamel' (1861), *Experiences of a Real Detective* 'by Inspector F' (1862) and *The Autobiography of an English Detective* (1863). By then he had competition from 'Charles Martel' (really Thomas Delf), who wrote *The Detective's Note Book* (1860) and *The Diary of an Ex-Detective* (1960), and 'Andrew Forrester, Jr.', who wrote *Revelations of a Private Detective* (1863), *Secret Service or Recollections of a City Detective* (1864) and, with great versatility, *The Female Detective* (1864).

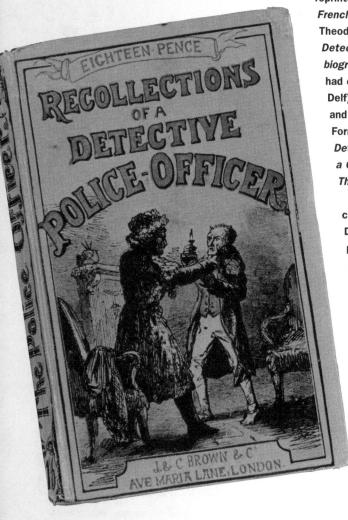

These books sought to capitalize on the press coverage which the Metropolitan Police's new Detective Department was attracting and on the popularity which Vidocq's *Mémoires* continued to enjoy. So it was fitting that the original *Recollections* by Waters should have crossed the Channel to France, where it appeared as *Mémoires d'un policeman*, apparently in 1868, as well as the Atlantic to the United States, where it joined the tradition of 'dime novels' which appeared under Allan Pinkerton's name from the 1870s onwards. Waters also gives a good idea of how people in Britain had come to view police detectives by the middle of the nineteenth century.

The FEMALE DETECTIVE

At first sight, not much has changed since Vidocq. Waters, like Vidocq, reforms or discovers his vocation only after a misspent youth, though he is at pains to stress that his peccadilloes before joining the police were only mild extravagances, unlike the crimes which earned Vidocq his sentences in prison. Being a detective, it appears, still requires mastery of disguise more than any other skill. Waters has colleagues who can feign drunkenness or otherwise transform themselves at a moment's notice, and in the course of the *Recollections* he himself appears as a 'heavy and elderly, well-to-do personage' with 'a flaxen wig, broad-brimmed hat, green spectacles, and a multiplicity of waistcoats and shawls', a fashionable dandy, a Cockney dog-stealer complete with stolen dog, and even a convict's wife. He can get away with cross-dressing only in a dim light, but his impersonation of the dog-stealer is so convincing that 'my own wife, when I entered the breakfast parlour just previous to starting, screamed with alarm and surprise.'

This theatrical flair may remind the reader of Vidocq, but the context in which it is exercised does not. Vidocq the detective, quite as much as Vidocq the criminal, had been an adventurer risking his life among other adventurers. He had no family life and no room for what the Victorians called the 'domestic sentiments'. Waters does. When a case requires him to set off in the morning carrying his pistols, he kisses his wife a particularly fond goodbye. When he is captured by criminals, he thinks immediately of her and his children. In fact, he is every bit as domesticated as his contemporary, Inspector Bucket in *Bleak House*. Becoming a police detective after a reckless youth involves not switching from one kind of excitement to another but settling down into domesticity and middle-class respectability.

That indicates a very different attitude to detection, untainted by greed. Though Waters is available for private hire (like other early policemen in fiction and real life), he sees himself as working not for money but for the public good. 'Police or Peace Officers are the life-guards of the sleeping realm, without whom chambers would not be safe, nor the strong law of more potency than a bulrush,' says the motto on the title page of the *Recollections*. Though Waters likes to spring traps for cunning criminals, he does not see himself as the zealous predator. Instead, he delights in uniting young lovers, defending helpless women and, particularly, exonerating the falsely accused. 'My duty,' he insists, 'was quite as much the vindication of innocence as the detection of guilt.' His words proclaim a sympathetic, potentially even sentimental, view of the detective's work which other Victorians would be quick to exploit – not just writers of later yellowbacks but playwrights like Tom Taylor, in *The Ticket-of-Leave Man*, and after them, of course, Sir Arthur Conan Doyle.

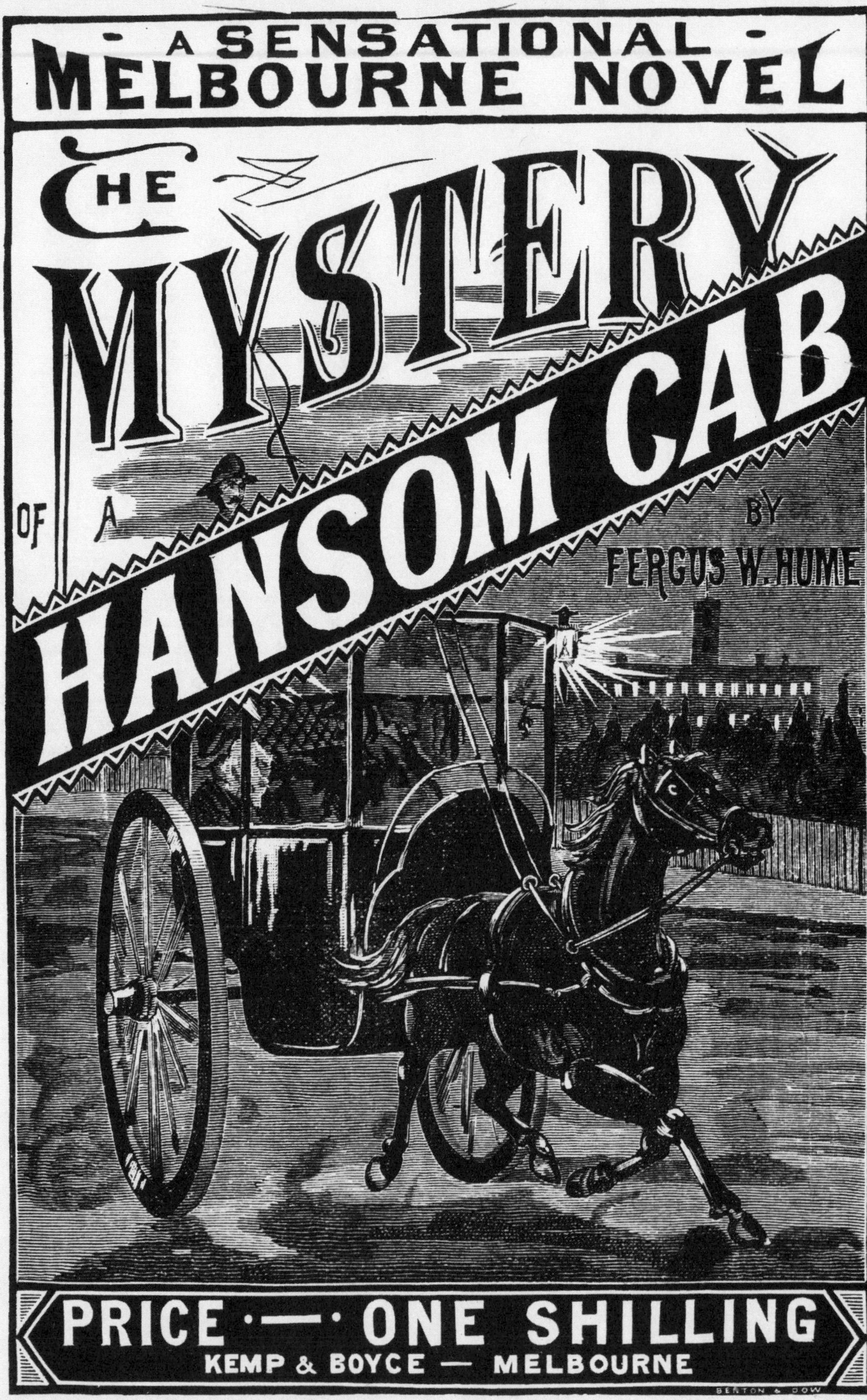

- A SENSATIONAL -
MELBOURNE NOVEL

THE MYSTERY
OF A
HANSOM CAB

BY
FERGUS W. HUME

PRICE · — · ONE SHILLING

KEMP & BOYCE — MELBOURNE

A Surprise Bestseller

THE MYSTERY OF A HANSOM CAB

By the 1880s novels dealing with crime and mystery appealed to a growing appetite among readers, but (then as now) even publishers found it hard to predict which particular title lightning would actually strike. Certainly, nobody could have foreseen that the big bestseller in the years immediately before Sherlock Holmes would come from an obscure writer in Australia. Fergus Hume had emigrated from Britain to New Zealand, where he trained as a lawyer, before moving on to Melbourne. There he abandoned his original hope of making his mark as a playwright and, noticing how well Gaboriau's novels were selling in the local shops, turned his hand to crime fiction instead. But booksellers were no more interested in local work than theatre managers, early Australians preferring to get their culture (or at least their reading) from Europe. So Hume published *The Mystery of a Hansom Cab* himself in 1886.

The first edition of about 5,000 copies sold quickly enough to justify several more printings which brought the sales up to an impressive 35,000. A group of speculators bought the rights to the novel and, under the imprint of The Hansom Cab Publishing Company, issued it the following year in London. There its success was immediate and resounding: by the time he came to write a new preface in 1898, Hume could point to sales of 375,000 copies in Britain, without taking several American editions into account. However, he himself had hardly profited from his success, since he had sold the rights for a mere £50. Nor, though he moved back to Britain and published well over a hundred more thrillers, did he manage to repeat it, not even with the hopefully titled *The Mystery of a Motor Cab* (1908).

Critics and historians have often been at a loss to explain why *The Mystery of a Hansom Cab* should have been a bestseller. This certainly had little to do with literary merit or even technical skill, for Hume had difficulty achieving his goal of providing readers with 'a mystery, a murder, and a description of low life in Melbourne'. The murderer's identity, he confessed engagingly in his 1898 preface, was so obvious in his first draft that he had been forced to cobble together a new ending with a new murderer. (And even then he still had not learned the arts of concealment, since he mentioned both names in his preface.) But outside Australia, the novel's origin and location were a selling point rather than a setback: they lent it novelty. And above all, the book had a striking title. It conjured up the same urban romance that Conan Doyle would exploit with Sherlock Holmes, whose first published adventure, *A Study in Scarlet,* also involves a mystery of a hansom cab.

BEETON'S CHRISTMAS ANNUAL

A STUDY IN SCARLET

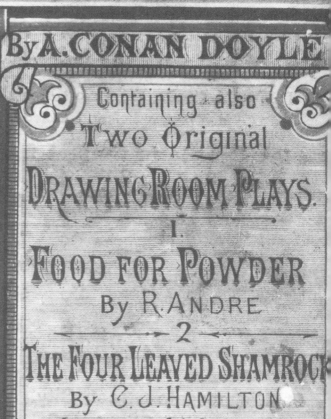

By A. CONAN DOYLE

Containing also
Two Original
DRAWING ROOM PLAYS.
I.
FOOD FOR POWDER
By R. ANDRE
2
THE FOUR LEAVED SHAMROCK
By C. J. HAMILTON
With ENGRAVINGS

Chapter 2
THE GREAT DETECTIVE

THE DEBT TO DUPIN

'You have been in Afghanistan, I perceive,' Sherlock Holmes remarks on first meeting Dr Watson at the beginning of *A Study in Scarlet.* Throwing out arresting little deductions about people on the basis of a casual encounter will turn out to be part of his stock-in-trade, as well as a natural consequence of his restless curiosity. It establishes his authority with clients – and readers too, of course – even before the case gets underway. But in *A Study in Scarlet* readers have to wait a chapter and a half, which Watson spends puzzling over the mysterious habits of his new flatmate and wondering what his profession might be, before Holmes reveals how he made the deduction about Afghanistan. Watson, he explains, has the look of both a medical and a military man, so he was no doubt an army doctor. He is suntanned, and he bears the mark of a recent injury. Where else could an army doctor then have seen active service in a hot climate but in Afghanistan?

The logic is compelling, or at least compelling enough to pass muster in a novel. But that is not quite how Watson chooses to put it:

'It is simple enough as you explain it,' I said smiling. 'You remind me of Edgar Allan Poe's Dupin. I had no idea that such individuals did exist outside of stories.'

Sherlock Holmes rose and lit his pipe. 'No doubt you think that you are complimenting me in comparing me to Dupin,' he observed. 'Now, in my opinion, Dupin was a very inferior fellow.'

This is in fact Conan Doyle's oblique way of paying tribute to Dupin's creator. Dupin disparaged his most famous predecessor, Vidocq, in a similar manner. For good measure Conan Doyle has Holmes continue with a few words dismissing Gaboriau's Lecoq as well: apart from his energy, the French policeman was, it seems, 'a miserable bungler' whose slow-wittedness could spin a case out to unnecessary length. That is more than a little unfair, particularly since *A Study in Scarlet* itself – like all the Sherlock Holmes novels except *The Hound of the Baskervilles* – unwisely follows Gaboriau in adopting a broken-backed structure which divides the narrative into two halves: the detective investigates and solves the case in the first, while the second gives a lengthy flashback of the past events which led to the crime.

Holmes is always at his best in the short stories. There, no reader could fail to be struck by how much Conan Doyle has borrowed from Poe and how happily he has enriched it. The debt begins with the central premise: a brilliant but eccentric detective who practises his own distinctive methods and an admiring friend who tells the story of their adventures together. Yet one only has to look at how Conan Doyle has transformed the character of the friend to appreciate the enrichment. Dupin's friend and chronicler does not even have a name: he is just a pallid version of Dupin himself, like Dupin in his nocturnal habits and his bookish tastes but without a genius for detection. After a

Sherlock Holmes may be world-famous but his career began modestly with *A Study in Scarlet*, first published in *Beeton's Christmas Annual* for 1887, and *The Sign of Four* (1890). His reputation was made by the short stories which appeared in *The Strand Magazine* from July 1891 onwards.

**Examining the body
of the victim in *A
Study in Scarlet*: a
bowler-hatted
Holmes** (above)**,
portrayed by George
Hutchinson, and a
top-hatted Holmes,
by James Greig.**

shaky-sounding start under the dandified
name of 'Ormond Sacker' in Conan
Doyle's notes for *A Study in Scarlet*,
Watson quickly becomes distinctive in his
own right, as Holmes' temperamental
opposite: solid in his conventionality, his
predictability and his loyalty, his average
intelligence untouched by imagination
or genius. It is as impossible to imagine
Sherlock Holmes without Dr Watson as
to imagine Cervantes' Don Quixote
without Sancho Panza or Dickens' Mr
Pickwick without Sam Weller.

The possibilities latent in this
marriage, or mismarriage, of opposites
sustained Conan Doyle in giving his
creations a far longer career than Poe
ever gave his. Poe published three stories
in four years. Conan Doyle published
four novels and fifty-six short stories
over some forty years. And he announced
his transformation of the bloodless and
theoretical world of the Dupin stories
even as he deliberately invoked the
memory of them in that early exchange
about Afghanistan. Holmes' description
of Dupin as 'inferior' – others might
have called him insufferable – signals
the arrival of not just another genius on
the scene but another arrogant genius.
His arrogance, however, makes him
potentially comic in a way that was
inconceivable of Dupin. All Poe's jokes

(never very funny and sometimes
gratingly unfunny) are at the expense of
Dupin's detractors, but Holmes himself
has just been made the butt of a joke
that will run and run throughout his
adventures. When he explains how he has
reached one of his startling deductions,
he is always liable to receive not the
admiration which greets Dupin but the
reaction conjurers get when they explain
how they pulled the rabbit out of the hat:
it's easy when you know how it's done.

From the start, then, Conan Doyle
located Holmes in a human and social
comedy which has room for sly little
jokes. He soon realized that the essence of
such jokes does not stale with repetition,
and he added various familiar routines to
his stock: the moments when Holmes'
vanity is wounded by compliments to
his greatness failing to materialize, for
example, or when Watson's hope that he

Holmes and Watson on their way to Dartmoor to investigate the disappearance of the racehorse Silver Blaze. Illustration by Sidney Paget for *The Strand Magazine*.

has learned to imitate Holmes' methods is dashed yet again. As time went by, Conan Doyle found room for affection, too. The early Holmes can be savage in his contempt for Watson's ineptness at detection, but the late Holmes comes close to tears when his friend is wounded. Affection had no more place than good jokes in the coldly intense atmosphere of Poe's art, but jokes and affection are as much a part of the fabric of the Holmes stories as mysteries and their solution. Quite as much as the plots, these are what have made the stories endure.

ART AND REASON

The forty years Conan Doyle spent writing the Sherlock Holmes stories brought about more changes than a growth in affection between, and sometimes towards, his characters.

NAPOLEONS OF CRIME

'He is the Napoleon of crime, Watson. He is the organizer of half that is evil and of nearly all that is undetected in this great city. He is a genius, a philosopher, an abstract thinker. He has a brain of the first order. He sits motionless, like a spider in the centre of its web, but that web has a thousand radiations, and he knows well every quiver of each of them.'

So Holmes describes Professor Moriarty near the beginning of 'The Final Problem', the story which ended *The Memoirs of Sherlock Holmes* (1894). Moriarty was, of course, Conan Doyle's device for killing Holmes off and freeing himself to pursue more serious writing (or so he hoped). But Moriarty could not remain just a device. If the great detective had to die, he had to die at the hands of a worthy foe. So Conan Doyle, prompted by memories of Dupin's opponent the Minister D— in Poe's 'The Purloined Letter' and of the suave Count Fosco in Wilkie Collins' *The Woman in White*, created in Moriarty a criminal who is to crime what Holmes himself is to detection. Moriarty (we are told) is a subtle strategist, a scientific genius and a master of disguise. In short, he is Holmes' *alter ego* or deformed twin, a symbiotic relationship dramatically embodied in the deadly embrace which plunges them over the Reichenbach Falls together.

Moriarty played a disproportionate role in the popular mythology which quickly grew up around the Sherlock Holmes stories – through, for example, William Gillette's stage melodrama (1899) and the silent films derived from it. Indeed, Moriarty's influence was almost as wide as that of Holmes himself. It became the fashion for the master-detective to have a master-criminal opposing him. G.K. Chesterton, for example, pitted Father Brown against Flambeau, a 'colossus of crime ... as statuesque and international as the Kaiser'. The metaphysical logic of the Father Brown stories required that Flambeau should quickly repent of his ways and become the priest's friend and assistant. Other writers had already spotted the advantages of making the master-criminal a series character in his own right, forever scheming and forever avoiding defeat, like Dr Nikola in the series of five novels Guy Boothby began with *A Bid for Fortune, or Dr Nikola's Vendetta* (1895).

Holmes had compared Moriarty to a spider. Invoking witches and their familiars, Boothby gave Dr Nikola a black cat as his constant companion. Sinister pets became a standard motif as villains grew more and more exotic in their perversity. In fact, they grew far more colourful than the heroes, no longer portrayed as eccentric geniuses, like Sherlock Holmes, but as bluff English gentlemen with stiff upper lips and strong right hooks. In Sapper's novels Bulldog Drummond still manages to hold the stage against Carl Peterson, but in Sax Rohmer's novels Nayland Smith looks pale and unmemorable beside Dr Fu-Manchu. These villains are extravagant in their goals too, aiming not just to control the criminal underworld but to destroy civilization as we know it. Such ambitions reflect the popular fear of Bolshevism and the Yellow Peril between the two World Wars, just as the villains of Ian Fleming's James Bond stories spoke to the anxieties of the Cold War.

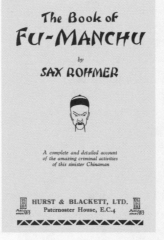

The Book of
FU-MANCHU
by
SAX ROHMER

*A complete and detailed account
of the amazing criminal activities
of this sinister Chinaman*

HURST & BLACKETT, LTD.
Paternoster House, E.C.4

Three arch-villains: Holmes' enemy Professor Moriarty (as depicted by Sidney Paget), Guy Boothby's cat-loving Dr Nikola, and Sax Rohmer's Dr Fu-Manchu, the personification of the Yellow Peril.

This was inevitable, if only because when he first conceived Holmes and Watson he had no means of knowing their adventures would grow to such proportions. When he wrote *A Study in Scarlet* he was still a young man, struggling in both his chosen professions as author and doctor. The novel attracted little notice, either on its appearance in *Beeton's Christmas Annual* in 1887 or on its reappearance in book form the following year, and Conan Doyle had every reason to suppose he was finished with Holmes. It was only the accident of a contract from the American publisher Lippincott which revived the detective for a second novel, *The Sign of Four* (1890).

Success came with the first series of short stories for *The Strand Magazine*, collected as *The Adventures of Sherlock Holmes* (1892). But by the time of the second series, collected as *The Memoirs of Sherlock Holmes* (1894), he had resolved to get rid of Holmes and invented Professor Moriarty for the purpose in 'The Final Problem'. Popular outcry, coupled with lavish financial offers from publishers, made him first produce *The Hound of the Baskervilles* (1901–02), an adventure set retrospectively before Moriarty's arrival on the scene, and then bring Holmes back from his watery grave at the Reichenbach Falls in 'The Adventure of the Empty House', the first of the stories collected in *The Return of Sherlock Holmes* (1905). Thereafter Conan Doyle turned intermittently and with professed reluctance to Holmes, like a man at once adding afterthoughts to a national monument and making deposits in his pension fund. The results were a novel, *The Valley of Fear* (1914–15), and two more collections of the stories which *The Strand Magazine* continued to publish, *His Last Bow* (1917) and *The Case Book of Sherlock Holmes* (1927).

There is a scholarly treatise yet to be written on the relationship which can develop between a writer and a character invented for a specific occasion but retained as a series character and grown into a near-lifelong companion. The history of detective fiction is particularly rich in examples: the names of Maigret and Lord Peter Wimsey immediately add themselves to the list which begins with Holmes. Weariness and impatience prevented Conan Doyle from simply growing old gracefully with his creation, as Simenon did, or trying to turn two flimsy dimensions into three solid ones, as Dorothy L. Sayers did. But he could not resist the obvious temptation (countless later writers have surrendered to it as well) of making his character more and more resemble himself. Inevitably, that meant making Sherlock Holmes nicer.

Despite the genial comedy which crept in from the start of *A Study in Scarlet*, Conan Doyle originally conceived his detective as a cold fish, in much the same way and for much the same reason that Dupin is a cold fish. When he does eventually get round to telling Watson he is 'a consulting detective', Holmes presents himself above all as the exponent of a theory and the practitioner of a method of detection. These do not require the sort of elaborate introductory essay Poe offered at the beginning of 'The Murders in the Rue Morgue' because they were less original to Conan Doyle and more familiar to his readers. The theory is essentially the theory of scientific rationalism, the method that of diagnostic medicine. Conan Doyle himself had learned both in his time at the University of Edinburgh, where he had been particularly impressed by Dr Joseph Bell, whom he no doubt had in mind as a rough model for Holmes when he sat down to write *A Study in Scarlet*.

Holmes awaits the final confrontation with Professor Moriarty at the Reichenbach Falls. 'It was the last that I was ever destined to see of him in this world,' wrote Watson, not foreseeing that Holmes would come back to life for further adventures. Illustration by Sidney Paget to 'The Final Problem'.

'He Takes My Mind from Better Things'

When the *Punch* cartoonist Bernard Partridge chose to portray Conan Doyle gloomily shackled to his most famous creation, he did no more than express a view the writer sometimes took of his own career. Conan Doyle had originally welcomed the success of Sherlock Holmes as an opportunity to give up the attempt to establish himself as a Harley Street oculist and throw himself into full-time writing: 'No longer would I have to conform to professional dress or to please anyone else. I would be free to live how I liked and where I liked. It was one of the great moments of exaltation of my life.' Yet even before the first series of *Strand* stories had run its course he was writing to his mother: 'I think of slaying Holmes in the last and winding him up for good and all. He takes my mind from better things.' She prevailed on him to hold his hand for the time being and, when he did kill Holmes off in 'The Final Problem', the plea to revive him was joined by the powerful voice of popular demand – that and the huge sums magazine editors were willing to pay for stories from best-selling writers.

Yet what were those 'better things' from which the success of Sherlock Holmes deflected, or was forever threatening to deflect, him? In an age which had inordinate respect for historical fiction – educational, even uplifting stuff by comparison to potboilers about detectives – he took particular pride in novels such as *Micah Clarke*, *Rodney Stone*, *The White Company* and *Sir Nigel*. He certainly put selfless energy, something he never lacked, into his histories of the Boer War and the campaign on the Western front in the First World War. But (since Scottish comparisons are always apt in understanding Conan Doyle) he was only a minor Robert Louis Stevenson as a historical novelist and only a minor John Buchan as an official historian of war. Of his other gifts, a talent for comedy enlivens the Brigadier Gerard and a talent for horror the Professor Challenger stories, but never so effectively or with such control as in the very work he most resented.

That is to speak only of his strictly literary achievements. But Sherlock Holmes had made Conan Doyle a public figure and given him the chance to exercise his gifts in other spheres. On the surface, the most conventional of Edwardian gentlemen – Dr Watson to a tee, one would say at first glance – he nevertheless had the quixotic passion and the ability to swim against the tide of popular opinion with which he had endowed Holmes. His opinions on criminal cases of the day naturally found a ready audience, but they were not delivered by a criminologist or a detective, much less by a man who confused himself with his own fictional creation. They were the work of a campaigner and a controversialist. It was in this spirit that he took up the cause of George Edalji, a half-Indian solicitor convicted in 1903 of maiming cattle but really a victim of racial harassment from his neighbours and prejudice from the police. And it was in the same spirit that he battled to vindicate Oscar Slater – another ready scapegoat, as a German Jew with a record as a pimp – when he was wrongfully convicted of the Glasgow murder of Marion Gilchrist in 1908.

If these two *causes célèbres* were Britain's equivalents of France's Dreyfus Affair, then Conan Doyle deserves to be remembered as the closest thing Britain had to Emile Zola. He himself explained his willingness to appear in the role by his belief in fair play, the cherished virtue of the Edwardian gentleman. But it also required qualities Edwardian gentlemen did not commonly possess: a lack of bigotry (or at least the ability to set bigotry aside, for Conan Doyle had the prejudices of his age and generation) together with a readiness to criticize the guardians of the Establishment in the harshest terms. So his campaigns against miscarriages of justice also prepared him for the ardent promotion of spiritualism which occupied the last years of his life, draining his energies as well as his purse, using up every ounce of credit the Holmes stories had won him, and excluding him from the safe role in public life which would otherwise have awaited him.

Conan Doyle enslaved by Sherlock Holmes:
Bernard Partridge's *Punch* cartoon.

Holmes insists on the principle of natural law as resolutely as any post-Darwinian scientist. 'From a drop of water,' he argues, 'a logician could infer the possibility of an Atlantic or a Niagara without having seen or heard of one or the other. So all life is a great chain, the nature of which is known whenever we are shown a single link of it.' In practice, his approach depends on observing those details about people which reveal their trades and callings or, like Watson's wound and suntan, speak of their past. To him the scenes of crimes – indeed, virtually any scene that life can present – are rich in evidence which goes far beyond bloodstains or footprints. Far-reaching conclusions can be drawn from apparently trivial discrepancies like the soiled knees of the shop assistant's trousers in 'The Red-Headed League', or the dog that did not bark in the night in 'Silver Blaze', or the contents of the dead man's room in *The Valley of Fear*. 'Dear me, Watson,' Holmes chides his long-suffering colleague in that novel, 'is it possible that you have not penetrated the fact that the case hangs upon the missing dumb-bell?'

In the early days, Holmes' commitment to scientific method is so consuming that he betrays near-total ignorance of anything outside his immediate concerns. Before he learns Holmes' profession Watson is left pondering the disparity between his new friend's grasp of chemistry ('Profound'), anatomy ('Accurate, but unsystematic') and sensational literature ('Immense') and the state of his information about politics ('Feeble'), literature ('Nil') and philosophy ('Nil'). Holmes even lectures Watson on the need to keep his mind unencumbered by irrelevant knowledge. Later, of course, he will be credited with expertise in all sorts of esoteric subjects: not just the hundred and forty varieties of tobacco ash or the different newspaper typefaces in common use, which have some passing relevance to his work, but (for instance) the ancient Cornish language and the compositions of Lassus. Eventually Holmes sets the fashion for later fictional detectives in showing a weakness for literary quotation.

Even after Holmes' character has been softened from its original severity, he is still given to insisting, like Dupin, that he pursues his inquiries in the name of science and his own pleasure, indifferent to any ideal of justice or to the niceties of other people's feelings. So single-minded is he that, at the beginning of *The Sign of Four*, he can trace the history of Watson's alcoholic brother from the evidence of the man's watch without any thought for the pain he might be causing. Quite late in his career, at the beginning of 'The Adventure of the Norwood Builder' in *The Return*, he can still lament the

Opposite **Holmes the aesthete, falling into a reverie over a rose in 'The Naval Treaty'. Illustration for** *The Strand Magazine* **by Sidney Paget.**

A dashing Holmes, accompanied by Dr Watson, discovers the body of Bartholomew Sholto in *The Sign of Four*.

absence of interesting criminals in London since the death of Moriarty. Clinical dispassion and egotism never entirely disappear from his nature, and the affection for Watson he occasionally betrays never quite eradicates the impression that he is a cold fish.

Dupin's dedication had been not just that of the scientist but also that of the artist practising art for its own sake. Conan Doyle began writing about Holmes in the 1880s, so it was almost inevitable that he should develop Poe's hint and make his detective look like one of the Aesthetes and Decadents who dominated the artistic world of the day. Even the title of *A Study in Scarlet*, which Holmes himself proposes to Watson, could be the title of a painting by Whistler or a poem by Oscar Wilde. The case itself resembles one of these works, since – like all Holmes' cases – it is striking and bizarre, and it induces in him a heightening of the senses. His pursuit of excitement, like the fear of boredom and the contempt for ordinary life that inevitably go with it, are entirely of a piece with the attitudes contemporary artists were proclaiming. By the same token, even Holmes' personal habits – his addiction to cocaine and his love of extemporizing wildly on the violin – echo the extravagant behaviour by which the artistic temperament then liked to announce itself.

THE LAST COURT OF APPEAL

Decadence, like scientism, never disappears entirely from Holmes' make-up, but it is greatly modified from the time of the first *Strand* series onwards. This was only prudent after Wilde's trials and public humiliation in 1895. But the real reason for the changes which overtake Holmes went much deeper.

SCIENCE AND
SHERLOCK HOLMES

'I've found it! I've found it,' cries Sherlock Holmes on
his very first appearance, in *A Study in Scarlet*. 'I have
found a re-agent which is precipitated by haemoglobin,
and by nothing else.' Too excited to go through the
motions of greeting his future chronicler Dr Watson
formally, he launches into an explanation of how his
new test for bloodstains will revolutionize crimino-
logical science. But that is the the last we hear of
it, even though *A Study in Scarlet* goes on to make
considerable play with the mysterious slogan found
written in blood on the wall beside Enoch J. Drebber's
corpse. Conan Doyle might have presented Holmes as
the embodiment of scientific rationalism and the
champion of its deductive method but he showed little
interest in scientific details and none in making them
essential to his plots. Like Holmes' violin-playing or
his monograph on the Chaldean roots of the ancient
Cornish language, they are incidental touches thrown
in to add to his glamour and authority. When they
are at all precise, they show both Conan Doyle and
Holmes to be distinctly out of touch with the develop-
ments of their day.

In fact, forensic science was less concerned with
finding a satisfactory test for human blood – which
would not come until decades later with the haemo-
chromogen test – than with criminal identification. This
was a far more urgent matter in an age when police
records still could not prevent habitual criminals from
appearing before the courts under a succession of
assumed names. The first great advance came from
Alphonse Bertillon (1853–1914) and the system he

called *anthropométrie*, but which the French public
preferred to call *bertillonage*. It consisted of an elaborate system of measurements – height, the length and
breadth of the head, the length of different fingers, the
length of forearms and feet, and so forth – all entered,
with photos of the subject's full face and profile, on
what Bertillon called a *portrait parlé* which in turn
became part of a card-index system. At first derided,
Bertillon's work was acknowledged when the French
police authorities adopted anthropometry in 1885.
Most other European countries were quick to follow
suit. So it comes as no surprise to be told in 'The Naval
Treaty', first published in 1893, that Holmes holds
Bertillon in 'enthusiastic admiration'. In *The Hound of
the Baskervilles* Holmes reacts with chagrin when Dr

Mortimer ranks him second to Bertillon in expertise, but this is more out of wounded vanity than any loss of regard for the Frenchman.

Yet by then Bertillon was on his way to being discredited. He had fatally wounded his reputation by testifying, as a handwriting expert, to the guilt of the accused in the Dreyfus affair. And anthropometry was already betraying its practical disadvantages: the measurements on which it depended were too complex to be entrusted to police and prison functionaries, and the card-index system that resulted could prove unwieldy. In Britain, where the system had been adopted only with cautious modifications, Sir Francis Galton (1822–1911) had lent his authority and his energy in the 1890s to reviving interest in the ancient practice of fingerprinting. Bertillon recorded fingerprints on his *portraits parlés* but without believing in their value. It was left to Sir Edward Richard Henry (1850–1931) to supply what had eluded Galton by proposing a convenient way of classifying fingerprints into plain arches, tented arches, radial loops, ulnar loops and whorls. The breakthrough persuaded Scotland Yard to make the decisive change from Bertillon's system in 1901, the very year when Conan Doyle began to publish the serialized version of *The Hound of the Baskervilles*.

So what does Holmes have to say about fingerprints? Nothing at all until 'The Adventure of the Norwood Builder', which appeared in 1903. 'You are aware that no two thumb-marks are alike?' asks Inspector Lestrade. 'I have heard something of the kind,' Holmes replies enigmatically. But the thumb-mark in question, not just the first but the only fingerprint to appear in the stories, is no vital clue pointing towards the solution. It is a deliberate red herring left by the criminal. Relying on fingerprint evidence, it seems, is part of the bureaucratic approach that so frequently leads dull policemen like Lestrade astray. When he exposes their error, Holmes also contrives to explain away in a mere sentence the burned corpse which the criminal has fabricated as well: 'I daresay that a couple of rabbits would account both for the blood and for the charred ashes.' R. Austin Freeman's Dr Thorndyke would have blushed to utter such airy nonsense. But, uniquely among Conan Doyle's imitators, Freeman set out to do precisely what the master did not attempt: to show not just the enthusiasm or single-minded dedication of the scientist but the detail of his working methods in the laboratory as well.

Arthur Wontner showing that the Great Detective can smoke his pipe and play the violin at the same time. Wontner first appeared on screen as Holmes in *The Sleeping Cardinal* **(1930, called** *Sherlock Holmes' Fatal Hour* **in USA), loosely based on 'The Adventure of the Empty House'.**

Conan Doyle himself had little in common with the pleasure-seeking Decadent, any more than he had with the cold-blooded scientist. He was a passionate and impulsive man, but he yoked his passions and impulses to the values of the conventional late-Victorian and Edwardian gentleman. When the later Holmes speaks of practising detection for its own sake he means simply that he is indifferent to public praise or reward, and he takes his language from the cricket field rather than the artist's studio: 'I play the game for the game's own sake'.

These words come from 'The Adventure of the Bruce-Partington Plans', which originally appeared in 1908 before being collected in *His Last Bow*. Holmes may begin the story by lamenting the dullness of London criminals but he is already human enough in his sympathies to respond to Watson's loyal assistance with 'something in his eyes which was nearer to tenderness than I had ever seen'. The adventure itself, with its background of politics and espionage, calls on his patriotism and rewards it with an audience at Windsor. Holmes, of course, is suitably discreet about what passed on that occasion or how it left him feeling: actually voicing warm and noble sentiment is still very much Watson's department. Yet Conan Doyle makes it perfectly clear that beneath the 'cold mask' the detective chooses to adopt there beats a heart generous and patriotic like his own.

In fact, Holmes has for some years been doing much more than practise detection for its own sake. Quite as much as a solver of puzzles in the name of science or his own amusement, he has long since been a defender of the helplessly endangered or the falsely accused. Indeed, such clients always make up the bulk of his practice. The most memorable ones, inevitably, are women in need of protection from men whose villainy shows no respect for the fairer sex: the list stretches from the wicked Dr Grimesby Roylott's stepdaughter in 'The Adventure of the Speckled Band' and the governess in 'The Adventure of the Copper Beeches' to the slandered wife, 'the best woman God ever made', in 'The Problem of Thor Bridge'. It may be Watson who voices the chivalrous impulse, as well as betraying a roving eye for a pretty woman, but it is Holmes who brings the real reassurance, rescue or vindication.

Holmes comforts a distressed female client in 'The Adventure of the Solitary Cyclist'. Illustration by Sidney Paget.

Mid-Victorian writers had first stressed this aspect of the detective's role as a way of reassuring their audiences that policemen, though bureaucrats and hirelings of the state, could still be impeccable in their sympathies and moral values. Conan Doyle likewise firmly identified the private detective as upholder of a private code, a code of justice above the law and outside its official machinery. Holmes himself grandly proclaims this function as early as 'The Five Orange Pips', where he tells a distressed client: 'I am the last court of appeal'. Being the last court of appeal often means that Holmes exposes the errors and rights the potential injustices of policemen such as Inspector Lestrade, whose role is still, as it had been in Poe's work, to get things wrong every time.

On occasion, though, Holmes takes the law into his own hands. He several times invites Watson to join him in a little high-spirited breaking and entering to advance the investigation, and Watson is always ready to tag along. Things go rather further in 'The Adventure of Charles Augustus Milverton', when the pair end up conniving at the murder of a blackmailer. In withholding his help from the authorities, Holmes firmly tells Lestrade: 'I think there are certain crimes which the law cannot touch, and which therefore, to some extent justify private revenge'.

Edwardian gentlemen (like Conan Doyle himself) were always willing to back their notion of what constituted fair play over what anybody else said, particularly a mere policeman or judge. And, of course, they did so in the reassuring knowledge that the authorities would usually be unable or unwilling to punish them for their stand. At the end of 'The Adventure of the Illustrious Client', which has seen one of Holmes and

Watson's illegal expeditions go disastrously wrong, Watson can report:

Sherlock Holmes was threatened with a prosecution for burglary, but when an object is good and a client is sufficiently illustrious, even the rigid British law becomes human and elastic. My friend has not yet stood in the dock.

These words may seem to smack entirely of the values of their time and place, and not in a particularly pleasant way. Yet the idea of the detective as chivalric knight-errant and, on occasion, private enforcer of rough justice long outlived Conan Doyle. American writers of hard-boiled fiction, from Chandler to Mickey Spillane and Andrew Vachss, would make it their continual theme.

By the end of his career Holmes can act not just as policeman or judge but also as ultimate spiritual authority. Conan Doyle never completely dropped Holmes' scientific rationalism: Holmes continues to scorn the supernatural, exploding superstitions about spectral hounds or vampires whenever he encounters them. But when one client speaks of his power to bring 'light into the darkness' she plainly has the relief of spiritual distress in mind rather than just scientific clarification or practical help. In 'The Adventure of Charles Augustus Milverton' Holmes lets a murderer go free. In 'The Veiled Lodger', among the last stories Conan Doyle ever wrote, Holmes does not even detect anything. He simply hears a murderer's unsolicited confession, counsels her and, implicitly, absolves her. What greater or more godlike heights of power could a detective aspire to?

The game's afoot! Holmes, Watson and the mysterious spy at the beginning of *The Hound of the Baskervilles*. Illustration by Sidney Paget.

THE SHERLOCK HOLMES BOOKSHELF

The cornerstone of any collection must surely be W.S. Baring-Gould's two-volume *The Annotated Sherlock Holmes* (1968), equipped both with early illustrations and a commentary that will engage even those who thought they already knew the novels and stories well. The vast attendant bibliography is provided in Ronald Burt De Waal's *The World Bibliography of Sherlock Holmes and Dr Watson: A Classified and Annotated List of Materials Relating to Their Lives and Adventures* (1974) and its companion volume, *The International Sherlock Holmes* (1980). Those who take pleasure in tongue-in-cheek Holmesian scholarship will want Baring-Gould's *Sherlock Holmes: A Biography of the World's First Consulting Detective* (1962), whose illustrations include photos of Watson and Moriarty in boyhood, or a more recent volume such as June Thomson's *Holmes and Watson: A Study in Friendship* (1995).

Holmesians (as they are known in Britain) or Sherlockians (as they are known in the USA) commonly neglect Conan Doyle himself, reduced in their language to being merely the 'literary agent' and not the author of the stories. A useful corrective is Peter Costello's *The Real World of Sherlock Holmes: The True Crimes Investigated by Arthur Conan Doyle* (1991), which can serve as an introduction to the various biographies, none of them very satisfactory, by Hesketh Pearson (1943), John Dickson Carr (1949), Pierre Nordon (in French, 1964; in English, 1966), Charles Higham (1976), Ronald Pearsall (1977) and Owen Dudley Edwards (1983).

PASTICHE, PARODY, PSEUDO-SCHOLARSHIP AND (inevitably) DECONSTRUCTION

Probably the dreariest accolade popular authors can receive is for the series characters they created to continue, after their death, in books by other hands. Sometimes they themselves even take the trouble to bequeath their creations to a successor, as a valuable part of their literary estate. Sapper did so with Bull-Dog Drummond and Ian Fleming with James Bond. Conan Doyle was too sensible, and cared too little for Sherlock Holmes, to make any such provision. But Holmes was a character for whom the public had an apparently bottomless appetite. Besides, Watson had a habit of referring in passing to cases left unnarrated, usually to avoid scandal or breaches of state secrecy. The world, it appeared, had not then been prepared for the affair of the Vatican cameos or the giant rat of Sumatra or the politician, the lighthouse and the trained cormorant. These hints were too tantalizing to ignore, so Sherlock Holmes survived Conan Doyle's death much as he had survived his creator's attempt to kill him at the Reichenbach Falls, though on both occasions in a rather weakened state. John Dickson Carr collaborated with Conan Doyle's son Adrian to produce the most carefully wrought addition to the canon, *The Exploits of Sherlock Holmes* (1954), while in recent years June Thomson has written *The Secret Files of Sherlock Holmes* (1990), *The Secret Chronicles of Sherlock Holmes* (1992) and *The Secret Journals of Sherlock Holmes* (1993).

These are pastiches, and pastiche is essentially a respectful art. Yet, by its attention to a writer's mannerisms, it lies close in the literary spectrum to parody, which is disrespectful, if usually affectionate. A spur to parody came from the tongue-in-cheek way Conan Doyle himself sometimes treated the myth of the great detective, and from the fun he openly poked at his own characters in the short story 'How Watson Learned the Trick' (1924). Long before Conan Doyle died the challenge had already been taken up by Mark Twain in 'A Double-Barrelled Detective Story' (1902), Bret Harte in 'The Stolen Cigar Case' in

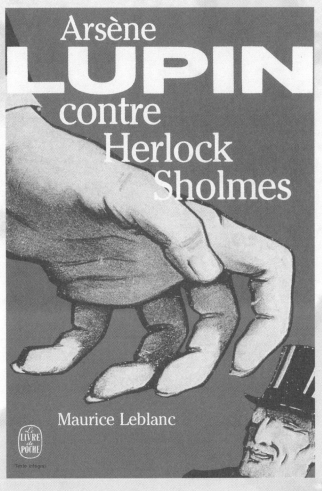

Arsène
LUPIN
contre
Herlock
Sholmes

Maurice Leblanc

Le Livre de Poche
Texte intégral

Maurice Leblanc's stories about a French gentleman crook, which first appeared in 1907, take an irreverent glance at Britain's Great Detective – Herlock Sholmes in French, but Holmlock Shears in the English translation.

Condensed Novels: Second Series (1902), O. Henry in two stories in *Sixes and Sevens* (1911), and Stephen Leacock in 'Maddened by Mystery, or the Defective Detective' in *Nonsense Novels* (1911) and 'An Irreducible Detective Story' in *Further Foolishness* (1916). These first parodies – is it just accident they come from North America? – are undoubtedly the best. Jokes about the great detective being fallible, imperceptive and even more vain than in the original stories quickly wear thin, though this has never deterred the parodists.

Both pastiches and parodies of the Sherlock Holmes stories tend to be written by the initiated for the initiated. They are a sort of fan literature. Another occupation – an industry, indeed – for fans was suggested by Ronald Knox in one of his *Essays in Satire* (1928). 'Studies in the Literature of Sherlock Holmes' applied to Conan Doyle's work the techniques of textual and historical scholarship which the Higher Criticism had brought to the study of the Bible. Why, for example, should John H. Watson's wife address him as James? Were there really two Watsons, as Baenecke had argued? And was 'The Final Problem' genuine, as Sauwosch had maintained? (The Higher Critics were usually German.)

Knox himself professed to believe there were in fact two cycles of stories: the real ones Watson narrated and the imaginary ones he invented. The targets of Knox's satire were the Higher Critics; the beneficiaries of his fun were the Holmesians. Accepting the great detective as a real-life figure, debating questions such as the university he had attended, highlighting and explaining discrepancies in Watson's accounts: these innocent pseudo-scholarly games have remained the staple of all the various Sherlock Holmes societies at their meetings and in their magazines.

For all except the fervently initiate, they pall as quickly as parody. A new direction was announced by Nicholas Meyer's *The Seven-Per-Cent Solution* (1974), a combination of pastiche, parody and pseudo-scholarship which exploited Holmes' cocaine addiction to put him in contact with his contemporary, Freud. Its successor, *The West End Horror* (1976), marked a descent into glib historical spin-off of a sort for which there continues to be a market: witness John Gardner's series beginning with *Moriarty* (1974; also called *The Return of Moriarty*) and M.J. Trow's series beginning with *The Adventures of Inspector Lestrade* (1985). Yet *The Seven-Per-Cent Solution* itself used the traditions of Holmesian writing and pseudo-scholarship to challenge their underlying assent to the myth of the great detective. By doing so it caught the same debunking mood of the times found in Julian Symons' *A Three-Pipe Problem* (1975), about an actor who starts to identify too closely with his TV role as Holmes. A similar notion informs Anthony Harvey's film *They Might Be Giants* (1971), starring George C. Scott.

From debunking it is only a short step to deconstruction as practised by Michael Dibdin in *The Last Sherlock Holmes Story* (1978). Its premise – Sherlock Holmes versus Moriarty, or Sherlock Holmes versus Jack the Ripper, or Sherlock Holmes versus Moriarty as Jack the Ripper – does not sound particularly original to anyone versed in the literature of Sherlock Holmes, to say the least. Moriarty had already reappeared and the detective had already pitted his wits against Jack the Ripper many times in pastiches and films. But Dibdin's premise serves only as the starting point for an investigation, at once learned and subversive, which gives us not just (perhaps) a pseudo-Watson but a pseudo-Moriarty, too, and a thoroughly deconstructed Sherlock Holmes.

Sherlock Holmes on his mind: George C. Scott with Joanne Woodward in *They Might Be Giants* (1971).

PENGUIN BOOKS

PARKER PYNE INVESTIGATES

AGATHA CHRISTIE

Chapter 3
THE GOLDEN AGE

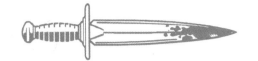

AFTER SHERLOCK HOLMES

The Sherlock Holmes stories soon had their imitators, at least after the success of the first two *Strand* series in the early 1890s. Arthur Morrison, otherwise known for realistic accounts of life in London's East End, created the amiable if deliberately colourless Martin Hewitt. Matthew Phipps Shiel took the Decadent touches in Holmes to extremes with Prince Zaleski. Most ingeniously, though to Conan Doyle's alarm, his own son-in-law E.W. Hornung used the partnership of Holmes and Watson as the model for the gentleman burglar Raffles and his companion Bunny. All these characters appeared on the scene before the turn of the century. None came close to rivalling Holmes in popularity – any more than they rivalled him in staying power – but together they demonstrated how large a public appetite Conan Doyle had stimulated.

The next generation of rivals, appearing before the First World War, was more formidable. Baroness Orczy's Old Man in the Corner and Ernest Bramah's blind Max Carrados deserve to be better remembered, but by any estimate two figures stand out: R. Austin Freeman's Dr Thorndyke and G.K. Chesterton's Father Brown. Where Conan Doyle had been content to deal in the principles of science, and to convey its glamorous aura, Thorndyke's cases involve its details: they depend on bench work and laboratory analysis. Some, notably the stories in the collection *The Singing Bone* (1912; later called *The Adventures of Dr Thorndyke* in USA), are 'inverted tales': they start by narrating how the crime was committed, converting the puzzle from the question of who did it to the question of how the detective will solve it.

Few, if any, writers had the expertise to follow Freeman so deeply into the technicalities of forensic science; many, besides, feared that the result would only strain the reader's patience. But they could all agree on the general lessons that there was no harm in making the technicalities in their stories subtle and that they had better get the details right. The happy days when Holmes could judge a man's intelligence by the size of his hat, or tell which direction a bicycle had travelled from its tyre marks, were numbered. By the same token, Freeman's 'inverted tale' was not often directly imitated but, instead, served as inspiration to those wanting to vary the terms of the puzzle.

The Father Brown stories had a more direct impact, not least in starting a tradition of clerical detectives which still continues. Their great strength lies in the way they embed the detective puzzle in a metaphysical-cum-theological fable without making it any less satisfying as a puzzle. Chesterton's sophistication finds an ideal vehicle in the character of Father Brown himself. With his meek manner, his umbrella and his brown-paper parcels, he is one of the few early detectives, if not the only one, to escape successfully the long shadow cast by Sherlock Holmes.

Agatha Christie, doyenne of the Golden Age writers, created Hercule Poirot and Miss Marple, as well as less memorable detectives such as Parker Pyne (in this 1934 collection of stories), Tommy and Tuppence Beresford, Superintendent Battle and Mr Quin.

The partnership of Holmes and Watson was echoed in the stories by E.W. Hornung, Conan Doyle's brother-in-law, about the gentleman burglar Raffles and his faithful friend Bunny.

Opposite **G.K. Chesterton's Father Brown was the first of a long line of priest-detectives who are not too unworldly to understand the workings of the criminal mind.**

A detective without charisma, without apparent distinction, seemingly without any of the qualities which make a detective: Chesterton's conception would prove as influential as Conan Doyle's.

With Freeman, Chesterton set a standard against which younger writers measured themselves. His influence was immediately felt, for example, in E.C. Bentley's *Trent's Last Case* (1913). Bentley brought something of Chesterton's playfulness to the form: the teasing brilliance of his ending earned the novel classic status. But he also had Chesterton's confidence that detective fiction could carry provocative ideas among its cargo. Not the least interesting aspect of *Trent's Last Case* is the implicit socialist bias informing the story, as indeed it informs the Father Brown stories themselves, which also like to take the murder of an unpleasant millionaire as their starting point.

The work of Freeman, Chesterton and Bentley confirmed the popularity that detective fiction would enjoy after the First World War. Though it would offer entertainment, and take pride in insisting it offered only entertainment, it would also insist that it was intelligent, even stringent and demanding. It could be written and read by people who looked down on 'shockers' like the romantic thrillers of E. Phillips Oppenheim and Sydney Horler or the serial adventures of Nick Carter, which had long since begun to appear in the USA. Detective fiction would take pride in being the preferred relaxation of the educated classes, the bedside reading of British prime ministers and American presidents.

Its flowering between the two World Wars is commonly known as the Golden Age of detective fiction. Historians (such as Howard Haycraft) who brought the label into use liked to confine the Golden Age proper to the 1920s. This, after all, was the decade when Agatha Christie first appeared on the scene with Hercule Poirot, Dorothy L. Sayers with Lord Peter Wimsey and Margery Allingham with Albert Campion. Their names stand out from a host of other writers who enjoyed a briefer fame: Freeman Wills Crofts, H.C. Bailey, Patricia Wentworth, Josephine Tey, Anthony Berkeley (later known under his other pseudonym of Francis Iles), Philip MacDonald, John Rhode, Christopher Bush and Henry Wade. All these writers were British. The USA produced Ellery Queen and S.S. Van Dine, a bigger name than Queen in his day but now forgotten when he is not despised.

The trends established during the 1920s continued in the next decade, though with modifications suggested by Dorothy L. Sayers' resolve to give Wimsey greater depth of character and by Agatha

Christie's introduction of Miss Marple, whom she soon came to prefer to her Belgian detective. The 1930s, too, saw the first appearance of other writers who still have their admirers: John Dickson Carr (under his own name and the pseudonym of Carter Dickson), Michael Innes, Ngaio Marsh and Nicholas Blake (the pseudonym of the poet C. Day Lewis). In the USA Rex Stout created the partnership of Nero Wolfe and Archie Goodwin in stories whose difference in flavour from S.S. Van Dine's Philo Vance novels is another way of marking the change from the 1920s to the 1930s.

Virtually all these authors were still writing after 1939, and new writers in essentially the same vein continued to emerge. Edmund Crispin, whose work breathes the spirit of the Golden Age, published his first novel near the end of the Second World War. The Golden Age was a long time a-dying. Indeed, one could argue that it still is not dead, since its mannerisms have proved stubbornly persistent in writers one might have expected to abandon them altogether as dated, or worse. Yet the Second World War marked a significant close, just as the First World War had marked a significant beginning. Only during the inter-war years, and particularly in the 1920s, did Golden Age fiction have the happy innocence, the purity and confidence of purpose, which was its true hallmark.

Max Carrados, the blind detective introduced by Ernest Bramah in 1914, being kidnapped. Illustration from *Pearson's Magazine* (1926).

Even by the 1930s its assumptions were being challenged. The Second World War, which swept so much else away, completed the rejection. Writers themselves may have shown a lingering fondness for Golden Age fiction, but Jacques Barzun was among the few critics to continue to defend it. Where it had once been commonplace to view the Golden Age as a high watermark of achievement, it became equally the fashion to denounce it. It had, so the indictment ran, followed rules which trivialized its subject. It had preferred settings which expressed a narrow, if not deliberately élitist, vision of society. And for heroes it had created detectives at best two-dimensional, at worst tiresome.

THE RULES OF THE GAME

'A detective story must have as its main interest the unravelling of a mystery; a mystery whose elements are clearly presented to the reader at an early stage in the proceedings, and whose nature is such as to arouse curiosity, a curiosity which is gratified at the end.' So Ronald Knox, a major arbiter of taste, wrote in 1929. His prescription sets the detective story apart from both the serious novel and the simple thriller. The serious novel may propose any number of narrative goals, and their interest is unlikely to depend on anything as technical as the unravelling of a mystery. The thriller may involve the unravelling of a mystery, but only incidentally, since its narrative interest depends more on suspense than curiosity.

By no means all the previous literature of crime and mystery satisfied Knox's severe standards, either. Many works had begun by posing a question and ended by answering it, but they had not always given readers the means of answering it by themselves. In 'The Murders in the

The distinctive green, white and black Penguin covers were familiar to generations of readers, not just of Golden Age mysteries but of hard-boiled novels and Simenon's Maigret series too.

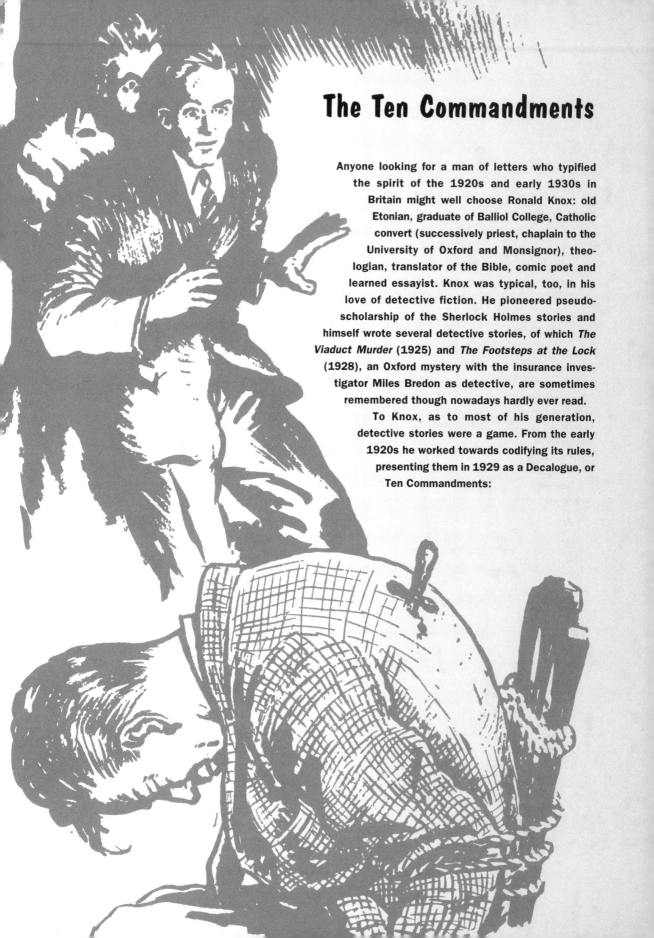

The Ten Commandments

Anyone looking for a man of letters who typified the spirit of the 1920s and early 1930s in Britain might well choose Ronald Knox: old Etonian, graduate of Balliol College, Catholic convert (successively priest, chaplain to the University of Oxford and Monsignor), theologian, translator of the Bible, comic poet and learned essayist. Knox was typical, too, in his love of detective fiction. He pioneered pseudo-scholarship of the Sherlock Holmes stories and himself wrote several detective stories, of which *The Viaduct Murder* (1925) and *The Footsteps at the Lock* (1928), an Oxford mystery with the insurance investigator Miles Bredon as detective, are sometimes remembered though nowadays hardly ever read.

To Knox, as to most of his generation, detective stories were a game. From the early 1920s he worked towards codifying its rules, presenting them in 1929 as a Decalogue, or Ten Commandments:

...according to Ronald Knox

1

The criminal must be mentioned in the early part of the story, but must not be anyone whose thoughts the reader has been allowed to follow.

2

All supernatural or preternatural agencies are ruled out as a matter of course.

3

Not more than one secret room or passage is allowable.

4

No hitherto undiscovered poisons may be used, nor any appliance which will need a long scientific explanation at the end.

5

No Chinaman must figure in the story.

6

No accident must ever help the detective, nor must he ever have an unaccountable intuition which proves to be right.

7

The detective himself must not commit the crime.

8

The detective is bound to declare any clues upon which he may happen to light.

9

The stupid friend of the detective, the Watson, must not conceal from the reader any thoughts which pass through his mind; his intelligence must be slightly, but very slightly, below that of the average reader.

10

Twin brothers, and doubles generally, must not appear unless we have been duly prepared for them.

Rue Morgue' Dupin kept a major clue to himself – a large tuft of ourang-outang hair, no less – and produced it with a flourish at the end. The Holmes stories were not always scrupulous either. But to Knox the matter was vital. The detective story should not just be a puzzle. It should be a game – a 'great battle of wits between the writer and the reader' – pursued with rigour and frivolity in more or less equal parts. It needed rules, as philosophy and cricket need rules, and above all it needed a spirit of fair play.

Most of Knox's 'Ten Commandments' enforce this requirement. He himself had little difficulty – and some innocent fun – spotting violations by well-regarded writers. The solutions in Freeman's stories sometimes depended on abstruse scientific knowledge that the reader was unlikely to share. A.A. Milne's *The Red House Mystery* (1922) – often taken as a supreme example of, according to taste, the weaknesses or the strengths of the Golden Age – gave a relatively modern house a secret passage whose existence the reader would hardly expect. But despite infringing the letter of Knox's rules, most writers accepted their underlying purpose. Writing detective stories required ingenuity in devising puzzles and equal ingenuity in presenting them without tipping readers off before the detective had gathered the suspects together in the library in the final chapter.

The mere fact that one can so readily characterize what is likely to happen in the final chapter shows how all-pervading the conventions were. Detective stories were not just any old puzzles played out according to certain rules: they were particular types of puzzle played out in particular types of place. The unspoken but near-universal agreement that they should involve murder is just one example of a convention which neither the spirit nor the logic of Knox's rules required. There is, of course, good reason why the puzzle should involve some sort of crime: it gives the perpetrator a motive for concealment, which is essential to the mystery. But Wilkie Collins sustained *The Moonstone* with no more than a theft, and some Sherlock Holmes stories deal only in minor crimes.

So why the insistence on murder in the Golden Age? Certainly not because of interest in its psychological origins or effects, or indeed in any form of psychology at all. W.H. Auden and others have suggested that the detective story enacts a primitive ritual of justice – of sin and its punishment – for which murder alone is sufficiently grave. But even if this is so, the ritual proceeds on a level so deep, so implicit, that neither reader nor writer need be aware of it. In practice, Golden Age writers followed each other in making their puzzles from murders

because they were the sort of writers who liked to follow each other. They obeyed familiar conventions as much as specific rules. So their murder puzzles also fell into obvious and acknowledged categories. Indeed, many writers specialized in a particular category. Freeman Wills Crofts, a former railway engineer, was master of the 'timetable alibi', John Dickson Carr of the 'locked-room puzzle'.

Agatha Christie, of course, liked to make the least likely person turn out to be the murderer. The daring with which she pursued this approach in *The Murder of Roger Ackroyd* (1926) did more than anything else to make her reputation. Originally the book was something of a *succès de scandale*: had she, after all, played fair with the reader? Later, it became a benchmark against which ingenuity was judged. Christie herself kept up the tricky task of finding less and less likely suspects, not just characters with seemingly unbreakable alibis or complete absence of motive but characters whom the reader automatically rules out from the start: the person who starts the hue and cry, one of the apparent victims, or the detective.

But what determines who is 'likely', not just in Agatha Christie's work but in Golden Age fiction generally? In life there is nothing which makes a butler a more or less likely murderer than anyone else. Yet readers of a detective story start by assuming the butler cannot be guilty because that would be too obvious, and they question the assumption only if they sense they are reading a writer – like Agatha Christie – capable of double-bluff or ironic refinement. Detective stories do not operate by the same rules as life: that is a truism. But they do not operate solely by their own declared rules, the rules of logic, either. They operate by convention, the accumulated practice of other

'Ackroyd was sitting as I had left him': the victim's body is discovered in Agatha Christie's classic puzzle, *The Murder of Roger Ackroyd* (1926).

The second victim is discovered in *The Murder of Roger Ackroyd*, filmed in 1931 as *Alibi* with Austin Trevor as Hercule Poirot, wearing a bow tie but lacking a moustache.

detective novels. This dictates not just that a murder will be committed and eventually solved, but also how it is likely to have been committed and who is likely or unlikely to have committed it. The world of the detective story is self-referential; it makes sense only in relation to other detective stories.

SNOBBERY WITH VIOLENCE?

W.H. Auden was specially qualified to speak of Golden Age fiction, being both an addict of it and the model for one of its detectives, Nicholas Blake's Nigel Strangeways. His summary of a typical plot is admirably precise: 'a murder occurs: many are suspected; all but one suspect, who is the murderer, are eliminated; the murderer is arrested or dies.' Or rather, the summary is precise

but for one clause: 'many are suspected'. Obviously there has to be more than one suspect for there to be a mystery at all, and obviously a handful of suspects, each passing under scrutiny in turn, helps the mystery achieve a proper length. But the list of suspects cannot be too long and it cannot, even potentially, be limitless, for that would open the door to unfair play.

The detective story requires a strictly limited cast of characters. Already 'closed' in its self-referentiality, its existence through rule and convention, the Golden Age detective story was also literally closed in its setting. The country house isolated by snow or the remoteness of its location was so ideal that it was to become one of the great clichés of the form in the 1920s. Oxbridge colleges offered the right combination of locks, keys and a quarrelsome community, too.

The Scene of the Crime: THE LOCKED ROOM

Poe's first detective story, 'The
Murders in the Rue Morgue' (1841), is prescient in all sorts of ways. The room in which the
murders are committed is apparently sealed, so Dupin has
to work out not just who the murderer is but how on earth he
escaped from the scene of the crime. In fact, Dupin quickly manages
to show that a window which looks as if it is nailed shut can in fact be
opened and closed. If modern readers find this solution disappointingly
simple, that is because the locked-room mystery – like all Poe's other ideas
for detective fiction – was so eagerly taken up by other writers. Israel
Zangwill tackled it in *The Big Bow Mystery* (1892). So did Gaston Leroux in
The Mystery of the Yellow Room (published in French in 1907 and translated
into English in 1908) and Jacques Futrelle in 'The Problem of Cell 13', the
best-known of his stories about Professor S.F.X. Van Dusen, included
in *The Thinking Machine* (1907; also called *The Problem of Cell 13*).
G.K. Chesterton's Father Brown tackled locked rooms and other situations making for apparently impossible murders or disappearances
in, for example, 'The Eye of Apollo', 'The Arrow of Heaven' and
'The Miracle of Moon Crescent'. 'The Invisible Man' has
a deliciously simple solution which has been
copied many times, while 'The Dagger With
Wings' was equally influential in presenting a
corpse found in snow unmarked by footprints.
Their love of ingenious puzzles and of closed
settings with a limited cast of suspects inevitably made writers of the Golden Age turn with
special enthusiasm to locked-room mysteries and
apparently impossible murders. The many contri-
butions from big names of the era include: S.S. Van
Dine's *The Canary Murder Case* (1927); Freeman Wills
Crofts' *Sudden Death* (1932) and *The End of Andrew
Harrison* (1938; called *The Futile Alibi* in USA); Ellery
Queen's *The Chinese Orange Mystery* (1934); Margery
Allingham's *Flowers for the Judge* (1936); and Agatha
Christie's *Murder in Mesopotamia* (1936) and *Hercule Poirot's
Christmas* (1938; called *Murder for Christmas* in USA). But no
author devoted himself to locked rooms with more concentration
than John Dickson Carr, whose taste for the eerie and the macabre
made him a direct descendant of Poe and Chesterton in other ways as
well. Locked-room mysteries feature in the bulk of his pre-war output,
which consisted of the stories about Henri Bencolin and Dr Gideon Fell
that he wrote under his own name and the stories about Sir Henry
Merrivale written under the transparent pseudonym of Carter Dickson.

One of Carr's best, *The Hollow Man* (1935; called *The Three Coffins* in USA), has a digressive chapter in which Fell lectures on all the various ways the problem of the locked room can be solved. He begins by ruling out the secret passage as a 'low trick' – a more extreme position than Ronald Knox had taken in the third of his 'Ten Commandments', which had limited detective writers to no more than one secret room or passage per book. Fell is particularly interested in deceptions which can make victims seem to be alive when they have in fact died or dead when they are still alive.

Such feats of illusion and impersonation ally the form not with the crossword puzzle or the board game – to which Golden Age detective fiction usually liked to compare itself – but with stage conjuring. After all, the readers who first made the locked-room mystery popular belonged to the same generation who admired the feats of Houdini. So it was only logical that a conjurer, Clayton Rawson, should have made his own stage identity as The Great Merlini into a fictional detective for a series of novels which rivals Carr's work. The first, *Death from a Top Hat* (1938), is the best. Another, much weaker, imitator of Carr was Clyde B. Clason, whose series of locked-room mysteries featuring Professor Theocritus Westborough began with *The Fifth Tumbler* (1936). Anthony Boucher, writing under the pseudonym of H.H. Holmes, took up Fell's lecture in *Nine Times Nine* (1940).

In his introduction to *All But Impossible!* (1981), an anthology of locked-room and impossible-crime stories, Edward D. Hoch reported on an informal poll he had conducted among writers, readers, editors and fans about the ten best locked-room mysteries. The resulting list is shown to the right:

Some readers might wish to substitute Ellery Queen's *The Door Between* (1937) for *The Chinese Orange Mystery*, but nobody could quibble with the generous representation of Carr/Dickson and everybody can be grateful for the prominence given to Hake Talbot's otherwise forgotten *Rim of the Pit*. All these books appear among the more than two thousand items in Robert Adey's enthusiastic *Locked Room Murders and Other Impossible Crimes: A Comprehensive Bibliography* (revised edition, 1991). Adey's list is particularly valuable in reminding readers of how the tradition of the locked-room mystery and the impossible crime has continued since the Golden Age in (to take several neglected classics by way of example) Joel Townsley Rogers' *The Red Right Hand* (1945), Derek Smith's *Whistle Up the Devil* (1953) and *The Woman in the Wardrobe* (1951) by Peter Anthony, the pseudonym under which the playwrights Anthony and Peter Shaffer jointly wrote detective stories. Recent examples include the stories of Edward D. Hoch and, from France, the work of Paul Halter.

JOHN DICKSON CARR
The Hollow Man (or *The Three Coffins*) (1935)

HAKE TALBOT
Rim of the Pit (1944)

GASTON LEROUX
The Mystery of the Yellow Room (1907)

JOHN DICKSON CARR
The Crooked Hinge (1938)

CARTER DICKSON (JOHN DICKSON CARR)
The Judas Window (1938)

ISRAEL ZANGWILL
The Big Bow Mystery (1892)

CLAYTON RAWSON
Death from a Top Hat (1938)

ELLERY QUEEN
The Chinese Orange Mystery (1934)

H.H. HOLMES (ANTHONY BOUCHER)
Nine Times Nine (1940)

CARTER DICKSON (JOHN DICKSON CARR)
The Ten Teacups (1937; called *The Peacock Feather Murders* in USA)

So did trains, cruise ships and eventually aeroplanes, as in Christie's *Death in the Clouds* (1935; called *Death in the Air* in USA). In fact, more or less any small and inward-looking group would do: the traditional English village, immortalized as St Mary Mead in the Miss Marple stories; the office or business, a recurrent favourite which allowed Dorothy L. Sayers to put her experience of advertising to use in *Murder Must Advertise* (1933); the theatre company or production, which gave Ngaio Marsh (herself a stage producer) the material for several novels and Michael Innes the setting for his masterpiece, *Hamlet, Revenge!* (1937); or just the eccentric family whose members live together or nearby, which always held particular fascination for Margery Allingham.

The convenience of such settings was obvious and the possible variants were apparently endless. Yet for all their

The flapper as detective: Miss Beryl Blackwood investigates in the 1931 radio serial 'The Scoop'.

fertility in coming up with new ones – the school, the hospital, the cathedral cloister, the millionaire's private island, the party of travellers in the desert – Golden Age writers stopped significantly short in ringing the changes. Lunatic asylums and prisons, wartime trenches or camps and slum neighbourhoods would have fitted their requirements. All turn up in Victorian fiction, and none is hard to find in 'mainstream' novels of the 1920s and 1930s. Yet they do not feature in detective stories. Once again Golden Age writers showed obedience not just to rules spelled out but to conventions silently agreed on.

This time the conventions are social. Detective writers needed closed settings but they also preferred respectably middle- or upper-middle-class milieus. There is, of course, nothing inherently wrong with this. Socially speaking, this world was more or less the same as the one Jane Austen had depicted: a few titled grandees at the top, a few servants at the bottom and a broad swathe of leisured or professional people in the middle. Altogether too much has been made of the failures in social attitude displayed by Golden Age writers, the snobbish or anti-Semitic remarks which they throw out in passing. These are failures for which their contemporaries in 'serious' literature could be convicted to roughly the same extent.

Yet there is a bias, social and eventually political, at work. It comes not so much from the convictions or prejudices of individual writers as from the form itself. Writers of left-wing views did turn to detective stories. Christopher St John Sprigg, who wrote Marxist criticism under the name of Christopher Caudwell, was one. Better known were G.D.H. and Margaret Cole, the husband-and-wife team of social historians.

The Scene of the Crime:

OXFORD, CAMBRIDGE – AND HARVARD HAS HOMICIDES, TOO

Lord Peter Wimsey in Oxford: Edward Petherbridge in the 1987 TV adaptation of *Gaudy Night*.

In an age when writers liked to make their detectives academic, by temperament if not actually by profession, universities were an obvious choice as settings. Oxbridge colleges made ideally enclosed environments, where only a limited number of people had access to the scene of the crime or jiggery-pokery with keys and secret entrances could be used to baffle the reader. Dons were portrayed as eccentrics locked in deadly rivalry with each other, ingeniously plotting murders or making deductions and, of course, endlessly given to harbouring guilty secrets. Their conversation was thick with allusion and quotation, and the mysteries they inhabited frequently hinged on literary manuscripts, usually forged. The solution often lay in the library – for academic libraries, unlike country-house libraries, were not just convenient places to leave a corpse but also, long

The Master was in his study at the Lodge. He rose courteously from his writing-table as the Inspector entered. In appearance everything that a Master should be, patriarchal and benevolent, he constantly gave the impression that he had just laid aside a treatise on the Hebrew gospels. He shook hands with his well-known hospitality and feebly motioned the Inspector to a chair.

'Well, Mr Inspector,' he said, 'this is a terrible shock to all of us. I hope you will be able to throw some light upon it.'

'I'm sure it's a dreadful thing to happen in a college,' replied the Inspector sympathetically.

T.H. White *Darkness at Pemberley*

before Eco's *The Name of the Rose*, as rich in concealment and revelation as a Piranesi drawing.

Together, these ingredients produced novels which critics have dubbed 'don's delights': at best learned and playful, at worst brittle and facetious. The tradition was pioneered by Ronald Knox, the apostle of Golden Age values, and the intelligence expert J.C. Masterman. Michael Innes (pseudonym of the critic and scholar J.I.M. Stewart) refined it to its sparkling best and Edmund Crispin (the composer Robert Bruce Montgomery) pushed it to its extreme. They all wrote about Oxford. Meanwhile Cambridge, after being honoured by a flying visit from Sherlock Holmes in 'The Adventure of the Missing Three-Quarter', had to make do with Glyn Daniel (the archaeologist, who began mystery-writing under the pseudonym of Dilwyn Rees) and, belatedly, V.C. Clinton-Baddeley, who wrote in the late 1960s.

The fact that Oxbridge could still serve as a setting in the late 1960s, not just after the Second World War but in a time of student revolution, is just one reminder of how many features of Golden Age fiction survived the death of the Golden Age itself. Some things needed toning down, of course: the wit and high spirits which marked the essential innocence of the 1920s and 1930s all but disappear. The detectives are more likely to be wary outsiders than snug insiders, and the plots are less college-bound, sometimes shifting from Gown to Town or mixing Oxbridge with more exotic locales. Probably the most significant spur to later writing came from Dorothy L. Sayers' *Gaudy Night*, a don's delight which nevertheless also began a debate about women in academic and professional life taken up by P.D. James, Amanda Cross (the pseudonym of Carolyn Heilbrun, writing about Harvard) and Joan Smith. Feminists have particular reason for being interested in Oxbridge, traditionally among the most prestigious male bastions of the English Establishment. Other mystery writers have turned their attention to provincial universities, following the lead given (though in a less than completely democratic spirit) by Michael Innes in the 1940s and 1950s.

OXFORD

T.J. BINYON
Greek Gifts (1988)

ANNA CLARKE
The Deathless and the Dead (1976; called *This Downhill Path* in USA)

GWENDOLINE BUTLER
Coffin in Oxford (1962) and *Coffin for Pandora* (1988; called *Olivia* in USA)

CAROL HIGGINS CLARK
Decked (1992)

EDMUND CRISPIN
The Case of the Gilded Fly (1944; called *Obsequies at Oxford* in USA) and *The Moving Toyshop* (1946)

AMANDA CROSS
No Word from Winifred (1986). See also Harvard, below

COLIN DEXTER
Last Bus to Woodstock (1975) and the rest of the series featuring Inspector Morse

P.C. DOHERTY
An Ancient Evil (1994). A medieval mystery

KATHARINE FARRER
The Missing Link (1952) and *Gownsman's Gallows* (1957)

ANTONIA FRASER
Oxford Blood (1985)

DAVID FROME
Mr Pinkerton Finds a Body (1934; called *The Body in the Turl* in UK). David Frome was the pseudonym of Mrs Zenith Brown, an American who also wrote as Leslie Ford

TIM HEALD
Masterstroke (1982; called *A Small Masterpiece* in USA)

HAZEL HOLT
The Cruellest Month (1991)

MICHAEL INNES
Death at the President's Lodging (1936; called *Seven Suspects* in USA), *Stop Press* (1939; called *The Spider Strikes* in USA) and *Operation Pax* (1951; called *The Paper Thunderbolt* in USA). All classics

RONALD KNOX
The Footsteps at the Lock (1928)

J.C. MASTERMAN
An Oxford Tragedy (1933). A classic

IAN MORSON
Falconer's Crusade (1994) and *Falconer's Judgement* (1995). Medieval mysteries

ANTHONY PRICE
Colonel Butler's Wolf (1973)

ROBERT ROBINSON
Landscape with Dead Dons (1956). The last of the Oxford 'don's delights'

DOROTHY L. SAYERS
Gaudy Night (1935)

JOAN SMITH
Masculine Ending (1987) and *What Men Say* (1993)

VERONICA STALLWOOD
Deathspell (1992), *Death and the Oxford Box* (1994), *Oxford Exit* (1994), *Oxford Mourning* (1995) and *Oxford Fall* (1996). The most promising Oxford mysteries since Colin Dexter's debut

PENNY SUMNER
The End of April (1993)

CAMBRIDGE

MARGERY ALLINGHAM
Police at the Funeral (1931)

HOSANNA BROWN
I Spy, You Die (1984)

DOUGLAS G. BROWNE
The May-Week Murders (1937)

V.C. CLINTON-BADDELEY
Death's Bright Dart (1967)

GLYN DANIEL
The Cambridge Murders (1945)

RUTH DUDLEY EDWARDS
Matricide at St Martha's (1994)

DORSEY FISKE
Academic Murder (1980)

ELIZABETH GEORGE
For the Sake of Elena (1992)

SUSANNA GREGORY
A Plague on Both Your Houses (1996) and *An Unholy Alliance* (1996). Medieval mysteries

RICHARD HUNT
Murder in Ruins (1991), *Death Sounds Grand* (1991), *Death of a Merry Widow* (1992), *Deadlocked* (1994), *A Cure for Killers* (1995) and *Murder Benign* (1995)

P.D. JAMES
An Unsuitable Job for a Woman (1972)

MARSHALL JEVONS
A Deadly Indifference (1995)

NORA KELLY
In the Shadow of King's (1984) and *Bad Chemistry* (1993)

JOY MAGEZIS
Vanishing Act (1988)

MARGARET MOORE
Forests of the Night (1987), *Dangerous Conceits* (1988), *Murder in Good Measure* (1990) and *Fringe Ending* (1991)

JILL PATON WALSH
The Wyndham Case (1993) and *A Piece of Justice* (1995)

Q. PATRICK
Murder at the 'Varsity (1933; called *Murder at Cambridge* in USA). The pseudonym Q. Patrick, here Richard Wilson Webb writing alone, had previously been used for Webb's collaboration with Martha Mott Kelley and would later be used for his partnership with Hugh Wheeler, which was also (and better) known under the pseudonym of Patrick Quentin

MICHELLE SPRING
Every Breath You Take (1994) and *Running for Shelter* (1995). About 'Eastern University', obviously Anglia University, Cambridge's former polytechnic

T.H. WHITE
Darkness at Pemberley (1932). An early venture into detective fiction by the author of *The Once and Future King*

DEREK WILSON
The Hellfire Papers (1995)

HARVARD

NICHOLAS BLAKE
The Morning After Death (1966)

AMANDA CROSS
Death in a Tenured Position (1981; called *A Death in the Faculty* in UK)

JEROME DOOLITTLE
Body Scissors (1990)

TIMOTHY FULLER
Harvard Has a Homicide (1936; called *J for Jupiter* in UK) and *Reunion with Murder* (1947)

JANE LANGTON
The Memorial Hall Murder (1978)

VICTORIA SILVER
Death of a Harvard Freshman (1984) and *Death of a Radcliffe Roommate* (1986)

Best known of all was Nicholas Blake, the poet C. Day Lewis. All might have been expected to write about prisons or slums; they were certainly more interested in them than in country houses. Yet they landed up writing like the rest, within the same agreed limits. No left-wing school of Golden Age fiction came into being.

Such is the power of literary convention, the power of the self-referential fictional world in perpetuating itself. The case of Nicholas Blake is particularly pertinent. His detective, Nigel Strangeways, was the creation of a left-wing poet modelled on the character of another left-wing poet. Yet he is an insouciant amateur with a few personal foibles, connections in the police and a fortuitous knack of being around when murders are committed. Many, if not

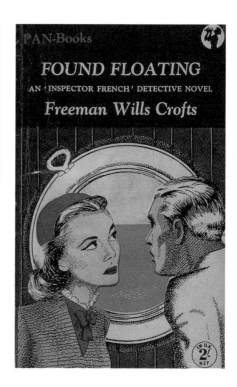

most, Golden Age detectives conform to this mould. Broadly speaking their personalities and way of life divide them into two main types: negligently aristocratic connoisseurs (like Philo Vance) and silly young asses (like Bailey's Reggie Fortune and Allingham's Albert Campion), with Lord Peter Wimsey bridging the gap between.

At least, that is how one remembers them. Yet the memory is only partly accurate. Strangeways is, in fact, not an amateur but a professional private detective. So are Christie's Poirot and a good number of the other Golden Age detectives listed in 'Careers and Day Jobs' (p. 86). This feature shows how many policemen flourished as well. Quite a few, like Crofts' Inspector French, are simply dull: not so much plausibly ordinary in the way a realist novelist might make them as colourless in the way a novelist concerned only with the puzzle is bound to make them. Others, like Marsh's

The interest of Freeman Wills Crofts' novels lay not in his detectives – usually the dull Inspector French – but in his fiendishly detailed plots.

Agatha Christie was not impressed by Margaret Rutherford as Miss Marple, but she might well have approved of Joan Hickson (below), **here in the 1987 TV adaptation of *4.50 from Paddington*.**

The Scene of the Crime:

THE ENGLISH COUNTRY HOUSE

'Even the exterior setting of the thing is in danger of becoming stereotyped,' Ronald Knox grumbled indulgently when he looked at classic detective fiction even before the 1920s had ended. He went on:

We know, as we sit down to the book, that a foul murder has almost certainly been done at a country house; that the butler will have been with the family for sixteen years; that a young male secretary will have been only recently engaged; that the chauffeur will have gone away for the night to visit his widowed mother.... We know that the victim, if he is a man, will have been killed either in the shrubbery or in his own study, with a wound at the back of his head; if she is a woman, she will be found in her bedroom, with an overdose of sleeping-draught to account for it all. We know that at least three members of the house-party will have been wandering about the passages in a suspicious manner during the small hours.

'If I walked into the detective-story house,' he confidently concluded, 'I believe I should be able to find my way about it perfectly; it is always more or less the same in design....'

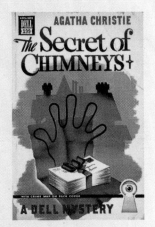

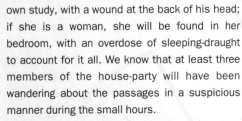

Alleyn and Innes' Appleby, are not dull but are not much like policemen either. They have something of Wimsey's suavity, and almost as good a social background too. Like Wimsey, and most other detectives of whatever nominal profession, they are as likely to happen on murders by accident as be assigned them in the line of work. Even when they are assigned, they deal with the suspects as equals, even in the best country houses, and have only the most discreet back-up to help with the mundane chores. As for their attitude to investigation, they seem to be doing it not for money but out of *noblesse oblige*.

THE CORPSE IN THE BLIND ALLEY

Golden Age fiction preferred its detectives to be gentlemen rather than players. They embodied the British tradition of the amateur: amateurishness not as bungling but as the personal flair which comes naturally to members of a certain class. This conformed with the determination to divorce crime and mystery from the realities it might assume in life, and to locate it in a fictional world as innocent and aloof as the world of pastoral. In the case of the detectives, though, the determination threatened to produce characters so flimsy they could scarcely pass muster in the most ephemeral West End comedy, much less sustain a continuing series of novels. Even Ronald

A villain is cornered by Albert Campion, the deceptively mild, bespectacled hero of Margery Allingham's novels.

Knox was troubled. The detective story, he admitted, could benefit from the depth of characterization in what he called 'the ordinary novel', though he still feared the day 'when the psychological crowd are let loose on it'.

In the 1930s writers came to share Knox's doubts and to adopt the remedy he tentatively proposed. Christie's Poirot was neither aristocratic connoisseur nor silly young ass, but his vanity and his moustaches, his little grey cells and his broken English, made him an embarrassingly crude cartoon. He could still just about serve when the plotting was sufficiently ingenious – as it undoubtedly was in *The ABC Murders* (1936), *Cards on the Table* (1936), *Death on the Nile* (1937), *Appointment with Death* (1938) and *Hercule Poirot's Christmas* (1938; called *Murder for Christmas* in USA) – but something still

had to be done. Christie later admitted as much in *The Clocks* (1963) through the character of Ariadne Oliver, a writer saddled with an implausible Finn as detective despite knowing 'nothing about Finns or Finland except possibly the works of Sibelius'.

Poirot himself was toned down and, after *Dumb Witness* (1937; called *Poirot Loses a Client* in USA), freed of Captain Hastings, a crass example of the Watson-like 'idiot friend'. (Hastings was, however, revived for *Curtain* (1975), the last Poirot novel, written in the 1940s but originally intended for publication after Christie's death.) Above all, Christie came to prefer Miss Marple, a more solidly conceived character – at least in her original incarnation as the vinegary spinster of *Murder at the Vicarage* (1930) and the early novels. Other writers, more

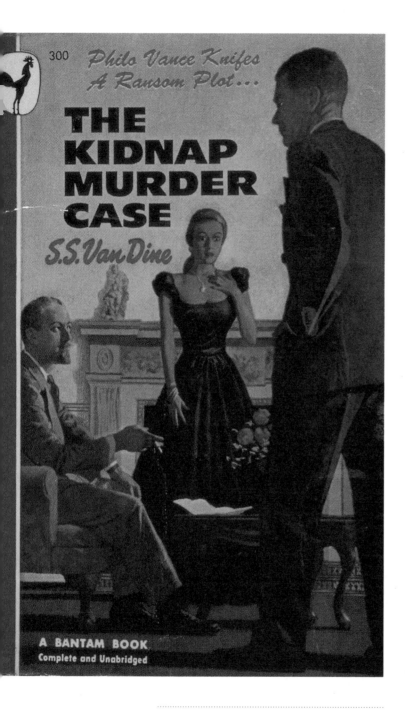

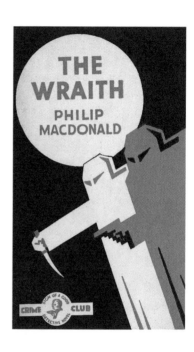

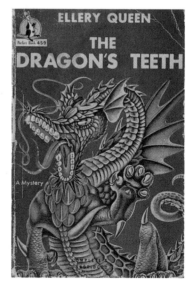

Some Golden Age writers – like Philip MacDonald –
have fallen almost entirely from fashion. Ellery Queen
is still gratefully remembered for his crime and
mystery magazine but S.S. Van Dine is now recalled
only as the creator, in Philo Vance, of a detective
who epitomized the snobbish affectations of the era.

AMBASSADORS THEATRE, West St. Cambridge Circus, **W.C.2**

Sole Proprietors: Ambassadors Theatre Ltd. Lessees: J. W. Pemberton & Co. Ltd.
Managing Directors: W. G. Curtis & H. J. Malden.

Licenced by the Lord Chamberlain to J. F. H. Jay.

Monday to Friday: 7.30   Saturday: 5.15 and 8.0   Tuesday: 2.30   BOX OFFICE
Stalls: 15/-, 10/6, 8/6;   Dress Circle: 15/-, 10/6, 8/6, 5/6;   Pit (unreserved): 3/6.   Temple Bar 1171

Peter Saunders presents

Richard Attenborough
Sheila Sim in

THE MOUSETRAP
by Agatha Christie

With
Jessica Spencer
Aubrey Dexter
Mignon O'Doherty
Allan McClelland
John Paul
and
Martin Miller

DIRECTED BY PETER COTES   *Décor by Roger Furse*

Not everything from the Golden Age has passed away. Agatha Christie's play, first produced in 1952 and still going, has broken all theatrical records by the length of its run.

thoroughly saddled with their original creations, made what shift they could. Strangeways and Alleyn grow subdued as their careers progress. Appleby, a rather shadowy figure at his first appearance, develops a richly Jamesian consciousness which helps put Innes' work virtually in a league of its own. Margery Allingham took active pleasure in aging Albert Campion – an unusual attitude for the creator of a popular series character – so that the pensive middle-aged man of the later novels bore little resemblance to the vacuous, bespectacled youngster who had first appeared.

Most famously, Dorothy L. Sayers set out to change Lord Peter Wimsey. With his monocle, his facetious remarks and breezily aristocratic slang, and his impossibly long list of accomplishments,

Parodying the Golden Age

Philo Vance Needs a kick in the pance. Ogden Nash

The more mannered a literary form becomes, the riper it grows for parody. In this respect the work of Christie, Sayers and their fellow writers of the Golden Age presented a target as tempting as the Holmes stories. Yet since Golden Age fiction, like the Holmes stories, is so mannered as to contain elements of self-parody, the line between the real and the spoof is sometimes hard to draw. E.C. Bentley, for example, neatly caught the tone of Sayers' Lord Peter Wimsey in 'Greedy Night', a piece which still sometimes turns up in anthologies. Yet his audience had largely missed the point of *Trent's Last Case* (1912; originally called *The Woman in Black* in USA), conceived not so much as a detective story as 'an exposure of detective stories'. Elliot Paul's *The Mysterious Mickey Finn: or, Murder at the Café du Dôme* (1939), aimed at S.S. Van Dine's Philo Vance novels, suffered a similar fate, and Paul went on to write eight more Homer Evans novels in which parody (though not humour) plays a diminishing part. The parody of Van Dine was unmistakable, however, in Corey Ford's *The John Riddell Murder Case* (1930), in which the victim turns out to have been bored to death. Agatha Christie also turned her hand to parodying her fellow-writers, though with unmemorable results, in *Partners in Crime* (1929), a collection of stories featuring Tommy and Tuppence Beresford.

Laurence Olivier as the spider and Michael Caine as the fly in the 1972 film of Anthony Shaffer's *Sleuth*.

However, two full-length parodies have secured a permanent niche for themselves: Leo Bruce's *Case for Three Detectives* (1936) and Marion Mainwaring's *Murder in Pastiche, or Nine Detectives All at Sea* (1954). Leo Bruce was the pseudonym under which Rupert Croft-Cooke went on to write crime and mystery novels without his tongue in his cheek. In *Case for Three Detectives* he introduced Sergeant Beef – 'burly, red-faced, heavy of hand and humour' and definitely 'not a man to appeal to the great public as an inspired investigator' – and allowed him to triumph over his rivals, Monsignor Smith, Lord Simon Plimsoll and Monsieur Amer Picon, in solving a locked-room mystery. Lord Simon is the first to concede defeat:

'I am not one to get excited about the jolly old police, but I'm climbin' down a peg.' Then he added, 'Lord, what a relief it is to have been wrong for once! You don't know the monotony of infallibility!'

'I also, the great Amer Picon, shall rest contented. At last I have made the faux pas. Hooray, as you say in English, it is a great change for me!'

And Mgr Smith murmured softly, 'I am so pleased. So pleased.'

In *Murder in Pastiche* the murder of a gossip columnist on a transatlantic liner – a nicely chosen victim and setting – receives the attentions of Atlas Poireau, Lord Simon Quinsey, Miss Fan Sliver (Patricia Wentworth's Miss Maud Silver), Sir Jon. Nappleby (Michael Innes' John Appleby), Broderick Tourneur (Ngaio Marsh's Roderick Alleyn), Mallory King (Ellery Queen), Trajan Beare (Rex Stout's Nero Wolfe) and, in acknowledgement of the changes which had taken place by 1954 (see Chapter 4, 'The Hard-Boiled School'), Jerry Pason (Erle Stanley Gardner's Perry Mason) and Spike Bludgeon (Mickey Spillane's Mike Hammer). The puzzle is solved by the murderer making an unprompted confession.

Since Leo Bruce and Marion Mainwaring the business of parodying the Golden Age seems to have passed largely into the hands of playwrights (whose point of reference is as likely to be *The Mousetrap* as *The Murder of Roger Ackroyd*), notably Joe Orton in *Loot* (1966), Tom Stoppard in *The Real Inspector Hound* (1968) and Anthony Shaffer in *Sleuth* (1970) and *The Case of the Oily Levantine* (1979). All of them set out to debunk in a more hostile spirit than their predecessors, but they still feel a lingering affection for the forms they mock. Shaffer had previously written detective novels with his brother Peter Shaffer, published under their own names and under the pseudonym Peter Anthony.

**Dorothy L. Sayers'
Lord Peter Wimsey
before she set
out to modify his
breeziness.
Illustration by John
Campbell for
Pearson's Magazine
(1926).**

Wimsey had at his inception been burdened with mannerisms which would return to haunt their creator's dreams. His courtship of Harriet Vane was meant to reveal new depths and to chart his growing maturity, and contemporaries heaped extravagant praise on the result. Yet at best, in *Gaudy Night* (1936), the serious preoccupations develop independently of the detective and his detection. At worst, in *Busman's Honeymoon* (1937), he remains alarmingly lightweight and the detective plot falls to pieces. Sayers was not the last British writer to work herself into this particular impasse. As much as embarrassment at popular success or the desire to pursue other interests, the realization of where she stood might well account for her abandoning both Wimsey and detective fiction altogether.

Knox followed the fashion in admiring the later Wimsey novels, but they did not answer his real fears about the future of the form – fears which, ironically enough, were stimulated by adherence to his own rules and formulae. This might have encouraged the technical rigour he judged essential, and it might even have produced the classical severity he admired in art. But the permutations on any given set of rules and formulae are not infinite, and even before they are exhausted the law of diminishing returns sets in. Already by the

end of the 1920s he could lament that 'while the public demand remains unshaken, the faculty for writing a good detective story is rare, and the means of writing one with any symptom of originality about it becomes rarer with each succeeding year'.

Most of the good ideas had been used, and the obvious ones had been used again and again. It was hardly surprising that Agatha Christie should have pulled the trick solution she had used in *The Murder of Roger Ackroyd* again in *Endless Night* (1967); indeed, it was some tribute that it took over forty years before she was reduced to this expedient. Readers, moreover, had got more sophisticated, and not just in recognizing the same old country house or knowing what they should expect of butlers. They knew the victim had not really been killed where the corpse was found, and had probably died at a different time from the time everybody supposed. They knew the first suspect was likely to become the second victim. They knew the character with an unshakable alibi was probably lying and the character with no alibi was probably innocent.

'The game,' Knox feared, 'is getting played out'. There was a tinge of desperation in his tone when he went on to ask: 'But in what possible way are we to enlarge the possible horizons of this … intriguing game, the solving of detective problems?' He had no answer, since none could be attempted without challenging his original precepts. Others who did not feel his attachment to those precepts did have an answer, or at least were interested in exploring new possibilities and seeking out new horizons. Before the Golden Age itself had ended, this is just what the hard-boiled writers in the USA were busy doing.

The Golden Age Bookshelf

Though Golden Age fiction is treated in the histories of crime and mystery mentioned in the general booklist at the end of this book, the decline in its reputation since the heady pre-war days has discouraged critical study. Women writers have fared the best.

Janet Morgan's authorized biography of Agatha Christie (1984) is an invaluable supplement to the writer's autobiography (1977), which found her modest and business-like in her attitude to writing but otherwise reluctant to reveal much of herself – particularly about the background to her much-publicized disappearance in 1926. H.R.F. Keating's collection, *Agatha Christie: First Lady of Crime* (1977), includes contributions from Michael Gilbert, Emma Lathen and Julian Symons. Popular guides to her fiction have proliferated since G.C. Ramsey's *Agatha Christie: Mistress of Mystery* (1967); recent examples include Randall Toye's *The Agatha Christie Who's Who* (1980), Charles Osborne's *The Life and Crimes of Agatha Christie* (1982), Dennis Sanders and Len Lovallo's *The Agatha Christie Companion: The Complete Guide to Agatha Christie's Life and Work* (1985), and Anne Hart's *The Life and Times of Miss Jane Marple* (1985) and *The Life and Times of Hercule Poirot* (1990). In their standards of accuracy and critical discussion they are all inferior to Robert Barnard's sensible *A Talent to Deceive: An Appreciation of Agatha Christie* (revised edition, 1990), which includes a bibliography by Louise Barnard, as well as listings of stage and film adaptations.

Janet Hitchman led the way in biographies of Dorothy L. Sayers with *Such a Strange Lady* (1975). Its revelations about her personal life were confirmed by James Brabazon's *Dorothy L. Sayers: The Life of a Courageous Woman* (1981; republished as *Dorothy L. Sayers: A Biography*, 1988), written with the consent and cooperation of her son, Anthony Fleming. Other biographers – who have included Ralph E. Hone (1979), David Coomes (1992) and Barbara Reynolds (1993) – have fleshed out her career as woman of letters. Trevor H. Hall's *Dorothy L. Sayers: Nine Literary Studies* (1980) concentrates on the detective fiction but *As Her Whimsey Took Her*, a collection of essays edited by Margaret Hannay (1979), includes flattering accounts of her in fact rather modest achievements as translator and playwright. Bibliographies of Sayers' work have been compiled by Robert B. Harmon and Margaret A. Burger (1977) and by Colleen B. Gilbert (1978). Ruth Tanis Youngberg's *Dorothy L. Sayers: A Reference Guide* (1982) lists the secondary sources.

Margery Allingham's life has been written by Richard Martin (1988) and more persuasively by Julia Thorogood (1991). Margaret Lewis' life of Ngaio Marsh (1991) supplements the novelist's own memoir, *Black Beech and Honeydew* (1966), which dwells mostly on her career in the New Zealand theatre. In *Myself and Michael Innes* (1987) J.I.M. Stewart left a memoir of his joint careers as scholar and detective novelist. S.S. Van Dine's memoir, published under the embarrassed and embarrassing title of *I Used To Be a Highbrow But Look At Me Now* (1929), has been supplemented by John Loughery's biography, *Alias S.S. Van Dine* (1992), more expert on its subject's career as art critic and historian than as creator of Philo Vance. *Royal Bloodline* (1974) by Francis M. Nevins, Jr, is a study of Ellery Queen. *The Door to Doom and Other Deductions*, a posthumous collection of John Dickson Carr's work edited by Douglas G. Greene (1980), includes a valuable bibliography.

Careers and Day Jobs:

GOLDEN AGE DETECTIVES AND WHAT THEY DO (OR DON'T DO) FOR A LIVING

Policemen

Inspector (later Superintendent) Roderick Alleyn. Created by Ngaio Marsh (New Zealand). First appears in *A Man Lay Dead* (1934), last appears in *Light Thickens* (1982)

John (later Sir John) Appleby. Created by Michael Innes (UK). First appears in *Death at the President's Lodging* (1936), last appears in *Appleby and the Ospreys* (1986)

Inspector/Superintendent William Austen. Created by Anne Hocking (UK). First appears in *Old Mrs Fitzgerald* (1939; called *Deadly is the Evil Tongue* in USA), last appears in *Murder Cries Out* (1968; finished by Evelyn Healey)

Superintendent Battle. Created by Agatha Christie (UK). First appears in *The Secret of Chimneys* (1925), last appears in *Towards Zero* (1944), with occasional appearances in novels about Hercule Poirot (see 'Private Detectives' below)

Sergeant Beef. Created by Leo Bruce (UK). First appears in *Case for Three Detectives* (1936), last appears in *Cold Blood* (1952)

Henri Bencolin, French *juge d'instruction*. Created by John Dickson Carr (an American expatriate in Britain for much of his working life). Appears in *It Walks By Night* (1930), *Castle Skull* (1931), *The Lost Gallows* (1931) and *The Corpse in the Waxworks* (1932; called *The Waxworks Murder* in UK), then replaced by Dr Gideon Fell (see 'Amateurs' below)

Inspector Cheviot Burmann. Created by G. Belton Cobb (UK). First appears in *No Alibi* (1936), last appears in *Secret Enquiry* (1968)

Detective Sergeant (later Superintendent) Charlie Chan. Created by Earl Dell Biggers (USA). First appears in *The House Without a Key* (1925), last appears in *Keeper of the Keys* (1932)

Thatcher Colt, New York Police Commissioner. Created by Anthony Abbott (USA). First appears in *About the Murder of Geraldine Foster* (1930; called *The Murder of Geraldine Foster* in UK), last appears in *The Shudders* (1943; called *Deadly Secrets* in UK)

Sir Clinton Driffield, Chief Constable. Created by J.J. Connington (UK). First appears in *Murder in the Maze* (1927), last appears in *Common Sense is All You Need* (1947), always with Squire Wendover

Inspector Septimus Finch. Created by Margaret Erskine (UK). First appears in *And Being Dead* (1938), last appears in *The House in Hook Street* (1977)

Inspector (later Superintendent) French. Created by Freeman Wills Crofts (UK). First appears in *Inspector French's Greatest Case* (1925), last appears in *Anything to Declare* (1957)

Inspector Alan Grant. Created by Josephine Tey (UK). First appears in *The Man in the Queue* (1929; later called *Killer in the Crowd* in USA), last appears in *The Singing Sands* (1952)

Inspector Hanaud of the Sûreté. Created by A.E.W. Mason (UK). First appears in *At the Villa Rose* (1910), last appears in *The House in Lordship Lane* (1946)

Michael Lord, special officer on the staff of the New York Police Commissioner. Created by C. Daly King (USA). First appears in *Obelists en Route* (1932), last appears in *Bermuda Burial* (1940)

Inspector/Superintendent MacDonald. Created by E.C.R. Lorac (UK). First appears in *The Murder on the Burrows* (1931), last appears in *Dishonour Among Thieves* (1959; called *The Last Escape* in USA)

Inspector Christopher McKee, Manhattan Crime Squad. Created by Helen Reilly (USA). First appears in *The Diamond Feather* (1930), last appears in *The Day She Died* (1954)

Inspector Mallett (1). Created by Cyril Hare (UK). First appears in *Tenant for Death* (1937), last appears in *He Should Have Died Hereafter* (1958; called *Untimely Death* in USA). From *Tragedy at Law* (1942) onwards, he sometimes appears with Francis Pettigrew (see 'Amateurs' below)

Inspector/Superintendent Mallett (2). Created by Mary Fitt (UK). First appears in *Sky-Rocket* (1938), last appears in *Mizmaze* (1958)

Superintendent Meredith. Created by John Bude (UK). First appears in *The Lake District Murder* (1935), last appears in *The Constable and the Lady* (1951)

Bobby Owen. Created by E.R. Punshon (UK). First appears in *Information Received* (1933), last appears in *Six Were Present* (1956)

Chief Inspector Pointer. Created by A. (sometimes A.E.) Fielding (UK). First appears in *The Eames-Erskine Case* (1924), last appears in *Pointer to a Crime* (1944)

Chief Inspector Poole. Created by Henry Wade (UK). First appears in *The Duke of York's Steps* (1929), last appears in *Gold Was Our Grave* (1954)

Police Constable (eventually Superintendent) Richardson. Created by Basil Thomson (ex-Assistant Commissioner, Metropolitan Police; UK). First appears in *P.C. Richardson's First Case* (1933), last appears in *A Murder Arranged* (1937; called *When Thieves Fall Out* in USA)

Superintendent Anthony Slade. Created by Leonard Gribble (UK). First appears in *The Case of the Marsden Rubies* (1929), last appears in *Strip-Tease Macabre* (1967)

Superintendent Vachell, a Canadian serving as head of the CID in Chania, imaginary East African protectorate. Created by Elspeth Huxley (UK). Appears in *Murder at Government House* (1937), *Murder on Safari* (1938) and *Death of an Aryan* (1939; called *The African Poison Murders* in USA)

Lieutenant Valcour, of the New York Police Department. Created by Rufus King (USA). First appears in *Murder by the Clock* (1929), last appears in *Murder Masks Miami* (1939)

Superintendent Henry Wilson. Created by G.D.H. and M. Cole (UK). First appears in *The Brooklyn Murders* (1923), last appears in *Toper's End* (1942), sometimes with the Honourable Everard Blatchington (see 'Amateurs' below)

Private Detectives

Ronald Camberwell. Created by J.S. Fletcher (UK). First appears in *Murder at Wrides Park* (1931), last appears in *Todmanhawe Grange* (1937; finished by Torquemada; called *The Mill House Murder, Being the Last of the Adventures of Ronald Camberwell* in USA)

Peter Clancy. Created by Lee Thayer (USA). Appears in about sixty books, from *The Mystery of the Thirteenth Floor* (1919) to *Dusty Death* (1966)

Colonel Warwick Gore. Created by Lynn Brock (UK). First appears in *The Deductions of Colonel Gore* (1924; later called *The Barrington Mystery*), founds his detective agency in *Colonel Gore's Second Case* (1925), last appears in *Q.E.D.* (1930; called *Murder on the Bridge* in USA)

Jim Hanvey. Created by Octavus Roy Cohen (USA). First appears in *Jim Hanvey, Detective* (1923), a collection of stories, last appears in *Star of Earth* (1932)

Fergus O'Breen. Created by Anthony Boucher (USA). Appears *The Case of the Crumpled Knave* (1939), *The Case of the Baker Street Irregulars* (1940; later called *Blood on Baker Street*), *The Case of the Solid Key* (1941) and *The Case of the Seven Sneezes* (1943), accompanied by Detective Lieutenant Jackson of the Los Angeles Police Department

Hercule Poirot. Created by Agatha Christie (UK). First appears in *The Mysterious Affair at Styles* (1920), last appears in *Curtain* (1975), originally accompanied by Captain Hastings

Miss Maud Silver. Created by Patricia Wentworth (UK). First appears in *Grey Mask* (1928), last appears in *The Girl in the Cellar* (1961)

Nigel Strangeways. Created by Nicholas Blake (UK). First appears in *A Question of Proof* (1935), last appears in *The Morning After Death* (1966)

Philip Tolefree. Created by R.A.J. Walling (UK). First appears in *The Fatal Five Minutes* (1932), last appears in *The Corpse with the Missing Watch* (1949)

Nero Wolfe. Created by Rex Stout (USA). First appears in *Fer-de-Lance* (1934), last appears in *A Family Affair* (1975), helped by Archie Goodwin

Amateurs

Major Roger Bennion, property developer and, in novels during the Second World War, Intelligence officer. Created by Herbert Adams (UK). First appears in *Exit the Skeleton* (1928), last appears in *Death of a Viewer* (1958)

The Honourable Everard Blatchington, gentleman of leisure. Created by G.D.H. and M. Cole (UK). Appears in *The Blatchington Tangle* (1926), *Death in the Quarry* (1934), *Scandal at School* (1935; called *The Sleeping Death* in USA). Usually helped by Superintendent Henry Wilson (see 'Policemen' above)

Amateurs cont...

Mrs (later Dame) Beatrice Lestrange Bradley, consultant psychiatrist at the Home Office. Created by Gladys Mitchell (UK). First appears in *Speedy Death* (1929), last appears in *The Crozier Pharaohs* (1984)

Miles Bredon, insurance investigator. Created by Ronald Knox (UK). First appears in *The Three Taps: A Detective Story Without a Moral* (1927), last appears in *Double Cross Purposes* (1937)

Father Brown, priest. Created by G.K. Chesterton (UK). First appears in *The Innocence of Father Brown* (1911), last appears in *The Scandal of Father Brown* (1935)

Albert Campion, gentleman of leisure rumoured to be related to the royal family. Created by Margery Allingham (UK). First appears in *The Crime at Black Dudley* (1929; called *The Black Dudley Mystery* in USA), last appears in *Cargo of Eagles* (1968; finished by Youngman Carter), accompanied by his manservant, Magersfontein Lugg

Joshua Clunk, solicitor. Created by H.C. Bailey (UK). First appears in *Garstons* (1930; called *The Garston Murder Case* in USA), last appears in *Shrouded Death* (1950)

Peter Duluth, Broadway producer, and his wife Iris. Patrick Quentin (pseudonym of Hugh Wheeler, writing until 1952 with Richard Wilson Webb, both born in UK but working in USA). First appears in *A Puzzle for Fools* (1936), last appears in *My Son, the Murderer* (1954; called *The Wife of Ronald Sheldon* in UK)

Montague Egg, commercial traveller. Created by Dorothy L. Sayers (UK). Appears in short stories in *Hangman's Holiday* (1933) and *In the Teeth of the Evidence* (1939)

Dr Gideon Fell, lexicographer and historian. Created by John Dickson Carr (an American expatriate in Britain for much of his working life). First appears in *Hag's Nook* (1933), last appears in *Dark of the Moon* (1966)

Gervase Fen, Professor of English at Oxford. Created by Edmund Crispin (UK). First appears in *The Case of the Gilded Fly* (1944; called *Obsequies at Oxford* in USA), last appears in *The Glimpses of the Moon* (1978)

Reggie Fortune, pathologist. Created by H.C. Bailey (UK). First appears in *Call Mr Fortune* (1920), a collection of short stories, last appears in *Saving a Rope* (1948; called *Save a Rope* in USA)

Henry Gamadge, scholar and man about New York. Created by Elizabeth Daly (USA). First appears in *Unexpected Night* (1940), last appears in *The Book of the Crime* (1954)

Colonel Anthony Gethryn, unspecified connections with the police and intelligence services. Created by Philip MacDonald (UK). First appears in *The Rasp* (1924), last appears in *The List of Adrian Messenger* (1959)

Antony Gillingham, man of independent means. Created by A.A. Milne. Appears only in *The Red House Mystery* (1922)

Dr Eustace Hailey, 'the Harley Street giant'. Created by Anthony Wynne (UK). First appears in *The Mystery of the Evil Eye* (1925), last appears in *Death of a Shadow* (1950)

Jimmy Haswell, barrister. Created by Herbert Adams (UK). First appears in *The Secret of the Bogey House* (1924), last appears in *The Woman in Black* (1942)

Mr Jellipot, solicitor. Created by Sydney Fowler (pseudonym of the science-fiction writer S. Fowler Wright; UK). First appears in *The Bell Street Murders* (1931), last appears in *With Cause Enough* (1954)

Sir Bruton Kaimes, Director of Public Prosecutions, and Harvey Tuke. Created by Douglas G. Browne (UK). First appears in *Death Wears a Mask* (1940), last appears in *Death in Seven Volumes* (1958)

Craig Kennedy, Professor of Chemistry at Columbia University. Created by Arthur B. Reeve (US). First appears in *The Silent Bullet: Adventures of Craig Kennedy, Scientific Detective* (1912; called *The Black Hand* in UK), a collection of stories, last appears in *Enter Craig Kennedy* (1935), novelettes adapted by Ashley Locke

Miss Jane Marple, genteel spinster. Created by Agatha Christie (UK). First appears in *Murder at the Vicarage* (1930), last appears in *Sleeping Murder* (1976)

Asey Mayo, eccentric former sailor. Created by Phoebe Atwood Taylor (US). First appears in *The Cape Cod Mystery* (1931), last appears in *Diplomatic Corpse* (1951)

Desmond Merrion, former Intelligence Officer. Created by Miles Burton (Cecil John Street, who also wrote as John Rhode; UK). First appears in *The Secret of High Eldersham* (1930), last appears in *Death Paints a Picture* (1960), assisted by his valet, Newport, and Inspector Arnold

Sir Henry Merrivale, barrister and doctor. Created by Carter Dickson (John Dickson Carr; USA/UK). First appears in *The Plague Court Murders* (1933), last appears in *The Cavalier's Cup* (1953)

Francis Pettigrew, barrister. Created by Cyril Hare (UK). First appears in *Tragedy at Law* (1942), last appears in *He Should Have Died Hereafter* (1958; called *Untimely Death* in USA), often with Inspector Mallett (see 'Policemen' above)

Dr Lancelot Priestley, scientist.
Created by John Rhode (UK). First
appears in *The Paddington Mystery*
(1925), last appears in *The Vanishing
Diary* (1961)

**Ellery Queen, author of detective
stories and son of Inspector Richard
Queen.** Created by Ellery Queen (USA).
First appears in *The Roman Hat
Mystery* (1929), last appears in *A Fine
and Private Place* (1971)

**J.G. Reeder, vaguely connected with
Scotland Yard and Public Prosecutor.**
Created by Edgar Wallace (UK). First
appears in *Room 13* (1924), last
appears in *The Guv'nor and Other
Stories* (1932; called *Mr Reeder
Returns* in USA)

**John Ringrose, retired Scotland Yard
detective.** Created by Eden Phillpotts
(UK). Appears in *A Voice from the Dark*
(1925) and *The Marylebone Miser*
(1926; called *Jig-Saw* in USA)

Huntoon Rogers, Professor of English.
Created by Clifford Knight (USA). First
appears in *The Affair of the Scarlet
Crab* (1937), last appears in *The Affair
of the Sixth Button* (1947)

Sir John Saumarez, actor-manager.
Created by Clemence Dane and Helen
Simpson (UK). Appears in *Enter Sir
John* (1928), *Printer's Devil* (1930;
called *Author Unknown* in USA) and
Re-Enter Sir John (1932)

Roger Sheringham, novelist. Created
by Anthony Berkeley (Anthony Berkeley
Cox, who also wrote as Francis Iles;
UK). First appears in *The Layton Court
Mystery* (1925), last appears in *Panic
Party* (1934; called *Mr Pidgeon's
Island* in USA)

Dr John Thorndyke, medical jurist.
Created by R. Austin Freeman (UK).
First appears in *The Red Thumb Mark*
(1907), last appears in *The Jacob
Street Mystery* (1942; called *The
Unconscious Witness* in USA)

**Ludovic Travers, writer and
gentleman of leisure who, after the
Second World War, founds a
detective agency.** Created by
Christopher Bush (UK). Appears in
sixty-three books, from *The Plumley
Inheritance* (1926) to *The Case of the
Prodigal Daughter* (1968)

Philip Trent, artist. Created by E.C.
Bentley (UK). Appears in two novels,
Trent's Last Case (1913; called *The
Woman in Black* in USA) and *Trent's
Own Case* (1936; in collaboration with
H. Warner Allen), and a volume of
short stories, *Trent Intervenes* (1938)

Harvey Tuke: see Sir Bruton Kaimes
above

**Philo Vance, connoisseur and
gentleman of leisure.** Created by S.S.
Van Dine (USA). Appears in twelve
novels, from *The Benson Murder Case*
(1926) to *The Winter Murder Case*
(1939)

Charles Venables, journalist. Created
by Christopher St John Sprigg (UK).
Appears in *Fatality in Fleet Street*
(1933), *The Perfect Alibi* (1934) and
Death of a Queen (1935)

Malcolm Warren, stockbroker.
Created by C.H.B. Kitchin (UK). First
appears in *Death of My Aunt* (1929),
last appears in *The Cornish Fox*
(1949)

**Theocritus Westborough, scholar and
historian of Roman Empire.** Created
by Clyde B. Clason (USA). First
appears in *The Fifth Tumbler* (1936),
last appears in *Green Shiver* (1941)

**Dr Basil Willing, psychiatrist,
Intelligence Officer, Harvard
professor.** Created by Helen McCloy
(USA). First appears in *Dance of Death*
(1938), last appears in *Burn This*
(1980)

**Lord Peter Wimsey, connoisseur and
gentleman of leisure.** Dorothy L.
Sayers (UK). First appears in *Whose
Body?* (1923), last appears in
Busman's Honeymoon (1937),
accompanied by his manservant
Bunter, and sometimes from *Strong
Poison* (1930) onwards by his
eventual wife Harriet Vane

Dr David Wintringham, doctor.
Created by Josephine Bell (UK). First
appears in *Murder in Hospital* (1937),
last appears in *The Seeing Eye*
(1958), working with Inspector Steven
Mitchell, who occasionally appears
by himself

**Leonidas Witherall, retired academic,
owner of a boys' school and writer of
crime fiction.** Created by Alice Tilton
(Phoebe Atwood Taylor; US). First
appears in *Beginning with a Bash*
(1937), last appears in *The Iron Clew*
(1947; called *The Iron Hand* in UK)

Hildegarde Withers, schoolteacher.
Created by Stuart Palmer (US). First
appears in *The Penguin Pool Murder*
(1931), last appears in *Hildegarde
Withers Makes the Scene* (with
Fletcher Flora, 1969)

**Anthony Berkeley's amateur detective
Roger Sheringham in a spot of trouble.
Illustration by C. Fitzgerald.**

FAREWELL, MY LOVELY

RAYMOND CHANDLER

Chapter 4
THE HARD-BOILED SCHOOL

A CHEAP, SHODDY AND UTTERLY LOST KIND OF WRITING...

A world of difference separates the hard-boiled school from the writers of the Golden Age. Golden Age writers present puzzles in closed settings, such as country houses or villages. Whether grey policemen or stylish amateurs, their detectives work towards solutions which are triumphs of orderly method, as Holmes had done and Dupin before him. Hard-boiled novelists may devise plots no less convoluted, but they make their stories unfold by violent twists and turns. Their heroes embark on journeys through the city, taking in its extremes of glamour and sleaze. Though they need to solve mysteries, they usually do so by stirring up trouble and being tough enough to handle the consequences. Hard-boiled endings, rather than returning society to order or vindicating the power of reason, affirm their heroes' ability to survive against the odds.

In formal terms, the difference is between 'closed' and 'open' narrative. Socially, this corresponds to the difference between the small, settled community and the amorphous larger unit: the country and the city. Culturally, the difference is between Britain and the USA. The Golden Age novel is quintessentially British – or at least it embodies all the features which people used to like to regard as quintessentially British. The hard-boiled novel, on the other hand, embodies all the features which it is still fashionable to regard as quintessentially American. Certainly, the Golden Age novel never looked more British than when the Americans were attempting it, or the hard-boiled novel more American than when the British were attempting it.

So the differences between the two schools quickly resolve themselves into opposition: Golden Age novels versus hard-boiled novels. Virtually all hard-core fans, and many casual readers too, have a preference so strongly developed that it amounts to loyalty to one or the other school and indifference to its alternative. They like their mysteries cosy or they like them tough. These loyalties cut across national boundaries: cult appreciation of the hard-boiled may well be stronger nowadays in Europe than in the USA and cult appreciation of the Golden Age stronger in the USA than in Europe. Loyalty can also run counter to critical judgement. As a reviewer W.H. Auden heaped influential praise on the hard-boiled school, but in his private capacity as a reader he admitted he still had difficulty enjoying mysteries which were not set in English villages.

Auden made the admission rather shamefacedly, by way of illustrating his argument that the appeal of mysteries had less to do with the aesthetics of art than with the psychology of addiction. Yet his embarrassment also defers to what had become orthodoxy by the Second World War. By and large it remains orthodoxy today. People who prefer their mysteries cosy are usually slightly ashamed.

Raymond Chandler moved the crime and mystery novel from the country house to the mean streets of the city but still found room for wistful romance – like Moose Molloy's quest for Velma in **Farewell, My Lovely.**

However tenacious their preference, they fear it marks them out as frivolous escapists – limited, when it comes to critical defence, to praising mere cleverness of construction or felicity of style in their favourite works. Supporters of the hard-boiled school sound altogether more confident. Did not its pioneers spearhead a rebellion against the Golden Age, exposing the complacency and inadequacies of their predecessors? Did not they show the way to making crime and mystery fiction more adult, more serious?

This critical claim will need careful examination, if only because of the influence – by no means always happy or productive – it came to exert over hard-boiled writers themselves. But the reading of history underpinning the claim needs to be challenged from the start. Golden Age writers might themselves have been growing aware of the exhaustible limits of

With *Red Harvest* (1929) Dashiell Hammett and the new 'hard-boiled' school graduated from pulp magazines like *Black Mask* to hard covers ... and then to best-selling paperbacks.

their form by the end of the 1920s, but their realization did not give birth to the hard-boiled school. It had already been born. The hard-boiled school came about not in reaction against Golden Age fiction, or indeed as the result of any programme of rebellion, but simply as a separate and rival development in the USA – a country which was anyway bound to tire of borrowing from the Old World and to find its own voice.

Chronologically speaking, the Golden Age and the hard-boiled era are the same period. Agatha Christie introduced Hercule Poirot in *The Mysterious Affair at Styles*, which was published in 1921, the same year that saw, on the other side of the Atlantic, the birth of *Black Mask*, the magazine which would nurture the hard-boiled school. In 1923, when Dorothy L. Sayers introduced Lord Peter Wimsey in *Whose Body?*, *Black Mask* published the first of Carroll John Daly's stories of Race Williams, the prototype for the hard-boiled detective. In 1926, when Agatha Christie published *The Murder of Roger Ackroyd* and S.S. Van Dine introduced Philo Vance in *The Benson Murder Case*, *Black Mask* acquired its most influential editor, Captain Joseph T. Shaw. In 1929, when Ronald Knox codified his 'Ten Commandments', Dashiell Hammett graduated from the pages of *Black Mask* to his first full-length novel, *Red Harvest*.

Hard-boiled fiction would have happened anyway, even if Agatha Christie and Dorothy L. Sayers and S.S. Van Dine had not written the way they did or Knox had not formulated his rules. The impetus came from the conditions of American life and the opportunities available to the American writer in the 1920s. The economic boom following the First World War combined with the introduction of Prohibition in 1920 to

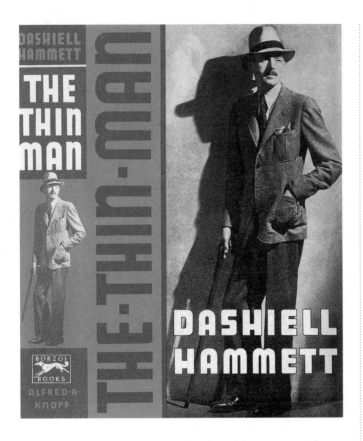

encourage the rise of the gangster. The familiar issues of law and lawlessness in a society determined to judge itself by the most ideal standards took on a new urgency. At the same time, the pulp magazines were already exploiting a ready market for adventure stories – what Ronald Knox would have called 'shockers' – which made heroes of cowboys, soldiers, explorers and masked avengers. It took no great leap of imagination for them to tackle modern crime and detection, fresh from the

Dashiell Hammett posing for the cover of his novel and sowing confusion about who 'the thin man' is. In the text he is the character whose disappearance prompts the mystery, but this photo and then the films starring William Powell and Myrna Loy encouraged people to identify the thin man with the boozy, sophisticated detective Nick Charles, and with Hammett himself.

newspaper headlines of the day, and create heroes with the same vigour as their well-established favourites.

From such cheap and fertile origins sprang the work first of Hammett, then a decade later of Raymond Chandler, and then of Ross Macdonald, the three writers whose work established the hard-boiled school and the legion of imitators and followers who still flourish today. Its popular appeal was obvious from the start. Its ability to achieve critical acceptance was another matter, though the need to undertake the task was spelled out by Chandler, always the school's most articulate theorist and polemicist. He celebrated his own success and, implicitly, that of Hammett before him in having taken 'a cheap, shoddy and utterly lost kind of writing and … made of it something that intellectuals claw each other about.' 'To accept a mediocre form and make something like literature out of it,' he added, 'is in itself rather an accomplishment.'

Or is that exactly a celebration? Perhaps the sentences are so hedged with qualification and trail off so vaguely because of uncertainty as much as modesty. Chandler, like Hammett before him, was always made uneasy by consideration of the ways in which hard-boiled fiction could develop, the achievements it could aspire to. Of course, he never lost an opportunity for shrewd, witty diatribe against the Golden Age. 'The Simple Art of Murder', the essay he published in 1944, radiates the justified confidence of a writer who knows that his brand of writing looks much healthier than its immediate rival. But just how much sophistication and self-consciousness could hard-boiled fiction develop before it lost touch with the crude vitality in which it had been rooted?

A NEW SAINT NOVEL By LESLIE CHARTERI

NOW 10¢

POPULAR DETECTIVE

JUNE

THRILLING PUBLICATION

THE CIVIC MURA

When Frank A. Munsey decided in the 1880s that good paper was less important than good writing and so began to issue his magazines on pulpwood paper, he gave a name to a whole era not just in American publishing but also in American popular culture. Its heyday came in the interlude between the two World Wars. By the mid-1930s there were about two hundred of these cheap magazines, published weekly, fortnightly or monthly, and sold largely by subscription at a cost of anything between a dime and twenty-five cents. Their brightly enamelled covers were as distinctive as their grey pages, which led people to call them 'grey paper' magazines (to distinguish them from 'white paper' or 'slick paper' magazines) or just the 'pulps'.

The writers, of course, were badly paid – often at a cent a word – and unsung, many of them big producers hidden behind a range of pseudonyms. Robert Leslie Bellem, for example, wrote perhaps three hundred stories in all (including the best-selling series about Hollywood detective Dan Turner) under his own name and as Jerome Severs Perry, Justin Case, Ellery Watson Calder and Harcourt Weems. Frederick C. Davis wrote at least a thousand, as Murdo Coombs, Stephen Ransome and Curtis Steele. Lester Dent, who also wrote as H.O. Cash, Kenneth Roberts, Tim Ryan and

Robert Wallace, was best known as Kenneth Robeson, the pseudonym under which he produced the Doc Savage novels. Such works made a bridge between the older tradition of the 'dime novel', which had given birth to Nick Carter and Dr Fu-Manchu, and the comic strips about Superman, Batman and the rest which would flourish in the 1940s. Before its brief hour in the sun was over pulp fiction had given America a long list of popular heroes which included the cowboys of Max Brand's Westerns, Tarzan, Zorro, The Shadow (alias millionaire Lamont Cranston) and Conan the Barbarian.

Pulp fiction also created the hard-boiled private eye. Alongside pulps devoted to romance, jungle or military adventure, the Wild West and the supernatural were titles such as *Crime Buster*, *Underworld Magazine*, *Greater Gangster*, *Ace G-Man*, *Private Detective*, *Real Detective*, *Super Detective*, *Double Action Detective*, *Thrilling Detective* and *Popular Detective*, not to mention *Candid Detective* and *Spicy Detective*, which changed its name to the more chaste *Speed Detective*. In this ephemeral and shifting market *Dime Detective* and *Detective Fiction Weekly* were particularly important, but pride of place was enjoyed by *Black Mask*. The distinguished journalist H.L. Mencken founded it in 1920 with the drama critic George Jean

Nathan to subsidize their up-market magazine *The Smart Set*. They were able to sell it off at a handsome profit after only six months, and *Black Mask* had a succession of editors before being finally absorbed by *Ellery Queen's Mystery Magazine* in 1951.

In the course of its career, *Black Mask* permanently changed the face of crime and mystery fiction in America. This achievement is associated above all with the names of Dashiell Hammett, who began publishing in its pages in 1923, and Raymond Chandler, who started his career in the magazine a decade later with 'Blackmailers Don't Shoot' in 1933. It was thus entirely appropriate that the only occasion when Hammett and Chandler met should have been at *Black Mask*'s dinner for its writers in 1936. (Hammett did not record his impression of Chandler; Chandler was struck mainly by Hammett's 'fearful capacity' for whisky.) To their names historians usually add that of *Black Mask*'s most famous editor, Captain Joseph T. Shaw. But Shaw had only a peripheral impact on Chandler's development and he did not become editor until 1926, when Hammett had already established himself as a contributor. Moreover, one of Shaw's predecessors, George Sutton Jr, had already labelled the magazine's special brand of fiction as 'daytime stories', so-called because readers with weak nerves should not tackle them at night.

Sutton had in mind the work not of Hammett but of Carroll John Daly, creator of heroes like Terry Mack ('Three Gun Terry'), Satan Hall and, above all, Race Williams. Williams first appeared in a *Black Mask* story in 1923 and in a novel, *The Snarl of the Beast*, in 1926. He is essentially a cowboy transferred, with little change, to the urban world of Prohibition and the Depression, standing somewhere in the middle between lawmen and gangsters. 'You can't make hamburger meat without grinding up a little meat,' he says in describing his approach to crime, an approach shared by the other detectives who flourished beside him in *Black Mask*. They included, for example, Jo Gar, the Manila detective whom Raoul Whitfield wrote about under the pseudonym of Ramon Decolta; Frederick Nebel's Donny Donahue and Cardigan of the Cosmos Detective Agency; and Erle Stanley Gardner's Ed Jenkins, the Phantom Crook. (The relentlessly productive Gardner also created a whole galaxy of heroes, such as Speed Dash and Lester Leith, for other pulps.)

But Shaw attached particular value to spare and idiomatic prose. When he took on the editorship of *Black Mask*, he found the sort of writing he most wanted to encourage less in Daly's rather stilted work – though Race Williams continued to be the magazine's biggest selling-point, always prominently announced on the cover – than in Hammett's stories about the Continental Op. In December 1928 Shaw formulated his requirements in what amounted to a manifesto of the hard-boiled school:

We do not care for purely scientific detective stories which lack action, and we are prejudiced by experience against the psychological story which is not very rugged and intense in its treatment and subject matter. We avoid the old formula type of so-called detective story, as well as the gruesome, the unnatural or supernatural. We stress plausibility in all details, and we wish swift movement and action.

As Chandler would later put it: 'When in doubt, have a man come through a door with a gun in his hand.' Nobody could doubt that a new school had emerged, or that *Black Mask* was its natural home, when Shaw attracted a second generation of writers. As well as Chandler they included now-forgotten figures like Willis Todhunter Ballard, Paul Cain, Norbert Davis and Cleve F. Adams, and a few who have kept some of their original reputation over the years: Horace McCoy, best known for his novel *They Shoot Horses Don't They?* (1935); George Harmon Coxe, with his Flashgun Casey series; and Cornell Woolrich (also publishing as William Irish and George Hopley), whose stories of lonely torment helped to forge a vital link between the world of the pulps and the *film noir*.

Frank Gruber's *The Pulp Jungle* (1967) is a rare autobiography by a pulp writer and Ron Goulart's *Cheap Thrills* (1972) an informal history of the pulps. Shaw himself compiled an anthology of stories from *Black Mask*, called *The Hard-Boiled Omnibus*, in 1946. Some (like Erle Stanley Gardner, who declined to be included) thought Shaw's introduction and selection exaggerated his own role in shaping the magazine. Ron Goulart supplemented it with *The Hardboiled Dicks* (1965), drawing on stories from *Dime Detective* and *Detective Fiction Weekly* as well as *Black Mask*, while Herbert Ruhm edited *The Hard-Boiled Detective: Stories from Black Mask Magazine 1920–1950* (1977) and Maxim Jakubowski *The Mammoth Book of Pulp Fiction* (1996).

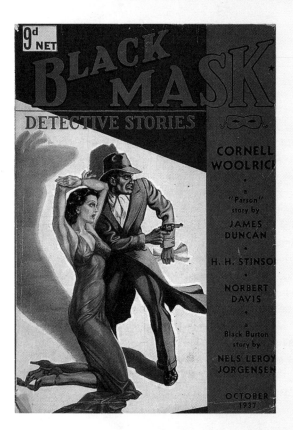

Cornell Woolrich was a prolific pulp author. His *The Bride Wore Black* was filmed by François Truffaut in 1967 as *La mariée était en noir*, starring Jeanne Moreau.

DETECTIVE
BOOK MAGAZINE
20c
The Bride Wore
BLACK
A BOOK WITHIN A MAGAZINE
ALSO A NOVELET & SHORT STORIES
"There is nothing more beautiful and honorable than killing."
FICTION HOUSE MAGAZINES
By CORNELL WOOLRICH

DASHIELL HAMMETT: STYLE AND SILENCE

Hammett made the answers look easy to everyone but himself. Other writers of crime and mystery fiction have been as influential, yet none has intervened in its history as briefly and decisively as he did. His real career lasted only eleven years, from the appearance of his first Continental Op story, 'Arson Plus', in *Black Mask* in 1923 to the publication of *The Thin Man* in 1934. During those years he published his Op stories and two novels, *Red Harvest* and *The Dain Curse* (both 1929), which apply the lessons of his apprenticeship to the demands of full-length narrative; two supremely controlled masterpieces, *The Maltese Falcon* (1930) and *The Glass Key* (1931); and *The Thin Man* (1934), a lightweight and cynical work which more or less declares his indifference not to writing but to his chosen form. Fundamentally, that indifference may have been there all along. Hammett did not die until 1961, but after *The Thin Man* he wrote

An illustration by Max Plaisted for Robert Leslie Bellem's *Dan Turner, Hollywood Detective*, a pulp magazine which flourished from 1942 to 1950. Bellem's stories pushed the tough-guy slang pioneered by Dashiell Hammett to comic extremes.

storylines for Hollywood, promised novels, stories and scripts which were never delivered, tinkered with fragments, and collected royalties from old work and old ideas. In effect he receded into silence.

Yet, even silent, Hammett remained a dominating presence. To understand why, one need only consider a typical passage from his work. This is how *Red Harvest* begins:

I first heard Personville called Poisonville by a red-haired mucker named Hickey Dewey in the Big Ship in Butte. He also called his shirt a shoit. I didn't think anything of what he had done to the city's name. Later I heard men who could manage their r's give it the same pronunciation. I still didn't see anything in it but the meaningless sort of humour that used to make richardsnary the thieves' word for dictionary. A few years later I went to Personville and learned better.

His assurance in summoning up the milieu in which the hero and the story will operate is almost nonchalant. The paragraph tells the reader that cities, apparently whole cities, can be corrupt and that the hero is too worldly to be surprised as well as too self-confident to be intimidated by the discovery. Plainly, he is already used to a criminal milieu which embraces characters with colourful names like Hickey Dewey, Brooklyn accents, specialized slang and obscenities which need to be rendered on the printed page by euphemisms like 'mucker'. Such experience is always a given in hard-boiled writing. It is there from the start in the narrative voice: spare and laconic, neutral enough to pick up the slang criminals use and examine it wryly, but not so neutral that it entirely avoids the same slang.

Before Hammett, no major crime writer had dared entrust the narrative to the detective himself, let alone entrust so much to the language he uses to tell his

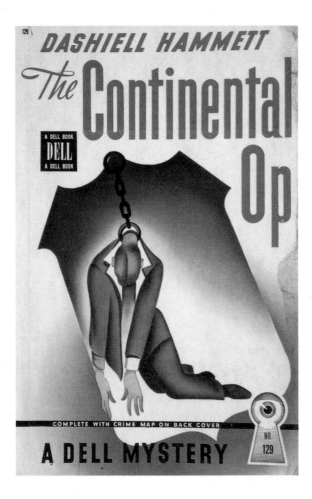

arbitrarily hidden from the reader – as by sudden discovery through adventure.

This is how the Continental Op, who tells the story of *Red Harvest*, does his work, and how most hard-boiled detectives do theirs. The adventures which yield discovery are usually confrontations, often physical ones, deliberately sought out and provoked. Stirring things up rather than thinking things out is always their method. Yet the confrontations are no simple opportunity for a show of physical strength. Being tough has little if anything to do with beating people up, at least not in Hammett and Chandler. In fact, their detectives win their spurs by being able to take a beating – or, better still, to avoid one with the right answer, the smart repartee that confounds the rich, the gangsters, the police and all the rest trying to obstruct their path. Being tough is a matter of attitude, not muscles and guns, the despised tools on which the detective's opponents usually rely.

World-weary and cynical, yet not too cynical to help a client in trouble, the Continental Op is the prototype of the fictional private eye, though Hammett himself dismissed *The Dain Curse* as a 'silly story'.

story. Together, these changes would transform the genre. For a start, just making the detective the narrator dramatically alters the detection. Doyle did not do it with Sherlock Holmes (or rather, he did it only once and in a weak story, 'The Lion's Mane') because it would have forced him either to give the game away or to cheat. That is the main reason why the 'idiot friend' from whom the detective conceals the real progress of his deductions is a favourite device in the classical detective story. When the detective becomes the narrator, his investigations cannot progress so much by detached reasoning – which would have to be either confided as he goes along or

Private Eyes in Fact and Fiction

When, near the beginning of *A Study in Scarlet*, Sherlock Holmes described himself to Dr Watson as a 'consulting detective', he was drawing a distinction between himself and the ordinary private detectives who, as he suggested, were almost as common as policemen. In Britain, as in other countries, reliance on freelance thief-takers had been lessened but not eliminated by the establishment of police forces in the nineteenth century. Even the men from the Detective Office, the predecessor of Scotland Yard, had been available for private hire – which was how Sergeant Cuff had got involved with the mystery of the missing diamond in Wilkie Collins' *The Moonstone*. Police detectives often left the force to set up in business for themselves, as Cuff's real-life prototype Jonathan Whicher had done, following in the footsteps of the famous Vidocq, who had established his own private inquiry agency after he finally retired from the Sûreté.

It was inevitable that private detection would cross the Atlantic to the United States, where the *laissez-faire* ethic and the state of frontier society offered special opportunities to the bounty-hunter. The pioneer was Allan Pinkerton, a Scottish immigrant who started his Pinkerton National Detective Agency in Chicago in 1850. By the time of the Civil War a decade later he was successful enough to become Lincoln's chief intelligence officer. After the war Pinkerton's specialized in solving bank robberies and railway theft, spending a great deal of fruitless energy in pursuit of the James brothers but managing to track Butch Cassidy and the Sundance Kid down to Bolivia. Pinkerton's also did security work for big companies, stamping out the terrorist activities of the Molly Maguires in the Pennsylvania coalfields and breaking strikes organized by the early labour unions.

By the early years of the twentieth century Pinkerton's had become a familiar institution, with imitators and rivals in the agencies founded by William Burns and Nick Harris. Its trademark, a wide-open eye with the motto 'We Never Sleep', was so universally known it had inspired the slang term 'private eye'. Its staff and resources rivalled the official police – particularly before the advent of an effective national police force, which had to await the reorganization of the FBI in answer to the threat from organized crime in the 1920s. In fact, Pinkerton's and the other big agencies were always careful to cultivate friendly relations with the police, as they were eager to do anything which would soothe memories of private detection's tainted past. Most did not do divorce work, which became the staple of smaller businesses. Pinkerton's frowned not just on the slangy 'private eye' but even on the word 'detective', insisting on calling its employees by the bureaucratic term 'operatives', soon abbreviated by the public to 'ops'. Later generations of private detectives would prefer to call themselves 'private investigators', which conveniently abbreviated to 'PIs'.

Yet for all his insistence on creating a respectable image for himself and his agency, Allan Pinkerton understood the value of self-publicity as well as Vidocq had ever done. *The Expressman and the Detective* (1874) was the first of the fictionalized accounts of the agency's cases that he lent his name to. It is impossible to determine what basis, if any, these books have in fact. What is certain, though, is that they were written by hack writers with the aim of promoting Pinkerton's reputation. And in this they succeeded, if their popularity is anything to go by: the series ran to more than a dozen titles before Pinkerton's death in 1884, and was imitated by other writers claiming to set down their authentic experiences. These books used the format of the 'dime novel' to do for private detectives in the United States what 'yellowback' reminiscences had done – and were still doing – for police detectives in Britain. Like the modern policeman, the modern private eye had no sooner emerged in real life than he was being transformed into fiction. Virtually from the start, fact and fiction flourished in the same ground.

They continued to do so in the 1920s and 1930s, when hard-boiled writers mythologized the private eye with particular intensity. Hammett, in particular, derived his status not just from his fresh approach to literary form but from the fact he had started out as a Pinkerton's man himself, working for the agency in Baltimore, Spokane and San Francisco for most of the years between 1915 and 1922.

By all accounts he was a good detective, employed on several well-known cases, including the scandal which destroyed the career of 'Fatty' Arbuckle, one of Mack Sennett's Keystone Cops, in the early 1920s. His experiences left him with a fund of wry anecdotes – 'I know a man who once stole a Ferris-wheel' was one – which he delighted to air during his years of fame. Most of his reminiscences are downbeat, often at the expense of the glamour other people attributed to private detectives: 'In 1917, Washington D.C., I met a young lady who did not remark that my work must be very interesting'.

His experience also gave Hammett the right to lecture readers and fellow writers on technical detail: 'a pistol, to be a revolver, must have something on it that revolves', silencers do not work, bullet and stab wounds do not hurt at the moment of impact, you do not follow a suspect by dodging from doorway to doorway. He made these points in an article which began with a laconic rebuke:

It would be silly to insist that nobody who has not been a detective should write detective stories, but it is certainly not unreasonable to ask any one who is going to write a book of any sort to make some effort at least to learn something about his subject.

When he began publishing his stories in *Black Mask*, Hammett was not a writer learning about detection but a detective learning about writing. And he always kept the special authority of a man who had really walked the mean streets of which he wrote. That was something no previous detective novelist could boast and something any hard-boiled novelist could envy.

THE
Maltese
Falcon

BY

Dashiell Hammett

First-person narrative is a vital instrument in conveying this view of toughness. Yet even in Chandler, where it reaches its ultimate refinement in dialogue bristling with wisecracks and narrative spiked with similes, the result is anything but confessional. Significantly, Philip Marlowe's reticence is at its most strongly defended when it comes to his emotional life. In Hammett's fiction, severe and classical by comparison, the reader knows almost nothing about the Continental Op, not even his name. He is unmarried, balding, middle-aged and, to judge from the way he tackles his cases, experienced and dogged. But that is really all the reader knows, or needs to know, of a character whose function is to be, as narrator, a trustworthy observer and, as character, a catalyst of the events which bring the plot to a head.

Hammett, said Chandler, took murder out of the hands of people who committed it with rare oriental daggers. These are just some of the new alternatives.

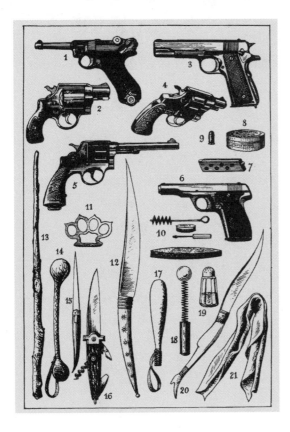

Given the slam-bang pace of *Red Harvest* and *The Dain Curse*, the reader would hardly have time to know more about the Op. Hammett built these early novels out of episodes modelled on, or actually taken from, the short stories he had been writing for Joseph T. Shaw at *Black Mask*, an editor determined to pack his pages with as much action as possible. As it was, Hammett still had to prune a few surplus bodies when he revised the serialized texts for publication as books. And in *The Maltese Falcon* and *The Glass Key* he settled, characteristically, for an altogether sparer form. In essence, each is a straightforward murder mystery depending on a few simple clues – daringly few and daringly simple, in fact. Hammett cleared as much space as possible in order to look more intently at the characters of his detectives, Sam Spade in *The Maltese Falcon* and Ned Beaumont in *The Glass Key*.

Significantly, he chose to do this by abandoning first-person narrative for the most detached and factual of third-person narratives. As John Huston discovered, one reason why *The Maltese Falcon* could be filmed so effectively was that the novel itself contained no more analysis of its characters' inner lives than a screenplay would. It is an old trick to make the detective as mysterious as the case he investigates, but Hammett managed to pull it off without burdening Sam Spade with the usual repertoire of puzzling or eccentric mannerisms. He simply made him enigmatic, and as a result readers spend as much time asking themselves questions about Spade as they do asking questions about who killed Spade's partner, Miles Archer. Does Spade really care about finding the murderer? Or is he just exploiting the intrigues of Gutman and his gang for his private advantage?

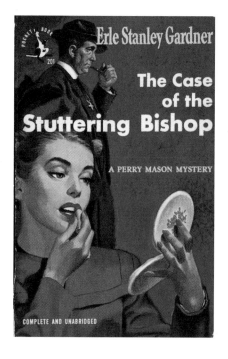

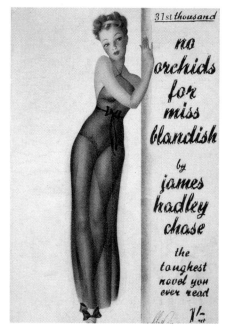

The glamour and dangerous passions of the hard-boiled school.

It turns out that Spade does care about finding the killer and is willing to turn her in, despite all the blandishments she has thrown his way. Yet the speech in which he explains his action – a classic set-piece both of detective fiction and cinema – almost bewilders in the sheer number of reasons he gives and the questions still left unanswered. Some considerations are merely prudential: Spade has to protect himself and his professional reputation. More important, though, is the argument from nature and instinct: 'I'm a detective and expecting me to run criminals down and then let them go free is like asking a dog to catch a rabbit and let it go. It can be done, but it's not the natural thing.' The parallel between the detective and the predator had often been drawn before, and usually not to any reassuring purpose. Yet here Spade's obedience to what is for him 'the natural thing' amounts to a sort of integrity, a code which does not need to invoke the language of ethics or idealism. On such issues, of course, Spade is silent, just as he remains silent about whatever private cost the code may exact from him.

The same holds true of Ned Beaumont in *The Glass Key*. He begins the novel at home among gangsters and corrupt politicians, distinguished only by the sharpness of his intelligence. By the end, he has shown that loyalty to his friend Paul Madvig lay behind his enigmatic behaviour – that, and the desire to escape the milieu. He has a code and he has integrity to himself. Neither demand that he go in for making moral declarations or revealing himself to the other characters. Yet *The Glass Key* casts light on Hammett's sense of the hidden limitations and private difficulties behind the enigmatic façade. The hero is neither as completely tough nor as completely untarnished as readers might wish him.

A Hard-Boiled Dictionary ?

The slang in use among criminals is for the most part a conscious, artificial growth, designed more to confuse outsiders than for any other purpose, but sometimes it is singularly expressive...

Dashiell Hammett 'From the Memoirs of a Private Detective' (1923)

I'm an intellectual snob who happens to have a fondness for the American vernacular, largely because I grew up on Latin and Greek. I had to learn American just like a foreign language. To learn it I had to study and analyse it. As a result, when I use slang, solecisms, colloquialisms, snide talk or any kind of off-beat language, I do it deliberately. The literary use of slang is a study in itself. I've found that there are only two kinds that are any good: slang that has established itself in the language and slang that you make up yourself. Everything else is apt to be passé before it gets into print.

Raymond Chandler letter of 18 March 1949

BADGER GAME - blackmail practised on a man who is lured by a woman into a compromising situation and then threatened by her male accomplice

BANG-TAIL, PONY - racehorse

BEAN-SHOOTER, CANNON, GAT, HEAT, HEATER, ROD, RODNEY, ROSCOE - gun (usually pistol or revolver)

BEEF - to grumble

BERRIES - dollars

BIG HOUSE, CABOOSE, CAN, COOLER, HOOSEGOW, PEN, STIR - jail (see also BOOBY HATCH)

BIG ONE, CHICAGO OVERCOAT - death (THE BIG SLEEP was Chandler's own coinage, which he lived to see used by Eugene O'Neill in THE ICEMAN COMETH in the belief it was genuine gangster slang)

BIRD - guy (also YEGG)

BLIP OFF, BLOW DOWN, BOP, BUMP, BUMP OFF, CROAK, KNOCK OFF, POOP, POP, RUB OUT - to kill (BOP also = to punch or hit)

BOOB - fool (also MUG, RUBE, SAP)

BOOBY HATCH - psychiatric hospital or jail

BOOZE HOUND, JUICER, LUSH, SOUSE - alcoholic

BOP, SOCK - to punch or hit

BRACE - to grab

BRACELETS, CUFFS, NIPPERS - handcuffs

Cont...

Cont...

BREEZE, DANGLE, DRIFT, DUST, DUST OUT, FADE, GO TO READ AND WRITE, SCOOT, TAKE A POWDER, TAKE THE AIR - to leave, make oneself scarce, disappear (also TAKE A MICKEY FINN)

BROAD, DAME, DOLL - woman

BULL, BUTTON, COP, COPPER, FLATTY, JOHN - policeman (in contrast to its meaning in British slang, COPPER can also be used for a private detective)

BUM STEER - something worthless or misleading

BUNCO - fraud, confidence trick

BUNK, HOOEY - nonsense

BURG - town

BURN, PUMP, SQUIRT, THROW METAL OR LEAD, SNAP CAPS - to fire bullets

BUSTED FLUSH - literally, in poker an incomplete hand of cards of the same suit; more generally, a failure

BUZZER - police badge

C, CENTURY, YARD - a hundred dollars (C also = cocaine, for which see DOPE, etc.)

CHIPPY - flirtatious or promiscuous woman

CHIV, CHIVE, SHIV, SHIVE - knife

CHOPPER - machine gun

CINCH - something easy or certain

CLAMP, NAB, ROCK OFF - to arrest, catch (also PINCH)

CLIP JOINT bar or club which charges high prices or cheats customers

CLUBHOUSE - police station

CON - convict, person with criminal record

COP THE SNEAK, TAKE IT ON THE LAM - to escape

CRAP GAME, CRAPS - game of dice (see RATS AND MICE)

CRASH OUT - to break out, escape from jail

CROAKER - doctor

DARK MEAT, DINGE, JIG, SMOKE - black person (also SHINE)

DICK, GUM-HEEL, GUMSHOE, HAWKSHAW, OP, PEEPER, SHAMUS, SLEUTH, SNOOPER - private detective (DICK is also used for a police detective, and all these words can be qualified in terms such as HOUSE DICK, HOUSE PEEPER or HOUSE SHAMUS for a hotel detective;

a COPPER can be a private detective as well as a policeman; HAWKSHAW goes back to Victorian times: see the feature on 'Hawkshaw and THE TICKET-OF-LEAVE MAN', p. 22)

DINGUS - thing

DIP - pickpocket

DIVE - disreputable bar or club

DOPE - information

DOPE, HOP, JUNK - drugs, especially heroin (SNOW = heroin or cocaine; HOPHEAD, DOPE-FIEND, SNOWBIRD = addict)

DOUGH, JACK - money

DRILL - to shoot

DROPPER, GUN, HATCHETMAN, TORPEDO, TRIGGERMAN - hired killer or gunman (see also GOON, etc. and GUNSEL)

DRY-GULCH - to knock out

DUMMERER - beggar who poses as a deaf mute

FIN, FIVE SPOT - five dollars, five-dollar bill

FINGER - to identify, inform on, or betray

FINK, PIGEON, STOOL-PIGEON, STOOLIE (or STOOLY) - informer (see also RAT)

FLIMFLAM - swindle

FLIVVER - Ford car

FLOGGER - overcoat

FLOP HOUSE - cheap hotel

GEE - guy

GLAUM, GLOM - to steal (also PINCH)

GONIF - thief

GOON, HOOD, HOODLUM, PUNK - criminal thug

GRAB AIR - to put one's hands up in surrender

GRAND, LARGE - a thousand dollars

GRIFTER - confidence trickster or fraudster

GUNSEL - young or kept homosexual (Joseph T. Shaw, editor of BLACK MASK, failed to censor the word when Sam Spade used it of Wilmer in THE MALTESE FALCON, under the impression it simply meant 'gunman')

GYP - to cheat

HACK - taxi (HACKIE = taxidriver)

HASH HOUSE - cheap restaurant

HEAP - car

HEIST - theft or hold-up

HIGHBINDER - corrupt politician or official

HOOCH, HOOTCH - whisky, especially illicit whisky sold during Prohibition

ICE - diamonds

JOINT - place, especially a bar or club

KICK OFF - to die

KNOCKOVER raid or robbery

LAY - job or situation

LUG - bullet (also PILL), or ear

MARBLE - pearl

MEAT WAGON - ambulance

MICKEY FINN, MICKEY - drugged drink (but TAKE A MICKEY FINN, TAKE A MICKEY = run off, disappear)

MITT - hand

MOB - gang

MOLL - girlfriend

MOUTHPIECE, SHYSTER - lawyer

MUG - face, or fool (also BOOB, RUBE, SAP)

NEVADA GAS - cyanide

NEWSHAWK - newspaper reporter

NEWSIE - newspaper seller

NICK, TRIM - to con or defraud (see also SHAKE DOWN)

NIX - no, nothing

NOGGIN, NOODLE - head

PACK, PACK IRON, WEAR IRON - to carry a gun

PASTE - to punch

PETERMAN - safebreaker (also YEGG)

PIKER - vagrant (also VAG), small-time gambler, or poor sport

PILL - bullet (also LUG), or cigarette

PINCH - to arrest, or to steal (also GLAUM, GLOM)

PORTRAIT OF MADISON - five hundred dollars, five-hundred-dollar bill

PUG - boxer (from pugilist)

RAP - criminal charge, or information (RAP SHEET = criminal record)

RAT - to inform

RATS AND MICE - dice

RINGER - fake

RUBE - easy target, or fool (also BOOB, MUG, SAP)

SAP - blackjack, or fool (also BOOB, MUG, RUBE)

SAWBUCK - ten dollars, ten-dollar bill

SHAKE DOWN - to extort or defraud, or to search thoroughly (especially for concealed weapons)

SHINE - bootleg liquor (moonshine), or black person (see also DARK MEAT, etc.)

SHOOT THE WORKS - to risk everything on one throw, or to tell the whole truth

SNATCH - kidnapping

SOAK - to pawn (HOCK-SHOP = pawnbroker's shop)

SPEAKEASY, SPEAK - illicit bar

STIFF - corpse

TICKET - private investigator's licence

TWO BITS - twenty-five cents

TWO-TIME LOSER - twice-convicted criminal

VAG, WAG - down-and-out (from vagrant)

YAP - petty swindler

YEGGMAN - safebreaker (more generally, YEGG also = guy)

YOUSE = plural form of 'you' (or so Hammett insisted, rebuking writers who made their characters use it indiscriminately for the singular and plural forms)

For some examples of the equivalent argot used by French crime writers, see the feature on 'Exporting the Hard-Boiled: Léo Malet and the roman noir américain' (p. 120)

HAMMETT IN HOLLYWOOD

He carries his love in his iron fists! Publicity for the 1935 film of *The Glass Key*

Hollywood's best memorial to Dashiell Hammett's work is John Huston's 1941 version of *The Maltese Falcon*, a film sensible enough to take most of its script from the tightly written dialogue of the novel and blessed with an ideal cast. Bogart's portrayal of Sam Spade, together with his performance as Philip Marlowe in Howard Hawks' version of Chandler's *The Big Sleep* five years later, gave the tough private eye his most definitive screen image. Yet the achievement came about only with great difficulty. *The Maltese Falcon* had already been filmed twice, first with Ricardo Cortez inappropriately bringing the personality of a Latin lover to Sam Spade in 1931, and then with Sam Spade elbowed out to create a vehicle for Bette Davis, called *Satan Met a Lady*, in 1936. A remake did not look a promising idea in 1941, and the difficulties which the young Huston met began when his first choice, George Raft, turned down the part of Spade and continued with the studio wanting, until the last moment, to call the film *The Gent from Frisco*.

Such difficulties typify those Hammett himself, as well as his published work, had in Hollywood. Yet his fascination with the film business was enduring. It had begun in 1929 when he sent a Hollywood producer his first novel, *Red Harvest*, even before it had appeared between hard covers. And it could still be rekindled towards the end of his life when, in 1950, he agreed (but predictably failed) to write a screen treatment of Sidney Kingsley's play *Detective Story* for William Wyler. In the years between he had been lionized by an industry which could never resist putting an acclaimed writer on its payroll and was, besides, eager to produce tough crime stories to meet the mood of the times. For his part Hammett welcomed the easy money and threw himself into partygoing, womanizing and drinking with all the reckless gusto of a man who, as one friend remarked, seemed to have no particular intention of being around much beyond next Thursday.

Artistically, the results were meagre. *City Streets* (1931), *Woman in the Dark* (1934) and *Mister Dynamite* (1935) were all based on stories he devised for the studios, but his only credited script came when he adapted *Watchers on the Rhine*, an anti-Nazi play by his partner Lillian Hellman, for the screen in 1943. In the meantime his published novels were faring little better than *The Maltese Falcon* had in its first two adaptations. In the process of becoming *Roadhouse Nights* (1930) *Red Harvest* lost its political bite and landed up owing far more to Ben Hecht than to Hammett. *The Glass Key* was twice bungled, a failure made all the more tantalizing by the fact that Gary Cooper never got the chance he wanted to play Ned Beaumont. In a 1935 version which deliberately muted the novel's uncomfortable ambiguities the part went to George Raft, who turned in a strong performance despite being awed by Hammett when he met him on the set ('He'd read all these different books. Me, I was never much for reading – I didn't have a lot to say to him'). The 1942 version had a sharp script by Jonathan Latimer – on his way from writing the Bill Crane novels to adapting Perry

Mason for TV – but otherwise all the limitations to be expected of a vehicle for Alan Ladd and Veronica Lake.

The Thin Man was better suited to studios which, at least in the 1930s, were far more at home making suave comedy-thrillers than recreating the bleak world of Hammett's other novels. William Powell, who had already played S.S. Van Dine's Philo Vance, became Nick Charles and Myrna Loy his wife Nora in a popular series which, after *The Thin Man* (1931), quickly lost its fizz as the titles proliferated: *After the Thin Man* (1936), *Another Thin Man* (1939), *Shadow of the Thin Man* (1941), *The Thin Man Goes Home* (1944), *Song of the Thin Man* (1947). By this time, of course, the 'Thin Man' was identified with Nick Charles and not, as in the original novel, with the character whose disappearance begins the mystery. And by this time, Hammett was

contributing nothing beyond his name and the 'Thin Man' tag: his involvement had ceased with the third film, whose storyline he cobbled together from an old story about the Continental Op. He continued to collect his money (and the money from the radio rights to the 'Thin Man') but Nick and Nora Charles bored him. Mystery fiction itself had come to bore him. In Hollywood his drinking bouts and missed deadlines had become legendary. It was certainly no place for a writer sinking into false starts and incomplete fragments to find a new direction or a new sense of purpose.

John Huston's 1941 film of *The Maltese Falcon*: Bogart (Sam Spade) prepares to get tough with Elisha Cook, Jr (Wilmer), a familiar face in gangster movies and *films noirs*.

In *The Maltese Falcon* Spade's nature had demanded that he avenge his partner's murder, but it had not stopped him sleeping with his partner's wife. The closing sentences of the novel leave him shivering at the prospect of another meeting with her. In *The Glass Key* Ned Beaumont's loyalty to Madvig does not stop him going away with the woman Madvig had hoped to marry. He both saves and loses Madvig, and the closing sentence has him looking at the door through which his friend has just left.

Few writers have made the mystery novel a finer instrument of moral inquiry than Hammett. In pioneering the hard-boiled form, he also pushed it to its limit. He did not try to push it further in *The Thin Man*, which fell back instead on bright and witty comedy about a husband-and-wife team, Nick and Nora Charles. It spawned a series of popular 'Thin Man' films and a fashion for boozy, screwball humour. Hammett himself spoke harshly of it as a 'charming fable of how Nick loved Nora and Nora loved Nick and everything was just one great big laugh in the midst of other people's trials and tribulations.' He had already been equally harsh in giving the novel another of his undercutting, ironic endings, for in this case the irony is directed at the form itself, and the triviality of its overriding preoccupation with murders and the exposure of murderers. It serves as prelude to Hammett's own silence. Nora asks Nick what will happen to the other characters, what the events of the novel have really changed. Nothing, says Nick. People will go on the same as before:

'Murder doesn't round out anybody's life except the murdered's and sometimes the murderer's.'

'That may be,' Nora said, 'but it's all pretty unsatisfactory.'

RAYMOND CHANDLER: A QUALITY OF REDEMPTION

Chandler consolidated what was immediately usable in Hammett's achievement in the sequence of seven novels about Philip Marlowe that he began, some five years after Hammett had stopped writing, with *The Big Sleep* (1939) and finished, though less with a bang than a whimper, with *Playback* (1958). In particular, he took the Continental Op stories and *The Maltese Falcon* as his points of departure, elaborating the private eye Hammett had sketched with such neutral dispassion into an icon, easy to recognize and easy to admire. The bored afternoons in his dusty office when Marlowe opens the bottle in his desk drawer, the evenings he spends playing chess with himself in his apartment, the late-night phone calls that take him out on the latest stage in a case: Chandler makes these familiar routines. The city where Marlowe works becomes equally familiar, with its geography of contrasts between the smart apartments of the rich and the cheap hotels or rooming-houses of the failed. That geography, too, has its roots in the world Hammett evoked, though Chandler sharpens the contrast by adding more corrupt glitter and more pathetic seediness.

Everything, indeed, seems to have been sharpened in Chandler's world. It appears more vivid than Hammett's and promises, even on its introduction, to prove more memorable. Where Hammett's prose was bare and laconic, Chandler's is deliberately heightened. 'He had style, but his audience didn't know it,' Chandler said of his predecessor, knowing full well that nobody could fail to notice he had style. It was the dullness he most objected to in Golden Age fiction, the dullness of writers who loved

reader, Chandler presents pathos or corruption with those labels already attached. His vision is avowedly moral from the start of the narrative; solving the mystery and resolving the plot at the end will merely affirm the specifics, the technicalities of guilt or innocence. And since Marlowe is both narrator and detective, he occupies a special position as an authority not just on mysteries but on the society in which the mysteries happen.

In practice, this means that he has a code for living honourably as well as for doing a reasonably honest job as a private detective on a case. And it means that the code is a basic premise on which the novels depend, not (as in Hammett) something to be discovered in the course of the narrative and still open to challenge once discovered. Chandler states this as plainly as the language of hard-boiled fiction allows on the first page of *The Big Sleep*. Marlowe arrives at the Sternwood mansion for the interview with General Sternwood which begins the case. Left by the butler to wait in the empty hall, he notices a stained-glass panel showing an Arthurian knight who has presumably just killed the dragon and is freeing the maiden from the ropes tying her to a tree:

I stood there and thought that if I lived in the house, I would sooner or later have to climb up there and help him. He didn't seem to be really trying.

At first reading his remark sounds faintly like a leering joke about the pleasures of grappling with captive maidens – and certainly, leering jokes do play their part in the queazy sexuality which the novels go on to discover in Marlowe. But the remark is not just a joke. The plot about to unfold will involve dragons and maidens, and Marlowe's role will be that of Arthurian

thinking up plots but did not actually like writing. He applied himself conscientiously but without enthusiasm to the business of plotting and kept his real energy for the local intensity of the narrative: turning a passing character into an immaculately observed thumbnail sketch, a scene briefly glimpsed into a sharp vignette.

Yet the heightened effect of Chandler's work comes from something more than the sheer energy and care he put into his writing. Its vividness is not just that of things and people seen, but of things and people confidently assigned their place in a moral scheme. Where Hammett had been content to leave judgement to the

knight. Chandler had, after all, originally thought of naming him Malory. Making detection into a form of knight errantry, chivalry in action, was by no means a new idea when he wrote *The Big Sleep*: several Victorians had done it and so, more memorably, had Conan Doyle. What is remarkable about Chandler is the way he makes the idea look fresh and appropriate in its urban Californian setting.

Finding dragons and captive maidens in California proves no problem, though often Chandler's maidens turn out to be more dangerous than the dragons. His task is further eased by the way the 'open' form of hard-boiled narrative already resembles the quest: a journey and a series of encounters on the way to an ultimate goal. In Arthurian romance these encounters serve a double purpose, giving the knight an additional pointer to his route and testing his virtue, his fitness for the journey. The confrontations which make up the plot of Chandler's novels serve exactly the same double purpose. Chandler ritualizes the process, as he does the routines which make up Marlowe's daily life, and emphasizes what is unpromisingly shabby about his hero. Sam Spade at least had a partner and a loyal secretary, but Marlowe, merely because he is a private detective, is small-time and apparently almost friendless.

It was Chandler more than any other writer who established the convention that private detectives in fiction should be marginal, if not despised figures. Their bank accounts are low and their cars unreliable. Their clients lie to them and try to manipulate them. The rich people they deal with regard them with open contempt; even the poor react with sullen indifference. The police are often hostile, sometimes eager to pull their licence to operate and sometimes just brutal. Everywhere they go, private detectives are treated as people to be bought, to be used, to be leaned on. Marlowe endures these ordeals, living in a world where the common slang terms for people of his profession – 'shamus', 'peeper' and the rest – almost all carry a sneer. 'So you're a private detective,' Vivian Regan greets him in *The Big Sleep*, 'I didn't know they really existed, except in books. Or else they were greasy little men snooping around hotels.' 'A private detective,' ponders a visitor to his office in *The High Window*: 'I never met one. A shifty business, one gathers. Keyhole peeping, raking up scandal, that sort of thing.'

Marlowe triumphs not just eventually in solving the case but stage by stage, like the knight on his journey. In a society where money and power are almost always in the hands of the morally suspect, the shabby job, like the shabby office, becomes an emblem of the essential purity underlying his toughness. And, of course, he carries his toughness not in his fists but in his language. Interviews, which in the hands of other writers might be (and frequently are) just routine exercises in getting the details of the case across to the reader, come alive with wisecracks. His client in *The High Window* tells him: 'I don't think I'd care to employ a detective that uses liquor in any form. I don't even approve of tobacco in any form.' He replies: 'Would it be all right if I peeled an orange?' A client complains about his manners: 'I don't mind if you don't like my manners. They're pretty bad. I grieve over them during the long winter evenings.' The gangster Eddie Mars resents being questioned in *The Big Sleep*:

'Is that any of your business, soldier?'
    'I could make it my business.'

He smiled tightly and pushed his hat back on his grey hair. 'And I could make your business my business.'

'You wouldn't like it. The pay's too small.'

Chandler is always the most quotable of writers. But he also knew – unlike many of his imitators – that a hero and a novel cannot be built from wisecracks that sound amusing in isolation. They soon tire the reader or, worse, make the reader think the hero a smartass. Chandler's wisecracks work in context as well as out of it, showing how an apparently small man, without power or prestige, asserts his integrity and his code. Sometimes they help win Marlowe the respect or even friendship of those he talks back to, though on this point Chandler is uncertain and apparently indifferent. What matters is that Marlowe should keep the reader's respect and that, alone and powerless, he should begin his ordeal and triumph afresh in the next novel.

Marlowe reflects: a glimpse of Robert Montgomery as Chandler's private eye in the film *Lady in the Lake*.

Chandler in Hollywood

TAMED BY A BRUNETTE— FRAMED BY A BLONDE—BLAMED BY THE COPS!

Publicity for *The Blue Dahlia*

'You never know in Hollywood,' Chandler told a friend. He had good reason to be cagey, after being as closely involved with the film industry as any American writer of his generation, and often as unhappily. In all, he received credits for five screenplays, though the only one based on his own storyline was *The Blue Dahlia* (1946), with Alan Ladd and Veronica Lake. It came from an idea for a novel which had run into difficulties, and he offered to make it into a script as a favour to his friend, the producer and actor John Houseman. Even then, he had to change the ending he had planned when the Navy Department objected to a Second World War veteran turning out to be the murderer. The tight shooting schedule dictated by Ladd's imminent departure into the forces drove Chandler, a reformed alcoholic who had managed to stay sober for some years, to go on a binge to get the script finished in time.

His other four screenplays were adaptations. *And Now Tomorrow* (1944), another Alan Ladd vehicle, and *The Unseen* (1945), starring Joel McCrea, were of little consequence, but the remaining two were of the first importance. Chandler collaborated with Billy Wilder in adapting James M. Cain's *Double Indemnity* in 1944, making a decisive contribution to the *film noir*, and he adapted Patricia Highsmith's *Strangers on a Train* for Alfred Hitchcock in 1951. *Strangers on a Train* was Chandler's last and least satisfactory experience in Hollywood, largely because the director showed little interest in consulting him and eventually hired another writer to rework his script. Hitchcock, Chandler complained after seeing the finished result, lacked his own scrupulous concern for motivation and narrative logic, working instead on the principle 'that if you move fast enough and make enough noise, nobody will bother to ask where you're going or why.'

It was inevitable that the Marlowe novels would enjoy their own career in Hollywood, though it was also inevitable their career would be as bumpy as their creator's. It began unpromisingly in 1942, when the plot of *Farewell, My Lovely* was recycled in *The Falcon Takes Over*, in the series starring George Sanders, and the plot of *The High Window* was recycled in *A Time To Kill*, a Mike Shayne film starring Lloyd Nolan. Marlowe himself did not appear on screen until Edward Dmytryk's adaptation of *Farewell, My Lovely* as *Murder, My Sweet* (1944). The film made a vital bridge between hard-boiled fiction and *film noir*, using the detective as narrator as well as central character. Though it impressed the critics, Dick Powell's performance as Marlowe did not impress Chandler, who was inclined to class Powell with Alan Ladd as 'a small boy's idea of a tough guy'.

Surprisingly, Chandler's own ideal casting for Marlowe was Cary Grant, an actor known for suavity rather than toughness. Yet he could applaud Humphrey Bogart's performance in Howard Hawks' *The Big Sleep* (1946) – 'As we say here, Bogart can be tough without a gun' – and even defend the film despite the hash it made of his plot. (The studio, he pointed out, had insisted on cutting the scenes with Carmen Sternwood for fear that the actress, Martha Vickers, was overshadowing Lauren Bacall.) Hawks and Bogart set the standards by which he judged later film adaptations. He took a strong enough interest in Robert Montgomery's *Lady in the Lake* (1946) to write a first, uncredited version of the script, though he later dismissed the film's central device – using the camera as Marlowe, who is only glimpsed in mirrors – as 'old stuff'. He cordially despised John Brahm's *The Brasher Doubloon* (1947), based on *The High Window*, with George Montgomery miscast as Marlowe: 'poor acting, poor direction, wretched scripting.'

Four Chandler films have been made since his death. James Garner was a lightweight, witty Marlowe in *Marlowe*, an adaptation of *The Little Sister* directed by Paul Bogart (1969). Elliott Gould was rumpled and bewildered in Robert Altman's deliberately iconoclastic *The Long Good-Bye* (1973). Not even the fact that the film was scripted by Leigh Brackett, who had collaborated on the screenplay of Hawks' *The Big Sleep*, could make Chandler fans like the result. Robert Mitchum, past his prime but still better cast than anyone since Bogart, appeared in Dick Richards' *Farewell, My Lovely* (1975) and Michael Winner's *The Big Sleep* (1978). *Playback* is now the only Marlowe novel which has not been filmed.

Three screen Marlowes: Humphrey Bogart (with Lauren Bacall) in *The Big Sleep*, Robert Mitchum in *Farewell, My Lovely* and Dick Powell (with Claire Trevor) in *Murder, My Sweet*.

The repetition of this pattern is essential to the novels, just as the guarantee of Marlowe's moral authority is essential in his confrontation with the bleak society Chandler depicts. Without it, Chandler argues in 'The Simple Art of Murder', his books could not have aspired to being called art. Such moral authority he ultimately found lacking in Hammett's severe and unsparing vision. But in the portrait of Marlowe he created – and insisted on the need to create – a saving remnant of virtue it was still possible to celebrate, 'a quality of redemption':

Down these mean streets a man must go who is not himself mean, who is neither tarnished nor afraid. The detective in this kind of story must be such a man. He is the hero, he is everything.

THE HARD-BOILED LEGACY

Somewhere between the publication of *Red Harvest* in 1929 and *Playback* in 1958 a new realm of possibilities had been opened up. Moreover, this had happened at just the time when Golden Age writers themselves had begun to fear that the possibilities of their form were rapidly being exhausted. The hard-boiled school suggested a different milieu for the characters to inhabit and a different type of slang for them to talk, new kinds of murder for them to commit and a new kind of detective to solve the murders. More generally, the 'open' narrative which followed the detective on his quest could free writers from the confines of the 'closed' narrative in which the detective sat and brooded about the puzzle. American critics had particular reason for congratulating their writers on having produced crime fiction rooted more securely and centrally in their own culture than S.S. Van Dine's Philo Vance novels

had ever been. And readers from abroad – André Gide, for example, or W.H. Auden – could join in praise which implied that in Hammett or Chandler crime fiction had at last found writers whose work could be judged by the same standards of seriousness routinely applied to 'mainstream' novelists.

Yet the problems in the hard-boiled legacy quickly began to show, and not just in those failed English imitations which affirmed how difficult it was to translate the form out of an American setting. American hard-boiled writers had their successes: Jonathan Latimer, for example, in building his Bill Crane novels on the boozy, screwball comedy of *The Thin Man*; or Rex Stout in showing how some, at least, of the hard-boiled atmosphere could actually be reconciled with the Golden Age form through the partnership of his two contrasting characters, Archie Goodwin and Nero Wolfe. Yet these achievements were both

Rex Stout's novels juxtapose Nero Wolfe, a Great Detective in the British tradition, and his assistant Archie Goodwin, whose irreverent humour links him with the private eyes of hard-boiled fiction.

Opposite **Mickey Spillane's Mike Hammer** novels return to the raw violence of the early pulps but without recapturing their freshness.

early, and both were relatively modest. Elsewhere, a cruel irony was being exposed. Hard-boiled novels had developed enough sophistication to make a return to the cheap simplicity of their roots in the pulps impossible: the thuggery of Mickey Spillane's Mike Hammer novels has nothing innocent, much less refreshing, about it – only a sour decadence. Yet at the same time hard-boiled novels had not quite succeeded in standing up to the serious scrutiny they invited.

This failure arose directly from Chandler's achievement and legacy. On the one hand, Chandler had developed a claim to social realism. The Marlowe novels deliberately cultivate a contemporary authenticity which is meant to be immediately persuasive. They derive much of their power from appearing to be, as Auden thought they actually were, convincing portraits of what sin looked like in the USA. Yet on the other hand, Chandler had also made his novels depend on the logic of romantic fable, particularly in their insistence on Marlowe's unquestioned, unquestionable status as hero, his ability to stay magically untarnished in a society which tarnished everything it touched.

None of Chandler's successors grappled with the problem of this discrepancy more persistently or thoughtfully than Ross Macdonald in his Lew Archer novels. To be sure, the early books in the sequence – beginning with *The Moving Target* in 1949 – lie rather too easily in Chandler's shadow, but from *The Doomsters* (1958) and *The Galton Case* (1960) onwards they are bent on escaping it. Sensibly, Archer is freed from the sexual hang-ups Marlowe betrayed in his unpredictable oscillation between flirtation and misogyny: leering at women and fearing they were out to get him. In other respects too, Macdonald was determined his private eye should shed the last remnants of the schoolboy's fantasy hero and come of age. Physical violence, already a vestigial trait in Marlowe, virtually disappears. So does the habit of persistent wisecracking. No longer self-assertive, no longer really hard-boiled in the original sense, Lew Archer has become instead an ideally sympathetic listener – a therapist with a private investigator's licence. And, like a therapist, his aim is not to judge the people he encounters but to heal their wounds:

'I know your type. You have a secret passion for justice. Why don't you admit it?'

'I have a secret passion for mercy,' I said. 'But justice is what keeps happening to people.'

Most of these modifications aim to get the private detective off the pedestal Chandler had put him on – to deny Archer the status so easily granted to Marlowe. Chandler might have been right to insist that art needed a quality of redemption, Macdonald conceded, but that quality could not simply be the hero's exclusive prerogative. Archer is tarnishable like any other character in the story, and he knows it. In fact, he continually examines himself: looking sideways at the emptiness of his private

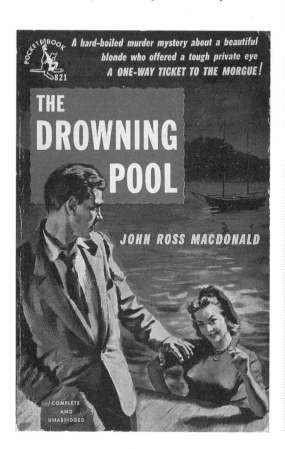

A hard-boiled murder mystery about a beautiful blonde who offered a tough private eye A ONE-WAY TICKET TO THE MORGUE!

THE DROWNING POOL

JOHN ROSS MACDONALD

COMPLETE AND UNABRIDGED

life, admitting the failures in his past, worrying about his motives for being a detective, feeling guilty about the money he takes from clients and fearing it could compromise him. Gone forever are the days when Spade and his partner, the other Archer, could cheerfully take on a client not because they believed her story but because they believed her money.

It is impossible not to feel that a lot of the fun has gone from hard-boiled fiction too. Macdonald toned it down with considerable skill and intelligence, but without actually making the result any more substantial. One effect of Archer's subdued personality is that greater emphasis falls on the convolutions of the plot, always the most transparently artificial element in hard-boiled fiction. Nor, when it comes to it, is Archer himself any more realistic than Marlowe. The private eye being a high-minded therapist is just as much a romantic dream as the private eye being a knight errant. The only difference is that Macdonald's romantic dream was more closely tailored to appeal to the liberal intellectual audience of the 1950s and 1960s, which was reading Erich Fromm when it was not reading Macdonald. In 1941 Philip Van Doren Stern, contemplating the sterile ingenuity of the puzzles in Golden Age novels, had spoken of the case of the corpse in the blind alley. In the USA by, say, 1971 – the year Eudora Welty praised Macdonald for *The Underground Man* in much the same language in which Gide had praised Hammett and Auden had praised Chandler – a cynic could instead have spoken of the case of the detective in the blind alley.

The Hard-Boiled Bookshelf

The enigmas of Hammett's life – which made him successively private eye, crime novelist, burnt-out alcoholic and victim of McCarthyism – have yet to be properly unpacked. The playwright Lillian Hellman, his partner in a long and stormy relationship, contributed vivid sketches of him in the introduction to her selection of his early and unpublished work, *The Big Knockover and Other Stories* (1966), and in three volumes of memoirs, *An Unfinished Woman* (1969), *Pentimento* (1973) and *Scoundrel Time* (1976). As Hammett's literary executor, she also impeded or breathed down the neck of would-be biographers. The books by Richard Layman (1981), William F. Nolan (1983) and Diane Johnson (1983) reflect the consequences in different ways. Johnson's biography is in general the best, but Nolan's gives the fullest account of Hammett's career as a private eye. Richard Layman has also published a useful descriptive bibliography (1979).

Chandler's biography has been written by Frank MacShane (1976), who has also edited a selection from his literate and witty letters (1981). This supplements but does not entirely replace *Raymond Chandler Speaking* (1962), edited by Dorothy Gardiner and Kathrine Sorley Walker, which also contains the short story 'A Couple of Writers' and the last, incomplete Marlowe novel, 'The Poodle Springs Story'. Minor items by Chandler also appear in *The Notebooks of Raymond Chandler and English Summer: A Gothic Romance*, edited by Frank MacShane (1976), and *Chandler Before Marlowe: Raymond Chandler's Early Prose and Poetry, 1908–1912* (1973), edited by Matthew J. Bruccoli, with a useful introductory essay by Jacques Barzun. Bruccoli has also produced a descriptive bibliography of Chandler's work (1979). *The World of Raymond Chandler* (1977), edited by Miriam Gross, contains reminiscences by those who knew him (Michael Gilbert, Dilys Powell and John Houseman).

John McAleer has written the life of Rex Stout (1977). Dorothy B. Hughes' life of Erle Stanley Gardner (1978) contains a bibliography by Ruth Moore running to more than a thousand items. Gardner's career as a best-selling writer is considered, along with the careers of Mickey Spillane and Ian Fleming, in J. Kenneth Van Dover's *Murder in the Millions* (1984). Ross Macdonald's *Self Portrait: Carelessly into the Past* (1981) gives some glimpse of the personal background which permeates his Lew Archer novels.

Four books mark the growth in academic study of hard-boiled detective fiction: Philip Durham's *Down These Mean Streets a Man Must Go: Raymond Chandler's Knight* (1963), William Ruehlmann's *Saint With a Gun: The Unlawful American Private Eye* (1974), Paul Skenazy's *The New Wild West: The Urban Mysteries of Dashiell Hammett and Raymond Chandler* (1982) and Edward Margolies' *Which Way Did He Go? The Private Eye in Dashiell Hammett, Raymond Chandler, Chester Himes, and Ross Macdonald* (1982). Other critical works are listed in Robert E. Skinner's *The Hard-Boiled Explicator: A Guide to the Study of Dashiell Hammett, Raymond Chandler and Ross Macdonald* (1985). Among the items it notes is 'The Violent Hero, Wilderness Heritage, and Urban Reality: A Study of the Private Eye in the Novels of Dashiell Hammett, Raymond Chandler and Ross Macdonald', an unpublished doctoral dissertation submitted to Boston University in 1971 by Robert B. Parker.

Exporting the Hard-Boiled: Léo Malet and the *roman noir américain*

IIIᵉ arrt.

Léo Malet

FIEVRE

AU MARAIS

Could hard-boiled fiction be exported? Or was it too deeply rooted in American myth and the American language, even in the landscape of the American city, ever to flourish outside the United States? The first British attempts to emulate the style, by James Hadley Chase and others, emphasized the problems and pitfalls. French attempts were more determined and more successful. France has always taken a close, though ambivalent, interest in American culture. The German Occupation of France, moreover, bred lawlessness and a reliance on the arts of individual survival (*le système D* to the French): conditions echoing those which had encouraged the birth of the hard-boiled school during the Prohibition era.

In France the pioneer was Léo Malet, cabaret singer, song-writer, poet and in the 1920s and 1930s a member of the Surrealist circle centred on André Breton and René Magritte. During the Second World War he turned to writing historical romance and crime fiction under various pseudonyms, including the resolutely Anglo-Saxon Frank Harding. In 1943 he published *120, rue de la gare* (translated into English under the same title) and introduced French readers to Nestor ('Dynamite') Burma, director of l'Agence Fiat Lux and 'le détective de choc'. In this and other early Burma novels, like *Le Cinquième Procédé* (1947; translated as *Mission to Marseilles*), collaborators and Resistance fighters, escaped prisoners of war and gangsters create an ideal milieu for the tough detective's adventures.

In 1948 *Le Cinquième Procédé* became the first novel to win the newly founded Grand Prix de Littérature Policière. In 1945 Marcel Duhamel had started publishing his Série Noire, which included French titles as well as translations of books by Hammett, Chandler, Horace McCoy and James M. Cain. The French had started their fascination with what they called *le hard-boiled*, or the *roman noir américain*, or just the *roman noir*, as opposed to the *roman d'énigme anglais*, or English mystery story, which had been practised in the 1930s by such writers as Stanislas-André Steeman, Jacques Decrest and Noêl Vindry. Malet himself produced well over fifty novels between 1941 and 1972, twenty-nine of them about Nestor Burma. They included fifteen of a projected twenty *Nouveaux Mystères de Paris*, each exploring a different arrondissement of the city, starting with *Le Soleil naît derrière le Louvre* (1954; translated as *Sunrise Behind the Louvre*) but abandoned in 1959.

Other books which helped to establish the hard-boiled style in France were Auguste le Breton's *Du Rififi chez les hommes* (1953), *Razzia sur la chnouf* (1954) and *Le Rouge est mis* (1954), Albert Simonin's *Touchez pas au grisbi!* (1953) and *Le Cave se rebiffe* (1954), and José Giovanni's *Le Deuxième Souffle* (1958). *Du Rififi chez les hommes* was memorably filmed by Jules Dassin in 1955; Jean Gabin, whose post-war career would fully revive when he took on the role of Maigret, appeared in the film versions of both *Razzia sur la chnouf* (by Henri Decoin, 1955) and *Touchez pas au grisbi!* (by Jacques Becker, 1954).

All these novels set out to construct a literary slang based on the *argot* of the criminal underworld. Simonin and le Breton even published dictionaries of it, Simonin in *Le Petit Simonin illustré par l'exemple* (1957) and le Breton in *Langue verte et noirs desseins* (1960; expanded as *L'Argot chez les vrais de vrais*, 1975). In the titles just mentioned, for example, *une razzia* is a raid; *la chnouf* (or *schnouf*) means drugs; *un rififi* is a fist-fight or, more generally, trouble; *le grisbi* (from *griset* or *monnaie grise*) is what Hammett or Chandler's characters would have called 'dough'; and *un cave* is a sucker.

Simenon

Maigret a peur

PRESSES DE LA CITÉ

Chapter 5
COPS AND KILLERS

THE CLUE OF THE BLOODSTAINED WILL

Tired of studying political economy, Charles Latimer turns to writing detective stories for light relief. To his surprise *A Bloody Shovel*, '*I*', *Said the Fly*, *Murder's Arms* and *No Doornail This* prove popular enough to allow him to resign his university post. In Turkey, where he is casually starting to plan his new novel, he meets Colonel Haki, a policeman as naïvely eager as any ordinary detective-story fan to confide his own idea for a plot. Lord Robinson is found murdered at his desk in the library of his country house, his blood soaking into the new will he was about to sign. Suspicion concentrates on the five previous beneficiaries the document would have excluded, all conveniently present in the house at the time. But the man from Scotland Yard eventually discovers that Lord Robinson had died by the hand of the butler whose wife he had seduced. Haki is particularly proud of this surprising revelation. He even offers Latimer a title, along with his permission to write the story up as his next book: *The Clue of the Boodstained Will.*

Latimer is used to such encounters. On this occasion he is saved further embarrassment by the genuine interest he can take in a real case which has just landed on Haki's desk. The body of a notorious criminal has been fished out of the Bosphorus. Haki is relieved to be able to close the man's file but Latimer, intrigued by his shadowy past, traces his career through the Balkans and eventually to Paris. There what he had undertaken in a spirit of idle academic speculation leads him into direct and present danger, for the criminal is still alive and ready to turn on anyone getting close to the truth. After narrowly escaping with his life, Latimer is still left with the problem of his new detective story. Wills and life insurance policies have been overdone of late; even his own work has been criticized on this score. Perhaps, for a change, he should write something set in a cosy English village?

All this, of course, comes not from real life but from fiction. It is the plot of *The Mask of Dimitrios* (called *A Coffin for Dimitrios* in USA), which Eric Ambler published in 1939. Even in so brief a summary, it shows the new spirit that led writers like Ambler to turn to the thriller, the previously despised 'shocker', in the 1930s. Ambler obviously believed – as Graham Greene did when he wrote 'entertainments' like *The Confidential Agent*, which also appeared in 1939 – that the thriller could tap into modern realities of crime and intrigue in ways that the Golden Age puzzle could not. Indeed, Ambler was confident enough to build his own oblique critical commentary into the story itself, making Latimer (like Ronald Knox) vaguely aware that the form he practises is approaching exhaustion yet still timidly determined to cling to it, blind to the richness of subjects right under his nose.

The spirit that animated *A Mask for Dimitrios* was not unique to Ambler, any

Maigret, surely the best-loved police detective of them all, had a fictional career spanning over forty years – from *M. Gallet, décéde* (1931; *The Death of Monsieur Gallet* or *Maigret Stonewalled*) to *Maigret et Monsieur Charles* (1972) – and more than eighty novels translated into many languages.

**An untidy ending:
Peter Lorre in the
1944 film of Eric
Ambler's *The Mask
of Dimitrios*.**

Opposite **Simenon,
pictured with just
some of his books.**

more than it was to a writer like Chandler, who also missed no opportunity to score points off the Golden Age. The desire to break with the old form and establish new territory was endemic in the 1930s. The results were various: not just the new school of hard-boiled writing in America but a new style of politically aware thriller in Britain, a new way of writing about police which critics would call the 'police procedural' and a new way of writing about criminals which critics would call the 'crime novel'. These attempts at classification do not, of course, satisfactorily encompass books which often rejected the whole idea of rules and formulae to which Knox and the Golden Age had been dedicated, seeking instead to be hybrid and eclectic. So it was appropriate that the period should have seen the emergence of

Georges Simenon, a major presence and a pervasive influence notoriously difficult to fit into any niche.

THE SIMENON CASE

It was Robert Brasillach who first spoke of *le cas Simenon* in the 1930s. The phrase stuck, and several generations of French critics and readers grew familiar with the Simenon case, and not merely the Simenon case but the Simenon phenomenon, the Simenon problem. For here was a writer gifted with a plain, clear style in the classic mould which, since Voltaire, the French have held in particular respect. Yet here also was a writer who could work carelessly, impatiently, with his eye fixed on profit rather than art. He was relentlessly productive, famous for being able to toss his novels off in days rather than weeks or months. Yet he was also a writer who seemed content to keep on doing just that as long as his energy allowed, with no desire to settle into the long, richly orchestrated works which, since Balzac's *Comédie humaine* in the nineteenth century, had marked the summit of ambition for the French novel. Here, in short, was a writer who came disconcertingly close to living up to his own self-description as *un imbécile de génie*: an idiot with genius.

In the simplest terms *le cas Simenon* reversed the usual rule which dictates that writers aiming for critical success had better make sure they achieve it before they become bestsellers. Simenon began

as a hack, in the same penny-a-line market which gave the American hard-boiled novelists their start. Between 1924, two years after arriving in Paris from his native Liège, and 1937 he wrote about a hundred and ninety erotic novels, cheap romances, adventure stories and crime stories about, among others, the detective Ansèlme Torres and the millionaire-adventurer Yves Jarry. He published them under various pseudonyms, regularly calling himself Jean du Perry and Christian Brulls, but also when occasion demanded Georges Sim (or Simm), Georges d'Isly, Georges-Martin Georges, Gom Gut, Luc Dorsan, Gaston Vialis (or Viallis), G. Violis (or Vialio), Jacques Dersonne, Jean Dorsage, Poum et Zette, Plick et Plock, Kim, Bobette and Germain d'Antibes.

Then, as if his apprenticeship was nearing its close, Simenon undertook something more ambitious. He invented Maigret. The novels about him were written at the usual headlong pace. The first batch of ten, beginning with *M. Gallet, décédé* (translated as *The Death of Monsieur Gallet* and later called *Maigret Stonewalled*), all appeared in 1931 and the total would rise to more than eighty by the time the last Maigret novel, *Maigret et Monsieur Charles,* appeared in 1972. By then Simenon had made himself equally known for non-Maigret novels, such as *L'Homme qui regardait passer les trains* (1938; *The Man Who Watched the Trains Go By*), *La Neige était sale* (1948; *The Stain in the Snow* and *The Snow Was Black*), *Le Président* (1958; *The Premier*) and *Les Anneaux des Bicêtre* (1963; *The Patient* and *The Bells of Bicêtre*) – to mention only a handful of the titles which brought the total number of books he published under his own name to about two hundred.

Manhunting

'I'm a detective and expecting me to run criminals down and then let them go free is like asking a dog to catch a rabbit and let it go. It can be done, but it's not the natural thing.' So Sam Spade says at the end of Hammett's *The Maltese Falcon* by way of explaining what makes him tick. However hard writers might have worked to present their detectives as heroes – making them disciples of science or reason or justice, or even of mercy – they could never completely remove the taint of the predator. Nor did they want to. The fact that the detective was not just a puzzle-solver but also a hunter helped make him different from other people, helped give him his authority.

Classic detective novelists largely reduced the predatory character of the detective to the level of metaphor. They gave their heroes hawk-like eyes or the nervous excitement of a bloodhound, and had them follow 'scents' or 'spring traps' without necessarily leaving the comfort of their armchairs; only

On the run: Robert Donat as Richard Hannay and Madeleine Carroll as his reluctant companion in Hitchcock's 1935 film of John Buchan's *The Thirty-Nine Steps*.

occasionally did they let them out into the field to follow footprints with the expertise of a Red Indian scout. Yet there was a
tradition of the thriller, or the adventure novel, which took the
idea of the chase much more literally. It goes back at least to
William Godwin's *Caleb Williams* (1794) and Robert Louis
Stevenson's *Kidnapped* (1886), though neither book had
anything like the influence of John Buchan's *The Thirty-Nine
Steps* (1915). It still carries quite a bit of the baggage of the
detective story: the hero, Richard Hannay, tackles cryptograms,
shows himself expert in disguise, and wrestles with the tantalizing clue embedded in the title. But, as Buchan admitted with
some embarrassment in the preface, his purpose had simply
been to write a 'dime novel' or 'shocker'.

In fact, he had put a new genre on the literary map, somewhere between detective story and thriller: the 'chase novel'.
Its hero may have the cerebral skills of the detective but he is
primarily a man of action, and his main goal is not to solve
riddles but to stay alive. In this ordeal he is usually alone, often
hunted by the authorities as well as the villains. (Sometimes, of
course, the authorities are the villains.) The twists and turns of
the hunt give the story its direction: the growing awareness of
threat followed by hairbreadth escape and flight and, eventually, role-reversals which transform the hunted into the
hunter. A good deal of local invention is needed to maintain the
suspense, and light comedy can offer a welcome relief – truths
which Alfred Hitchcock showed he had grasped rather more
firmly than Buchan when he transferred *The Thirty-Nine Steps* to
the screen in 1935.

It was no accident that Buchan had chosen to make
espionage the theme of his story. He sat down to write *The
Thirty-Nine Steps* during the First World War, when, as he said,
'the wildest fictions are so much less improbable than the
facts'. The chase novel flourishes amid war and the threat of
war. So crime writers were bound to turn to it again in the
1930s, particularly since they also had quite separate reasons
for discontent with the Golden Age puzzle in that decade. The
spirit in which they did so was epitomized by Eric Ambler in *The
Mask of Dimitrios* (1939; called *A Coffin for Dimitrios* in USA),
the novel which – more than any other single work – spelled out
both the political and formal preoccupations of its moment.
Charles Latimer, the academic and detective novelist, embarks
on his hunt for Dimitrios in the belief that this is merely a matter
of idle research, a paper chase. But Dimitrios is alive and real
and, as Latimer discovers, capable of biting back when cornered.

If *The Mask of Dimitrios* offers oblique commentary, Geoffrey
Household's *Rogue Male* (also published in 1939) tackled

the form with a directness which makes it a classic. A big-game hunter sets out to assassinate Hitler, misses his target and is pursued by Hitler's agents when he escapes and returns to Britain. From the start Household is sensibly brief in sketching in the political background – Hitler is not even named – and the hero's motives. His interest is in the psychology of a chase which ends with the hero, literally driven to earth like a fox, waiting to trap the hunter who stalks him. As the appurtenances of civilization, almost of humanity itself, are stripped away, only animal instinct is left. This was a timely story to tell in the year war broke out, but when Household continued it in post-war novels like *A Rough Shoot* (1951), *A Time to Kill* (1951) and *Watcher in the Shadows* (1960) he risked the law of diminishing returns. Of his later work, only *The Dance of the Dwarfs* (1968) recaptures the power of *Rogue Male*.

In the meantime the chase novel had served as a handy vehicle for capturing the propagandist mood of the war itself. Most of the Golden Age writers did their bit, though none more inventively than Michael Innes, whose *The Secret Vanguard* (1940) first mined a vein he continued to exploit in *From 'London' Far* (1946; called *The Unsuspected Chasm* in USA), *The Journeying Boy* (1949; called *The Case of the Journeying Boy* in USA) and *Appleby Plays Chicken* (1957; called *Death on a Quiet Day* in USA). Hollywood's wartime chase movies included Fritz Lang's 1941 film of *Rogue Male* as *Man Hunt* (the title under which the novel had appeared in the USA) and Hitchcock's *Saboteur* (1942), with its memorable climax on the Statue of Liberty. After the war Hitchcock again adopted, in *North by Northwest* (1959), the lighter touch he had perfected in his film of *The Thirty-Nine Steps*. So did the novelists who took up the chase novel, now indebted to Hitchcock as much as to Buchan. They have included Lionel Davidson in *The Night of Wenceslas* (1960), Paula Gosling in *A Running Duck* (1978) and Michael Gilbert in *The Long Journey Home* (1985).

Walter Pidgeon as the nameless hero, both hunter and hunted, of Fritz Lang's *Man Hunt* (1939), based on Geoffrey Household's *Rogue Male*.

These ironic fables, saved from bleakness by the same moments of unexpected gaiety that brighten the Maigret novels, confirmed his critical reputation. It had been in the making at least since 1936, when Simenon himself discovered that André Gide did not merely admire his novels but had annotated his copies of their slender texts so thoroughly as to make them 'almost more Gide than Simenon'. Highly regarded virtually from the start, the Maigret novels raised the recurrent question of whether crime and mystery fiction could aspire to be serious literature. Simenon himself took a prosaic view. His early hackwork, which the French would normally call *romans populaires* (popular novels), he called *romans alimentaires* (bread-and-butter novels). The non-Maigret novels were *romans durs, romans-roman, romans tout court*: hard novels, real novels, novels pure and simple.

But Maigret? Well, he was *semi-alimentaire*. Simenon had plucked his surname at random from his earlier hackwork (where he had used it for a character who did not anticipate the famous Maigret) and, in fact, he would always have trouble with the Christian name. It is usually given as Jules – though not even Madame Maigret calls him Jules – but also on occasion as Amédée, Anthèlme, Joseph and François. The same casual inadvertence led him to resurrect Maigret's assistant Torrence in later novels after he had died in *Pietr-le-Letton* (1938; *The Case of Peter the Lett* and *Maigret and the Enigmatic Lett*). As Conan Doyle had tried to kill Sherlock Holmes off in 'The Final Problem', Simenon was already firmly announcing Maigret's retirement as early as 1934 in *Maigret* (translated as *Maigret Returns*). The yearning to retire and the anticipated pleasures of the cottage at Meung-sur-Loire would go on to become a running joke. From the start Simenon had chosen to publish the Maigret novels under his own name – a big step for a man so much in the habit of hiding behind pseudonyms – and when he gave up writing them he also gave up writing novels altogether.

Some hint of Maigret's staying power was present at the moment of his conception, a moment Simenon elaborated into legend (like so much else about himself and his career) but without destroying an essential kernel of truth. In the autumn of 1929 he moored the boat on which he lived at the Dutch port of Delfzijl. One morning he went into a local bar, smoked his pipe, drank a few glasses of gin and fell to musing about his fellow-customers. Then the idea of Maigret occurred to him: a Commissaire working from the Paris headquarters of the Police Judiciaire on the Quai des Orfèvres, middle-aged (Simenon would specify his age as forty-five), big and bony with a strong physical presence, wearing a bowler hat and a heavy overcoat, forever smoking his pipe.

Perhaps the most striking thing about the way Simenon remembered the moment is that it was as much about a place (he even remembered the name of the bar where he had been sitting) as about a character. And that is how the novels work. All the critics agree that place and its atmosphere are everything in Simenon, though too many have casually succumbed to the blurb-writers' habit of presenting the Maigret novels as just a saga of Paris. Many of them, particularly the early novels in the series, take place outside the capital and the characteristic atmosphere they evoke is the atmosphere of northern France. A preoccupation with weather is not the unique preserve of

The Simenon Bookshelf

Of the many interviews he gave, Simenon's conversation with Carvel Collins for the *Paris Review* in 1955 casts the most light on his art; it is reprinted in the first series of *Writers at Work*, edited by Malcolm Cowley (1977). When Simenon gave up writing fiction, he turned to self-revelation (or self-mystification) and published many volumes of 'Dictées' – as he called his dictated diaries, memoirs and reflections – leading to the huge and embarrassing *Mémoires intimes* (1981). Concentrating on his relations with his dead daughter Marie-Jo and his feud with his second wife, Denise (or Denyse), it was his last book, and the only one of his autobiographical writings to be translated into English (as *Intimate Memoirs*). The fullest biography, Pierre Assouline's *Simenon* (1992), is available only in French. English readers should avoid Fenton Bresler's gossipy *The Mystery of Georges Simenon* (1983) in favour of Patrick Marnham's *The Man Who Wasn't Maigret: A Portrait of Georges Simenon* (1992).

Thomas Narcejac's *Le Cas Simenon* (1950), the first full-length critical study, appeared in English as *The Art of Simenon* (1952). Stanley G. Eskin's *Simenon: A Critical Biography* (1987) also offers a useful introduction to the fiction. Like Assouline, Eskin provides a bibliography of Simenon's work written under pseudonyms as well as his own name. Bibliographies have also been prepared by Trudee Young (1976) and R. Williams (1988). *L'Univers de Simenon: guide des romans et nouvelles (1931–1972) de Georges Simenon*, edited by Maurice Piron with Michel Lemoine (1983), is not available in translation.

British writers and Simenon, though he could take pleasure in exposing Maigret to the heat of the Midi, was above all a connoisseur of the uncertain climate of the north, which makes getting wet in the rain or warm and dry indoors experiences as sharp and memorable as any of the passions that drive the plot. His particular fondness was for canals, harbours and *rats de mer*, the types who hang about ports.

For Simenon, as for any novelist in the great realist tradition, place is never just a backdrop or a location: it cannot be reduced to the sort of diagrammatic ground plan which Golden Age writers were in the habit of supplying in their novels. It embraces all the characters and determines their destiny. Indeed, the point when Maigret has absorbed the spirit of a place is often the point when he begins to glimpse the truth of the mystery he is investigating, when he gets the *déclic* (click) that tells him he is on the right track. The setting of *Maigret en meublé* (1951; *Maigret Takes a Room* and *Maigret Rents a Room*), for example, is

just an ordinary stretch of street, with almost no passers-by, a pair of pavements, some houses, a few hundred people living in the houses, men who set out in the morning and came back in the evening, women who did their housekeeping, children squealing, old people enjoying the fresh air at their windows or on their doorsteps.

Maigret, however, abandons his office to haunt these mundane surroundings and, when he can 'sink back ... voluptuously into the atmosphere of his little back-street', the reader's anticipation quickens as palpably as it does when other fictional detectives discover a bloodstain or a footprint.

In fact, the first publisher of the Maigret novels, Arthème Fayard, feared he would lose money on the venture because, for all their physical presence,

Simenon's settings did not offer nearly enough bloodstains or footprints. As well as having a hero too stolidly unromantic to prove popular, Fayard thought, the books were not even proper detective stories with mysteries unravelled by logic. The commercial prediction was wrong, of course, but even the critical observation it stemmed from was slightly off target. The early novels in particular show that Simenon could weave a tangled web – from family tensions in the past and false identities in the present – when he wanted to, even if he usually had Maigret cut through it with intuition and luck rather than unravel it by analysis.

But usually Simenon did not want this sort of plot. His characteristic impatience led him to make the story up as he went along and sometimes to move it forward by hasty and implausible leaps. He had no time for the careful ingenuity of *le roman d'énigme anglais*, or English mystery story. He was not disillusioned with it, as some English novelists themselves had grown, or forever annoyed by it, as Chandler was. The Golden Age puzzle just bored a writer who, in middle age, could admit that he had not read the Sherlock Holmes stories since childhood.

Simenon's unease at being identified in the public mind as the creator of Maigret was never strong enough to stop him seeking all the publicity he could for the Maigret novels. His grandest gesture was the party he organized, and partly paid for, to launch the very first batch of novels published by Fayard in 1931: an extravagant *bal anthropométrique*, named with a backward glance at the nineteenth-century system of criminal identification devised by Alphonse Bertillon (see the feature on 'Science and Sherlock Holmes', p. 50). But the most enduring publicity image he created was the photograph taken in 1966 at the unveiling of the statue of Maigret at his 'birthplace', the Dutch port of Delfzijl. Simenon stands at the base of the statue

Simenon and four of the TV Maigrets of 1966 beneath the statue at Delfzijl.

Opposite **Jean Gabin** making the first of his three screen appearances as Maigret, in the 1957 film of *Maigret tend un piège* (*Maigret Sets a Trap*).

surrounded by four of the actors then portraying Maigret on TV: Rupert Davies in Britain, Heinz Ruhmann in Germany, Jan Teuling in Holland and Gino Cervi in Italy.

To be complete the photograph would have needed to include Boris Tenin from Russia, Kinya Aikawa from Japan and, of course, Jean Richard, who for several decades depicted Maigret in France itself (but who has now been succeeded by Bruno Cremer). Even in its diminished form, however, the group has the *trompe l'oeil* effect Simenon doubtless intended: adult quintuplets, or Simenon and four clones, standing in the shadow of a bronze representation of themselves. Yet on closer inspection the effect evaporates: the six figures do not actually look much alike. In the statue Maigret wears the bowler hat and heavy overcoat Simenon had endowed him with in the 1930s. Except for Gino Cervi, the actors copy the trilby hat and trench coat Simenon himself favoured in the post-war years, as well as carrying the straight pipe which, though absent from Simenon's hand on this occasion, was otherwise his inseparable companion. The statue's face is deliberately indistinct and the human faces have little in common with each other.

That is appropriate. Did not Simenon, who gave so many of his own personal habits to Maigret, also insist that he had never seen Maigret's face? And, of course, it was Maigret's facelessness which guaranteed that he could be incarnated on film and television so many times by so many different actors. The first was Pierre Renoir in 1932 in *La Nuit du carrefour* (*Maigret at the Crossroads* or *The Crossroads Murder*), just a year after the first batch of Maigret novels had appeared. The film was directed by Pierre's brother Jean Renoir, who made *Boudu sauvé des eaux* (*Boudu Saved from Drowning*) the same year and would go on to make *La Règle du jeu* (*The Rules of the Game*) on the eve of the Second World War. The project made Jean Renoir the writer's close friend. Simenon also helped with the scenario of *La Chien jaune* (*A Face for a Clue*) the same year, in which Jean Tarride directed his elderly and hammy father Abel as Maigret. After that, he took little interest in film versions of his work, not even when the part of Maigret attracted the distinguished Harry Baur (or Bauer), later to die at the hands of the German occupiers. Nor, Simenon would insist, did he have anything to do with the nine adaptations of his work produced during the Occupation by the German-controlled Continental studios, among them an anti-Semitic version of *Les Inconnus dans la maison* (*Strangers in the House*) directed by Henri Decoin and scripted by Henri-Georges Clouzot, and three films starring Albert Préjean as a wary, tight-faced Maigret who looked as if he had strayed from American hard-boiled cinema.

Post-war Maigrets included a wonderfully rumpled Michel Simon and Charles Laughton, the first English-language Maigret, giving an unsuccessful attempt at a bravura performance in *The Man on the Eiffel Tower* (1949). But, for the French at least, the role was dominated by Jean Gabin, the stocky working-class hero of pre-war films like *La Belle Equipe* and *Quai des brumes* (*Port of Shadows*). Gabin had the knack – is it a peculiarly French gift? – of aging into character-acting without losing his star presence. He helped to revive his post-war career in versions of Simenon's non-Maigret novels, like *La Marie du port* (*A Chit of a Girl* or *The Girl in Waiting*) and *Le Chat* (*The Cat*), and in three Maigret films. The first, *Maigret tend un piège* (*Maigret Sets a Trap*) in 1958, remains probably the best tribute French cinema has yet paid to Simenon's detective.

But not according to Simenon. He might have kept only a financial, rather than an artistic, interest in Maigret's fate beyond the printed page, but he could still have his opinions. And he spoke of Gabin with no more than mild respect: Gabin looked too sloppy and too little like a police *commissaire* in action. In some ways the first Maigret had been the best, because Pierre Renoir had grasped that he was above all a civil servant. Michel Simon had been extraordinary (in any part, he was an actor of special genius) but Jean Richard, the face of Maigret on French TV, was all wrong: too brisk, too rude, too tough. As for the non-French Maigrets, Laughton had been 'rather terrible' but Rupert Davies (in the British TV adaptations by Giles Cooper broadcast from 1960 onwards) had won Simenon's highest respect. Except for the embarrassment Davies betrayed at having to pat Madame Maigret's bottom, he had mastered the Frenchness of his character quite remarkably. Had he lived to make the judgement, Simenon might have lent mild approval to Michael Gambon in the British TV series launched in 1992, though he would have shuddered at its attempt to pass Budapest off as Paris. Of the 1988 made-for-TV movie with Richard Harris, he would undoubtedly have preferred not to speak.

French Maigret Films: A Checklist

La Nuit du carrefour (1932)
Starring Pierre Renoir, directed by Jean Renoir. Adapted from the novel of the same title (1931), translated as *Maigret at the Crossroads* and *The Crossroads Murder*

La Chien jaune (1932)
Starring Abel Tarride, directed by Jean Tarride. Adapted from the novel of the same title (1931), translated as *A Face for a Clue*

La Tête d'un homme (1933)
Starring Harry Baur (or Bauer), directed by Julien Duvivier. Adapted from the novel of the same title (1931), translated as *A Battle of Nerves*

Picpus (1943)
Starring Albert Préjean, directed by Richard Pottier. Adapted from the title novel in the collection *Signé Picpus* (1944), translated as *To Any Lengths*

Cécile est morte (1944)
Starring Albert Préjean, directed by Maurice Tourneur. Adapted from the novel of the same title, in the collection *Maigret revient* (1942), translated as *Maigret and the Spinster*

Les Caves du Majestic (1945)
Starring Albert Préjean, directed by Richard Pottier. Adapted from the novel of the same title, in the collection *Maigret revient* (1942), translated as *Maigret and the Hotel Majestic*

Brelan d'as (1952)
Starring Michel Simon, directed by Henri Verneuil. Partly based on a story, 'Le Témoignage de l'enfant de choeur', in the collection *Maigret et l'inspecteur malchanceux – puis malgracieux* (1947)

Maigret mène l'enquête (1955)
Starring Maurice Manson, directed by Stany Cordier. Partly based on *Cécile est morte*, in the collection *Maigret revient* (1942), translated as *Maigret and the Spinster*

Maigret tend un piège (1958)
Starring Jean Gabin, directed by Jean Delannoy. Adapted from the novel of the same title (1955); film and novel both called *Maigret Sets a Trap* in the UK and USA

Maigret et l'affaire Saint-Fiacre (1959)
Starring Jean Gabin, directed by Jean Delannoy. Adapted from *L'Affaire Saint-Fiacre* (1932), translated as *The Saint-Fiacre Affair* and *Maigret Goes Home*

Maigret voit rouge (1963)
Starring Jean Gabin, directed by Gilles Grangier. Adapted from *Maigret, Lognon et les gangsters* (1952), translated as *Maigret and the Gangsters* and *Inspector Maigret and the Killers*

Nor had he ever bothered to tackle anything by Agatha Christie. This indifference, moreover, agreed with the habit of radical simplification which led to his famously plain style of prose. His instinctive assumption that what crime and mystery novels needed was not more technical ingenuity but less – as little, indeed, as they could possibly get by on – made him throw more of the traditional paraphernalia of plot overboard than hard-boiled writers like Chandler or Macdonald in the USA ever dared to.

The first of the Maigret novels to appear in 1931 has at its centre an apparent murder victim who finally turns out to have killed himself. Simenon does not give this shopworn device any striking new twist (he handles it much less satisfyingly than, for example, Conan Doyle had done in 'The Problem of Thor Bridge') but simply uses it to help him concentrate on what most interests him. That, of course, is Maigret's contemplative reconstruction of the dead man's character. More than thirty years later, in a novel like *Maigret et le tueur* (1969; *Maigret and the Killer*), Simenon was still brazenly using the most clichéd devices – the killer who turns up at his victim's funeral, the killer who phones up the investigating policeman – simply because they offered the quickest way to allow Maigret to sit and brood about the characters of the victim and the killer.

Yet if understanding character is Simenon's consuming preoccupation, character itself is as sparely sketched as everything else in his books. The victims and their killers are constructed from a few suggestive hints. Even Maigret himself, when Simenon first glimpsed him in the bar at Delfzijl, was curiously elusive, almost anonymous. He came, of course, endowed with external attributes of the sort readers had grown to expect of fictional detectives: a pipe, a particular style of clothing, and so forth. As the novels multiplied, Simenon elaborated the circumstantial details of Maigret's life: his flat at 130 Boulevard Richard-Lenoir in the eleventh *arrondissement* (on the non-existent fourth floor of a real building), his domestic routines with Madame Maigret, his love of beer and white wine, his favourite meals, his pleasure in having in his office on the Quai des Orfèvres the only real old-fashioned stove in the building, his weakness for Western films, his refusal to learn how to drive, the interest in gardening which he hopes to indulge in retirement, and so on. Simenon almost embeds Maigret in such details, as Conan Doyle had done with Sherlock Holmes. Their repetition lends each new book the pleasure of familiarity, and makes Maigret himself seem like an old friend.

Yet still that first impression, not just of his reassuring ordinariness but of his anonymity, remains. Simenon himself insisted that he had never seen Maigret's face. In the early novels he is, above all, an observer: a sympathetic intelligence, acute but still fallible, through which the story is filtered. Later he grows in stature, while never entirely shedding his role as Everyman. He becomes, one could say, what Everyman aspires to be. Simenon's fellow-novelist Thomas Narcejac called Maigret 'a connoisseur of souls': a man who approaches mystery by trying to understand the people it engulfs and approaches people by exercising compassion, by insisting continually on a common humanity. His motto could well be the motto his creator adopted for his personal bookplate, *comprendre et ne pas juger*: 'understand and do not judge'.

Simenon himself eventually called Maigret 'a mender of destinies', but that surely oversteps the mark. In the novels,

Above and opposite: **from *Le Petit Simonin illustré par l'exemple* (1957), Albert Simonin's guide to the world of French police and crime.**

destiny is precisely the thing that cannot be mended, least of all by a civil servant who, for all his willingness to bend rules in the name of his conscience, is still constrained by his job. This limitation gives the novels their note of melancholy beneath the sensory freshness and wry comedy. Simenon never captured it better than he did in the last chapter of *Maigret et les vieillards* (1960; *Maigret in Society*). The passage comes as close to philosophical statement as a writer who always insisted he was just an observer would allow himself:

If he [Maigret] hadn't a very high opinion of men and their capabilities, he went on believing in man himself.

He looked for his weak points. And when, in the end, he put his finger on them, he didn't crow with joy, but on the contrary felt a certain sadness.

POLICE PROCEDURALS

Essentially unconcerned though he was for the future, as well as the past, of the form he found it convenient to adopt, Simenon was bound to have a wide influence. On the most general level, the Maigret novels made it difficult to conceive fictional policemen in quite the same way again. Policemen, of course,

LA POLICE

Préfet de police (période d'ordre) — Commissaire divisionnaire — Commissaire principal — Inspecteur principal

Motard — Suspect — Gendarme — Monsieur l'agent — Officier de police

Hirondelle — Garde champêtre — Poulet — Faux poulet — Gardien de prison

had played a despised and unenviable role in the tradition begun by Poe and developed by Conan Doyle, as mere foils to make the amateur or private detective shine more brightly. The policemen-heroes in Golden Age fiction had been either colourless ciphers, like Freeman Wills Crofts' Inspector French, or honorary gentlemen, like Ngaio Marsh's Inspector Alleyn.

Simenon had changed all that. He had given his policeman a convincing humanity which enhanced rather than reduced his role and a convincing ordinariness which made him admirable rather than negligible. Scarcely a fictional policeman since Maigret has not profited from that example. If one is looking for heirs in a more specific sense one has only to cite two examples: Friedrich

Dürrenmatt's Bärlach, the Berne policeman who appears in *Der Richter und sein Henker* (1952; translated as *The Judge and His Hangman*) and *Der Verdacht* (1953; translated as *The Quarry*) and, better known to English readers and an influential creation in his own right, Nicolas Freeling's Dutch detective, Inspector van der Valk, who first appeared in *Love in Amsterdam* (1962).

Quite without intending to, Simenon's portrait of Maigret had also given a boost to the rise of the 'police procedural'. The form would have flourished anyway and Simenon, if he had noticed it, would probably have despised it. Yet he had in passing lent it some of his authority by dethroning, more effectively than any predecessor, the myth of the Great Detective: making Maigret not just a fallible human but a bureaucrat dependent on the support of his colleagues. The novels thus sketch in the various *inspecteurs* who assist him – Lucas, Janvier, Lapointe and the rest – so that they become, like Maigret himself, familiar figures in the series.

Or rather they become familiar names. Only Lognon, the misfit and loser, really engages Simenon's attention. The others interest him so little that he could manage to kill and resurrect Torrence without apparently noticing or caring. They are there to give a superficial impression of police routine and to handle the dull or technical aspects of the investigation – looking up records, watching suspects, interrogating minor witnesses – which Simenon does not wish to trouble the reader with. Maigret is essentially a loner, more involved in the moral dilemmas of police work than its formal procedures. His solitary imaginative communion with the spirit of the crime and the criminal is at the heart of the novels.

'Police procedurals' from Sweden and (opposite) **the USA, concentrating on routine and team-work rather than the deductive leaps of a brilliant individual.**

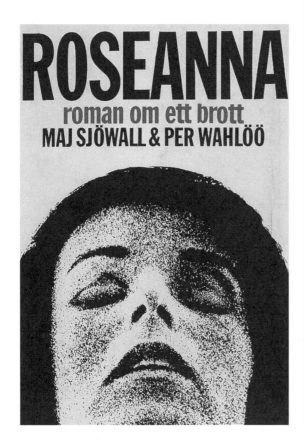

The police procedural shifts the emphasis to the team work and routine which Simenon left largely unexplored. Typically, it does not deal in mysteries or puzzles which require flashes of individual brilliance but in ordinary-looking cases which require stubbornness and tenacity to crack bit by bit. And the ending is not usually a solution in the Golden Age style – a lucid, astounding explanation presented to the group of suspects gathered in the library – but the accumulation of enough evidence to point to a suspect, justify an arrest and stand up in court. This is how a pioneer American work such as Hillary Waugh's *Last Seen Wearing …* (1952) gains its effects. An undergraduate goes missing from a small women's college. The police examine her past for any motive that might make her wish to disappear, or any reason why someone might want to kill her. They find her body after a long and frustrating search. As they sift all the evidence again and again, the identity of her killer slowly begins to emerge, like a photograph taking on recognizable features in the developing fluid.

Waugh went on to write a series, started in *Sleep Long, My Love* (1959; also called *Jigsaw* in UK), which featured Chief Fred Fellows of the imaginary small town of Stockford, Connecticut. Yet neither he nor any other crime novelist so clearly demonstrated both the strength and the limitations of the police procedural as he did in *Last Seen Wearing* …. Its strength is that the intricacies of more or less any technical process can hold narrative interest. Even the temporary failures and frustrations encountered by the police heighten suspense, while the small moments of triumph which mark the progress towards a solution come to seem like great victories. The problem, however, is that

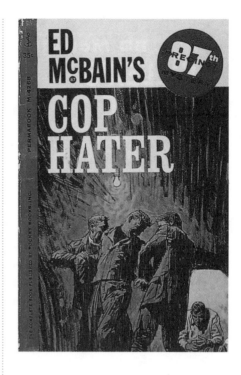

such narrative concentration squeezes out most of the other things that novels, even Golden Age puzzles, usually hope to embrace, if only in passing. Dialogue, characterization and setting at best are reduced to being functional; at worst they sink into cliché.

The police procedural always threatens just to return the crime and mystery novel to the scrupulous, immaculate dullness it possessed in the hands of Freeman Wills Crofts. Its best practitioners have anticipated the danger and approached the form in the knowledge that purity would quickly kill it. The Swedish writers Maj Sjöwall and Per Wahlöö had from the start a deliberate, if hidden, agenda in their novels about Inspector Martin Beck and his colleagues. They began the series, in *Roseanna* (1965), by mixing police procedure with comedy before gradually moving on to a radical critique of contemporary society.

Just the Facts, Ma'am

Until the 1940s it was fair to speak of crime and mystery films as deriving from fiction. The printed word led the way and the cinema simply followed – albeit quickly and enthusiastically, producing the first Sherlock Holmes film in 1900 and the first (French-made) Nick Carter film in 1909. But with the rise of the *film noir* the cinema assumed a new role, pioneering crime and mystery in its own right and becoming an influence on literature, not just a reflection of it. Though Hollywood would never again create anything as distinctive as the *film noir,* its influence continued, joined in the 1950s by the influence of television. And nothing television produced has had as much impact as *Dragnet*: the archetypal TV police series, the first American police series to be shown on British TV and (though usually unacknowledged) the inspiration for countless 'police procedural' novels written in its wake.

Dragnet had its first airing in 1949 on radio – radio already being the home to more or less all the popular fictional detectives, often played by the same actors who had played the parts in Hollywood (Rathbone and Bruce as Holmes and Watson, Powell and Loy as Nick and Nora Charles). The radio series lasted until 1956, overlapping with the first NBC TV series which ran from 1952 to 1958, making the show familiar to millions outside as well as inside the USA. Its formula was simple and memorable, right from the opening phrases of its signature tune and the voice-over announcing: 'Ladies and gentlemen, the story you are about to see is true. Only the names have been changed to protect the innocent.' The stories themselves were equally simple, striving for the feel of records taken directly from the police blotter, as they followed Sergeant Joe Friday and his various partners from the Los Angeles Police Department about their work. Each episode ended with a brief résumé of the sentences handed out to the criminals, a much-borrowed device whose familiarity is just one proof of how much the conventions of TV police shows owe to *Dragnet*.

The low budget – everywhere apparent in the cheap sets, the small cast and the limited repertoire of camera angles – helped its documentary atmosphere. So did its short, half-hour format, as the unsuccessful full-length *Dragnet* film of 1954 served only to underline. A second *Dragnet* series of 1967–68 also had its problems, this time emphasizing how its naïvely admiring stance towards policemen belonged essentially to the 1950s rather than to the age of radical protest. But the second series also introduced Friday's most famous partner, Officer Bill Gannon, played by Harry Morgan. Morgan went on to become a

familiar face on TV (in *M*A*S*H*, for instance) and one of the features of *Dragnet* that people of a certain generation love to reminisce about.

Most memorable of all, though, was Friday himself, with his wonderfully Brylcreemed hair, his sallow features, his respectable but cheap sports jackets and his catchphrase, 'Just the facts, ma'am'. He was played by Jack Webb who, as writer and director of *Dragnet* as well, was in a special sense the show's creator. And as the author of novels about the LAPD homicide detective Sammy Golden (the first was *The Big Sin* in 1952), Webb also helped confirm the connections that now linked 'police procedurals' with TV police shows.

Jack Webb as Joe Friday (right), with Harry Morgan as Officer Bill Gannon (centre), in 'The Hammer', an episode of *Dragnet* first screened in 1967.

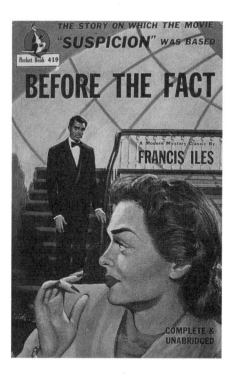

THE STORY ON WHICH THE MOVIE "SUSPICION" WAS BASED

Pocket Book 419

BEFORE THE FACT

A Modern Mystery Classic By
FRANCIS ILES

COMPLETE &
UNABRIDGED

A change of names
and a change of
style: Anthony
Berkeley's novels
belonged to the
Golden Age, but the
work which the
same author
published as Francis
Iles heralded the
'crime novel'.

Ed McBain has no such systematic agenda, but his 87th Precinct novels about Steve Carella and his team have always been rooted in the knowledge that police procedure was not enough. In the early novels – the series started with *Cop Hater* in 1965 – his interest lay in using his policemen's viewpoint to create a kaleidoscopic impression of violence in the big city. Later he devoted himself to exploiting the possibilities of the team itself as a microcosm of the city's variety: from Meyer Meyer, the disgruntled and worldy-wise Jew, to Dick Genero, the New York equivalent of Simenon's Lognon. In practice, McBain has come close to attempting a marriage between police procedural and situation comedy – by no means an impossible union, since situation comedy has frequently taken fellow-workers and the workplace as its subject. But, like the pure police procedural, situation comedy is an essentially repetitive, exhaustible form:

most TV sitcoms run into the ground after the first couple of series. McBain's attempts to vary his brand of entertainment – particularly by making a series character of the Deaf Man, a villain from the world of Marvel Comics – serve only to underline the problem.

CRIME NOVELS

The police procedural soon showed itself to be as limited as the Golden Age puzzle. The crime novel never ran this risk so actively, because it did not lend itself so easily to formulae. Its flexibility is what attracted Simenon when he wanted, in the 1930s, to venture beyond the *littérature semi-alimentaire* of the Maigret series and establish a more serious reputation for himself. Many of what he called his *romans durs*, and others have called 'psychological thrillers' or the like, are 'crime novels' in the simple and specific sense that their central character is not a detective but a criminal. Typically, the crime novel tells 'the story of a murder rather than the story of the detection of a murder'. When it wishes to suggest the potential that such a story may hold, it has only to point to Dostoevsky's *Crime and Punishment* as its great precedent and prototype.

The definition of the crime novel just quoted does not come from Simenon but from another writer, now half-forgotten but with his own historical importance. His real name was Anthony Berkeley Cox and, as Anthony Berkeley, he contributed to the Golden Age with his series about an amateur detective, Roger Sheringham, who made his début in 1925. Yet by 1930, in the preface to *The Second Shot*, Cox was voicing discontent with the traditional detective story more urgently and more creatively than Ronald Knox had done: 'I personally am convinced that the days of the old crime-puzzle pure and simple, relying entirely upon plot and without any added attractions of character, style or even humour, are, if not numbered, at any rate in the hands of the auditors.' *The Second Shot* did not really fulfil the promise of 'the story of a murder' that Cox went on to proffer, but he made it good in two novels he went on to publish under the pseudonym of Francis Iles, *Malice Aforethought* (1931) and *Before the Fact* (1932).

'It was not until several weeks after he had decided to murder his wife that Dr

Hitchcock's psychological thriller, released in 1958, derived from *D'entre les deux morts* (*The Living and the Dead*, 1954) by Pierre Boileau and Thomas Narcejac.

Bickleigh took any active steps in the matter. Murder is a serious business.' The opening sentences of *Malice Aforethought* still carry some of the refreshing shock they had at the time. Yet their tone also suggests the limited goals which Iles proposed in his story of how Dr Bickleigh's oh-so-clever scheme for murdering his wife turns out not to be quite so clever after all. The book is an ironic fable, witty but slight, finally content to look back to the 'inverted tales' of R. Austin Freeman (which the preface to *The Second Shot* had specifically mentioned) rather than to explore uncharted water.

Before the Fact is different, and says so in its opening paragraph:

> Some women give birth to murderers, some go to bed with them, and some marry them. Lina Aysgarth had lived with her husband for nearly eight years before she realized that she was married to a murderer.

As its title emphasizes, the novel maintains its predecessor's concentration on what happens 'before' rather than 'after', on crime rather than detection. But here Iles' focus on the crime itself is total and relentless. It excludes interest in how fate might undo the criminal, much less in how human investigation might expose him. The novel is enclosed by the possibilities latent in its opening: a woman realizing her husband is a murderer in the process of realizing that she is his next target. The space between is preoccupied with the relationship between killer and victim, the ambiguities of domination and submission.

The crucial word here is 'psychology'. Ronald Knox had breathed it with horror when he looked at what might happen to the detective story if its confines were enlarged: 'Heaven help us, when the psychological crowd are let loose on it.'

A KISS BEFORE DYING

STARRING
ROBERT WAGNER · JEFFREY HUNTER · VIRGINIA LEITH · JOANNE WOODWARD WITH MARY ASTOR

Colour by
TECHNICOLOR

A CinemaScope PICTURE

CinemaScope is the registered trade mark of
20th-Century Fox Film Corporation

Screenplay by LAWRENCE ROMAN · From the novel by IRA LEVIN · Produced by ROBERT L. JACKS · Directed by GERD OSWALD
CROWN PRODUCTIONS PRESENTATION

Psychos and Serial Killers

In Agatha Christie's *The ABC Murders* (1936) her
Belgian detective Hercule Poirot dealt with the case of a
murderer who was apparently working his way through
the alphabet, choosing victims solely on the basis of the
letter that began their surnames. In the end, of course,
Poirot established that the serial killer was doing
nothing of the sort: he had a particular victim in mind
and committed the other murders merely as a smoke-
screen. This was only to be expected in a Golden Age
puzzle. Its world was enclosed, and hence rational.
However bizarre or perverted the ingenious means they
chose, its murderers had material motives for their
crimes and tangible links with their victims. There was

no room for random killing, any more than for any other sort of random event.

By challenging the structure of the traditional story and by shifting the emphasis from the detective to the criminal, the crime novel changed all that. Yet it did so only slowly. At first, its preoccupations could often seem as enclosed as those of the Golden Age puzzle itself. Writers as different as Francis Iles, James M. Cain and Simenon still dealt in tales of husbands who murder wives and wives who murder husbands: enclosed people making their bid for freedom. But Iles' portrait of Johnnie Aysgarth, the weak but charming husband in *Before the Fact*, hinted at something different and more disturbing.

At any rate, it was too disturbing for Hollywood and, when he came to film the novel as *Suspicion* (see the feature '*Film Noir*', p. 150), Hitchcock had to make Johnnie an innocent and misunderstood man. Cary Grant, after all, could not be a murderer. Or could he? In the richly textured camera work of *film noir* his familiar, amiable features certainly took on a sinister aspect. The suave psychopath, the man who would equally marry or kill his way to money, became a recurrent figure in *film noir* and in thrillers, of which Ira Levin's *A Kiss Before Dying* (1953) was probably the best known. And soon after Levin's novel appeared Patricia Highsmith would begin chronicling the unsettling career of Tom Ripley. Morbid psychology – not just the desperation of normal people under pressure – was firmly on the agenda.

This led crime fiction to tackle more extreme characters, characters in whom the veneer of normality was thinner and the abnormality more shocking. Works like Graham Greene's *Brighton Rock* (1938), Jim Thompson's *The Killer Inside Me* (1952) and *Pop. 1280* (1964), and Hitchcock's highly influential film *Psycho* (1960) all helped to make the crazy killer a familiar figure. The sheer diversity of these examples is suggestive – they cover the full range from social realism to American Gothic – yet all admit to lying somewhere in Freud's shadow. *Psycho* even produces a psychiatrist to explain matters at the end. The explanation might be inadequate and the ending ironic but still, for those in the audience wanting explanation and closure, Freud was all there was to offer.

Since the era of *Psycho* popular crime novels and films – following in the wake of the Boston Strangler, the Yorkshire Ripper, Ted Bundy and the rest – have shifted their attention specifically to the serial killer. Any list of recent examples would have to include: Thomas Harris' novels about Dr Hannibal 'The Cannibal' Lecter, *Red Dragon* (1981; later called *Manhunter*) and *The Silence of the Lambs* (1988), and their screen adaptations; Bret Easton Ellis' *American Psycho* (1991); Helen Zahavi's *A Dirty Weekend* (1991); Caleb Carr's *The Alienist* (1994); and Patricia Cornwell's recent novels about Dr Kay Scarpetta. It could easily be extended, but the result would still look less like an intellectual tendency than a commercial bandwagon in full career. The serial killer, it could be argued, epitomizes the anxiety of our times: an anxiety not to be explained in Freudian terms, or indeed by any intellectual system, but simply as representing what is unsettled and randomly threatening in the shape society has assumed. Sadly, recent fiction has not attempted this argument. Instead of creating a symbol, it rests content with a made-for-TV cliché. Fashion will soon move on, urged by the tabloid headlines. Stalkers are already getting quite popular, and paedophiles are not far behind.

Richard Attenborough as Pinkie the teenage gangster in the 1947 film of Graham Greene's *Brighton Rock*; distributors in the USA retitled it *Young Scarface*.

Clearly Knox wanted to get no closer to psychology than the truisms about people's foibles which pass for psychological truths in the mouths of Hercule Poirot or Miss Marple. Indeed writers from various quarters remained wary of psychology, as a new and suspect discipline. Until the advent of Ross Macdonald, hard-boiled writers kept their distance, and even Macdonald followed his predecessors in giving hostile portraits of psychiatrists themselves. The Maigret novels show a similar ambivalence. Despite the fact that Maigret had originally studied medicine in the hope of becoming a doctor – one of the facts about his past which Simenon mentions most often – and despite the fact that he has in his way become an analyst of the human heart, Maigret is bewildered by clinical jargon and ready to dismiss it.

Yet, like Iles, Simenon also wanted to explore the same territory psychologists were exploring, albeit as observer rather than analyst; he wanted to take a direct look at those hints about human perversity which are sketched, but only sketched, in the course of the Maigret novels. His characteristic setting – in, for example, novels like *Dimanche* (1958; translated as *Sunday*) and *Le Chat* (1967; *The Cat*) – is the same world of the family that Iles had chosen in *Malice Aforethought* and *Before the Fact*. Long-nursed hatred between husband and wife, the desperate attempt to escape from suffering in small rooms behind closed curtains, the discovery that entrapment is final: such bleak experiences make up the stuff of Simenon's contribution to the crime novel.

These claustrophobic themes might sound both entirely European and almost Victorian, still identifiably in touch with Emma Bovary and Victorian wife-poisoning. Yet they could convincingly be

GREAT PAN

THE TALENTED Mr RIPLEY
Patricia Highsmith

'One of the most brilliant dissections of the criminal mentality I have ever read.'
DAILY EXPRESS

2'6

Patricia Highsmith's novels typify the dangerous territory explored by the 'crime novel'. Her *Strangers on a Train* was filmed by Hitchcock in 1951.

transplanted, with surprisingly little modification, to other times and other places. James M. Cain's *The Postman Always Rings Twice* (1934) had already located them in the USA of the Depression. Here the character's helplessness and entrapment gains power for being played out against the backdrop of the country's dream of limitless freedom and mobility. In Cain's hands the crime novel merges with the distinctively American tradition – that of Theodore Dreiser, John Dos Passos and John Steinbeck – which examines the disparity between grandiose hope and shabby circumstance.

Cain is usually put first on the list of those American writers whose crime novels, without adopting the conventions of the hard-boiled school, breathe a distinctly hard-boiled atmosphere. The other names on such a list – lesser talents like Cornell Woolrich and Jim Thompson, whom it is periodically fashionable to

revive – in fact specialized in pulp Gothic, which never looked so good on the printed page as it did in the American *film noir*. Always dangerously in love with overheated language, pulp Gothic needed the cool detachment of the camera lens to create some equivalent to the plain style which Iles, Cain and Simenon all wisely took to be essential to the low-key effects of the crime novel.

If the tradition of the crime novel continued, and broke significantly new ground, it was thanks largely to Patricia Highsmith. She first made her reputation with *Strangers on a Train* (1950), and what everybody remembers, or knows, about the novel is that it describes how two chance acquaintances decide to swop the murders they each have reason to commit. This is a beautifully simple premise which could equally well serve as the premise for an old-fashioned puzzle or an old-fashioned thriller. But these are precisely what Highsmith chose not to write. Instead, she wrote a novel about people meeting anonymously but impinging violently on each other, exposing how little they know themselves, and how much that is frightening and unfamiliar the familiar self contains. In so doing, Highsmith staked out the territory she would explore throughout her long career – though probably never to better effect than in the first of her novels about the charmingly psychopathic Tom Ripley, *The Talented Mr Ripley* (1955). The result is more bleak and chilly even than it had been in Simenon, but challenges comparison with his work in showing what, at the full extent of its power, the crime novel can do.

YOU'LL BE IN THE GRIP OF LOVE'S STRANGEST TRIP!

It begins with the shriek of a train whistle and ends with shrieking excitement! Young America's idol — a good looking stranger in search of sensation — and a girl in love. These are the people around whom Alfred Hitchcock spins his wonderful new web of suspense and surprise. **WARNER BROS.** bring a pounding new tempo to motion picture entertainment.

IT'S OFF THE BEATEN TRACK!

ALFRED HITCHCOCK'S
"Strangers on a Train"

STARRING FARLEY **GRANGER** RUTH **ROMAN** ROBERT **WALKER**

FILM NOIR

People don't want to see this in a film, the way they really are. And maybe they're right. They were expecting a cocktail and I gave them vinegar instead. Billy Wilder, of his film *Ace in the Hole* (1951)

Every story is a tall story. François Truffaut

Despite their differences, virtually all the writers mentioned in this chapter and in the chapter about the hard-boiled school have one thing in common: in one way or another, deliberately or accidentally, they contributed to *film noir*. That is itself hardly surprising. Crime and mystery fiction had been linked to the cinema since Sherlock Holmes first appeared on screen – and that had been in 1900, long before the days of sound or the dominance of Hollywood. But with the emergence of *film noir*, the relationship between cinema and literature ceased to be simply a matter of adaptation. It grew more complex, and more creative.

For one thing, cinema had itself become an influence on writing: Simenon and Graham Greene are just two examples of novelists whose concept of narrative was partly shaped by their experience of film. The desire to tell on the printed page a story as it could also be told on film was one impulse that sounded the death-knell of the Golden Age puzzle. All the various literary tendencies which bear separate and sometimes unsatisfactory generic labels ('thriller', 'hard-boiled novel', 'crime novel' and so forth) declared their cinematic affinity as *film noir*. This affirmed the status of major figures like Hammett, Chandler and Cain, but it also created a new perspective on (for example) a figure like Cornell Woolrich. He became an essential presence in the cinema, not just through Hitchcock's *Rear Window* (1954), derived from one of his short stories, but through other films of his work which, in a very direct way, put the *noir* in *film noir*.

Inevitably, though, *film noir* remains eclectic and eludes definition; one critic prefers to call it a 'generic field' rather than a genre. Most historians point to its origins in Europe, and to the importance of European directors like Fritz Lang, Jean Renoir, Julien Duvivier, Robert Siodmak and Jacques Tourneur, who went to Hollywood before or during the Second World War. There they could influence and be influenced by other *émigrés*, such as Alfred Hitchcock, and Americans such as Orson Welles and John Huston. German expressionism and the 'poetic realism' of the French cinema were thus brought into vital contact with home-grown Hollywood forms like the gangster movie and the prison movie, as well as hard-boiled writing.

The style of film which emerged declared its debts to this fertile mix most obviously in its characters and settings: tough detectives, brutal cops, mobsters, small-time criminals, crazed killers, men on the run, *femmes fatales* and (from the mid-1940s) war-tortured veterans playing out their destinies in confined interiors and the anonymous streets of the city. Their characteristic inner state is confusion, fear or obsession, and their characteristic relationship with others is intrigue or betrayal. The characteristic outcome is defeat. The route to defeat is often traced through flashback and first-person narrative, devices which lend themselves to representing dreams, nightmares and hallucinations.

Yet perhaps what most defined *film noir* was simply its look. It was above all a cameraman's cinema and its cameramen (John Alton was the master) specialized in *chiaroscuro*. Everywhere the play of light and shade finds ambiguity in a face, menace in a staircase and fear in a city street. Those effects belong essentially to black-and-white, and it was no accident that the rise of colour coincided with the decline of *film noir* in the late 1950s. Some historians see a whole series of contrasts: black-and-white versus colour, narrow screen versus wide screen, confinement versus openness, *film noir* versus Western, the anti-heroic versus the heroic myth of the USA. But it is wrong to grant *film noir* too exclusively American a character. It partly owed its existence to directors from Europe and continued to flourish there long after Hollywood *film noir* had begun its downward path towards the pastiches and remakes of the 1980s. France, in particular, maintained its own tradition, feeding partly on native contributions to Marcel Duhamel's Série Noire but also helping to revive interest in American writers like David Goodis and Jim Thompson, much as earlier *film noir* kept alive Cornell Woolrich's reputation.

Glenn Ford as the honest cop, with Gloria Grahame, in Fritz Lang's film *The Big Heat* (1953), based on William P. McGivern's novel about corrupt politics.

A Brief Filmography

This list concentrates on films obviously connected with crime and mystery fiction, or crime and mystery writers, and so excludes many other works mentioned in studies such as Robert Ottoson's *A Reference Guide to the American Film Noir, 1940–1958* (1981), Robin Buss' *French Film Noir* (1994), *The Movie Book of Film Noir*, edited by Ian Cameron (1992) and Bruce Crowther's *Film Noir: Reflections in a Dark Mirror* (1988).

THE BIG CLOCK (1948)
Directed by John Farrow, screenplay by Jonathan Latimer from Kenneth Fearing's novel (1946), with Ray Milland and Charles Laughton

THE BIG HEAT (1953)
Directed by Fritz Lang, from William P. McGivern's novel (1953), with Glenn Ford and Lee Marvin

THE BIG SLEEP (1946)
See 'Chandler in Hollywood', p. 114

THE BURGLAR (1957)
Directed by Paul Wendkos, adapted by David Goodis from his novel (1953), with Dan Duryea and Jayne Mansfield. (The novel was also the basis for *La Casse*, or *The Burglars*, directed by Henri Verneuil in 1971, with Omar Sharif and Jean-Paul Belmondo)

CONFIDENTIAL AGENT (1945)
Directed by Herman Shumlin, from Graham Greene's novel (1939), with Charles Boyer, Lauren Bacall and Peter Lorre

COUP DE TORCHON (*Clean Slate*; 1981)
Directed by Bertrand Tavernier, from Jim Thompson's *Pop. 1280* (1964), with Philippe Noiret

DARK PASSAGE (1947)
Directed by Delmer Daves, from David Goodis' novel (1946), with Humphrey Bogart and Lauren Bacall

DEADLINE AT DAWN (1946)
Directed by Harold Clurman, screenplay by Clifford Odets from Cornell Woolrich's novel (1944; published under the pseudonym of William Irish), with Susan Hayward and Paul Lukas

DETECTIVE STORY (1951)
Directed by William Wyler, from Sidney Kingsley's play, with Kirk Douglas. (See 'Hammett in Hollywood', p. 108)

LES DIABOLIQUES (1954)
Directed by Henri-Georges Clouzot, from Pierre Boileau and Thomas Narcejac's *Celle qui n'étais plus* (1953; translated as *The Woman Who Was*, *The Woman Who Was No More* and *The Fiends*), with Simone Signoret and Vera Clouzot

DOUBLE INDEMNITY (1944)
Directed by Billy Wilder, screenplay by Billy Wilder and Raymond Chandler from James M. Cain's novel (1936), with Barbara Stanwyck, Fred MacMurray and Edward G. Robinson. (See 'Chandler in Hollywood', p. 114)

DU RIFIFI CHEZ LES HOMMES (*Rififi*; 1955)
Directed by Jules Dassin, from Auguste le Breton's novel (1953), with Jean Servais, Carl Mohner, Robert Manuel and Jules Dassin. (See 'Exporting the Hard-Boiled: Léo Malet and the *roman noir américain*', p. 120)

FEAR IN THE NIGHT (1947) and **NIGHTMARE** (1956)
Both directed by Maxwell Shane, both from Cornell Woolrich's story 'Nightmare' (published under the pseudonym of William Irish), the latter with Edward G. Robinson

THE GLASS KEY (1942)
See 'Hammett in Hollywood', p. 108

I WAKE UP SCREAMING (1941)
Directed by H. Bruce Humberstone, from Steve Fisher's novel (1941), with Betty Grable, Victor Mature and Laird Cregar

IN A LONELY PLACE (1950)
Directed by Nicholas Ray, from Dorothy B. Hughes' novel (1947), with Humphrey Bogart and Gloria Grahame

JOURNEY INTO FEAR (1943)
Directed by Norman Foster (with uncredited contributions by Orson Welles), from Eric Ambler's novel (1940), with Joseph Cotten, Dolores Del Rio and Orson Welles

KISS ME DEADLY (1955)
Directed by Robert Aldrich, from Mickey Spillane's novel (1952), with Ralph Meeker

LADY IN THE LAKE (1946)
See 'Chandler in Hollywood', p. 114

LAURA (1944)
Directed by Otto Preminger, from Vera Caspary's novel (1943), with Dana Andrews, Gene Tierney and Clifton Webb

THE LODGER (1944)
Directed by John Brahm, from Marie Belloc Lowndes' novel (1913), with Laird Cregar. (Hitchcock directed the British silent film of the novel in 1926, starring Ivor Novello, who was also in the 1932 British talkie)

LA LUNE DANS LE CANIVEAU (*The Moon in the Gutter*; 1983)
Directed by Jean-Jacques Beineix, from David Goodis' novel (1953), with Gérard Depardieu and Natassia Kinski

THE MALTESE FALCON (1941)
See 'Hammett in Hollywood', p. 108

MAN HUNT (1941)
Directed by Fritz Lang, from Geoffrey Household's *Rogue Male* (1939), with Walter Pidgeon and George Sanders

LA MARIÉE ÉTAIT EN NOIR (1967)
Directed by François Truffaut, from Cornell Woolrich's *The Bride Wore Black* (1940), with Jeanne Moreau

THE MASK OF DIMITRIOS (1944)
Directed by Jean Negulesco, screenplay by Frank Gruber from Eric Ambler's novel (1939), with Peter Lorre, Sydney Greenstreet and Zachary Scott

MILDRED PIERCE (1945)
Directed by Michael Curtiz, from James M. Cain's novel (1941), with Joan Crawford, Jack Carson and Zachary Scott

MINISTRY OF FEAR (1944)
Directed by Fritz Lang, from Graham Greene's novel (1943), with Ray Milland and Dan Duryea

MURDER, MY SWEET (1944)
See 'Chandler in Hollywood', p. 114

NIGHT AND THE CITY (1950)
Directed by Jules Dassin, from Gerald Kersh's novel (1938), with Richard Widmark

NIGHT HAS A THOUSAND EYES (1948)
Directed by John Farrow, screenplay by Barré Lyndon and Jonathan Latimer from Cornell Woolrich's novel (1945; published under the pseudonym of George Hopley), with Edward G. Robinson and Gail Russell

NIGHTFALL (1956)
Directed by Jacques Tourneur, from David Goodis' *The Dark Chase* (1947), with Aldo Ray, Brian Keith and Anne Bancroft

OUT OF THE PAST (1947)
Directed by Jacques Tourneur, screenplay by Daniel Mainwaring (with uncredited contributions from James M. Cain) from his novel *Build My Gallows High* (1946; published under the pseudonym of Geoffrey Homes), with Robert Mitchum, Kirk Douglas and Jane Geer

PANIQUE (*Panic*; 1946)
Directed by Julien Duvivier, from Simenon's *Les Fiançailles de M. Hire* (1936; translated as *Mr Hire's Engagement*) with Michel Simon. (The novel was filmed again as *Monsieur Hire* by Patrice Leconte in 1989)

PHANTOM LADY (1944)
Directed by Robert Siodmak, from Cornell Woolrich's novel (published under the pseudonym of William Irish; 1942), with Ella Raines and Franchot Tone

PLEIN SOLEIL (*Purple Noon*; 1959)
Directed by René Clément, from Patricia Highsmith's *The Talented Mr Ripley* (1955), with Alain Delon

THE POSTMAN ALWAYS RINGS TWICE (1946)
Directed by Tay Garnett, from James M. Cain's novel (1934), with Lana Turner and John Garfield. (The novel had previously been filmed in France, by Pierre Chenal as *Le Dernier Tournant* in 1939, and Italy, by Visconti as *Ossessione* in 1942)

QUE LA BÊTE MEURE (*This Man Must Die* or *Killer!*; 1969)
Directed by Claude Chabrol, from Nicholas Blake's *The Beast Must Die* (1938), with Michel Duchaussoy

RAZZIA SUR LA CHNOUF (1955)
Directed by Henri Decoin, from Auguste le Breton's novel (1953), with Jean Gabin. (See 'Exporting the Hard-Boiled: Léo Malet and the *roman noir américain*', p. 120)

THE RECKLESS MOMENT (1949)
Directed by Max Ophuls, from Elizabeth Sanxay Holding's *The Blank Wall* (1947), with James Mason and Joan Bennett

RIDE THE PINK HORSE (1947)
Directed by Robert Montgomery, from Dorothy B. Hughes' novel (1946), with Robert Montgomery

SÉRIE NOIRE (1979)
Directed by Alain Corneau, from Jim Thompson's *A Hell of a Woman* (1954), with Patrick Dewaere, Marie Trintignant and Bernard Blier

THE SPIRAL STAIRCASE (1946)
Directed by Robert Siodmak, from Ethel Lina White's *Some Must Watch* (1933), with Dorothy McGuire, George Brent and Ethel Barrymore

STRANGERS ON A TRAIN (1951)
Directed by Alfred Hitchcock, screenplay by Raymond Chandler and Czenzi Ormond from Patricia Highsmith's novel (1950), with Robert Walker and Farley Granger. (See 'Chandler in Hollywood', p. 114)

SUSPICION (1941)
Directed by Alfred Hitchcock, from Francis Iles' *Before the Fact* (1932), with Cary Grant and Joan Fontaine. (See also the text of this chapter and the accompanying feature on 'Psychos and Serial Killers', p. 144)

THE TALL TARGET (1951)
Directed by Anthony Mann, from a story by George Worthington Yates and Daniel Wainwaring (Geoffrey Homes), with Dick Powell

THIS GUN FOR HIRE (1942)
Directed by Frank Tuttle, screenplay by W.R. Burnett and Albert Maltz from Graham Greene's *A Gun for Sale* (1936), with Alan Ladd and Veronica Lake

TIREZ SUR LE PIANISTE (*Shoot the Piano Player*; 1960)
Directed by François Truffaut, from David Goodis' *Down There* (1956), with Charles Aznavour

TOUCH OF EVIL (1958)
Directed by Orson Welles, from Wade Miller/Whit Masterson's *Badge of Evil* (1956), with Charlton Heston, Orson Welles and Janet Leigh

TOUCHEZ PAS AU GRISBI! (*Grisbi* and *Honor Among Thieves*; 1954)
Directed by Jacques Becker, from Albert Simonin's novel (1953), with Jean Gabin. (See 'Exporting the Hard-Boiled: Léo Malet and the *roman noir américain*', p. 120)

VIVEMENT DIMANCHE! (*Finally, Sunday* and *Confidentially Yours*; 1983)
Directed by François Truffaut, from Charles Williams' *The Long Saturday Night* (1962), with Jean-Louis Trintignant and Fanny Ardant

ELMORE LEONARD'S

Bandits

A NOVEL BY THE AUTHOR OF GLIT

Chapter 6
THE STATE OF THE ART

CHOOSING A FORM

Golden Age detective puzzles, stories about hard-boiled private eyes, 'procedural' novels about policemen and thrillers focusing on crime and the psychology of the criminal: all these different types came into being at some point between the two World Wars. They were all still being written in the years after the Second World War, for that matter: historians who like to classify the phases of literature neatly into decades often forget that in the 1950s the names of (for example) Christie, Chandler, Simenon and Patricia Highsmith were all current with the reading public, vying for sales and awards. But that was forty years ago. What distinctive types have been added to the list since then? And which types dominate crime and mystery fiction today?

If no simple, let alone single, answer to these questions presents itself, that is because of the way literary history works. It does not progress, like a train stopping at different stations and then continuing on its journey. Nor does it evolve, though a lot of mistaken writing about literary history still takes its model from evolutionary theory. Literary genres do not replace each other in clean and distinct succession. Nor do they always start out crudely, crawling on to the dry land of the printed page dripping the slime of their primitive origins, and then refine themselves to a pitch of formal perfection from which they can then only decay into extinction.

That was the mistake writers and critics made in the Golden Age when they devised rules to preserve the form, like a fly in amber, exactly as their generation were practising it. Such purism merely encouraged the rise of the hard-boiled school in reaction against them. This would have happened anyway, if without the edge of polemical zeal from which hard-boiled writing took so much of its momentum. Yet when Chandler wrote of the Golden Age detective novel as something to be overthrown, or which had been overthrown during his writing career, he too was misunderstanding how literary history works. Golden Age novels continued to be written alongside hard-boiled novels and, while Chandler was still writing, they had in turn been joined by police novels and crime novels.

Rather than succeeding or replacing each other, all these variants overlapped and co-existed. They could even reach across the ideological divisions that apparently set them at odds and modify each other, to the despair of polemicists and theoreticians alike. Hard-boiled writers never abandoned puzzles, and so could still learn from the Golden Age in devising them. They also had a good deal to teach other writers, of whatever complexion, in how to tell the story which springs from the puzzle. Nobody could entirely ignore the interest in police procedure, any more than they could ignore the long-awaited impact of psychology which the crime novel finally unleashed. So writers grew increasingly eclectic rather than increasingly pure,

Elmore Leonard's portrayal of urban sleaze in all its varieties has set the tone for much recent crime and mystery fiction in the USA.

taking advantage of the opportunity to pick and choose from the various possibilities which the history of the form had put at their disposal. And they still do. As a result, no single form dominates, though reviewers still regularly announce the triumph of one or other and the death of the rest. Nor, despite the predictions of reviewers, has any new form emerged to typify the contemporary approach. Now, more than ever, variety holds sway.

This implies that a certain ground-breaking energy, even a certain innocence, has gone out of the business of writing crime and mystery fiction. Such is the price of coming of age. But it does not mean that the present scene looks muddled or indeterminate by comparison to the clarity of purpose, even the clarity of oppositions, which often governed in the past. Writers still have choices to make, even if the way such choices now present themselves has little to do with the way they used to. Nobody can sit down to write a Golden Age novel or a hard-boiled novel, or for that matter even a police novel or crime novel as such, except in a spirit of pastiche. But the writer still has to decide, whether deliberately or instinctively, between a 'closed' or an 'open' form: a closed cast of

characters and a mystery enclosed within the past, or an open cast of characters and a mystery which unfolds in the present. Though not absolute, this distinction at least has kept its meaning, however much the practice of recent years may have rubbed off the sharp edges of the different approaches to crime and mystery fiction.

But is crime or mystery writing inevitably just 'genre literature' or 'paraliterature', the terms critics now like to use for works of entertainment which follow set formulae and so are excluded from the canon of serious literature? That is how publishers, bookshops and libraries view the matter when they issue, sell and circulate some books under the label of 'crime fiction' and others simply as 'fiction'.

Or can 'crime fiction' aspire to be 'fiction' pure and simple? That is what some committed critics have wished to argue, even if they have usually been forced to make their plea from the ghetto of the special columns to which reviewing crime and mystery novels is still confined. Most of them, like Julian Symons, have based their argument on the belief that such novels could aspire to the same virtues of social and psychological realism which distinguish serious literature.

Around the World Today

Since the foundation of the Série Noire in 1945 announced its fascination with the hard-boiled style, France has kept up a habit of reviving neglected foreign writers, such as Jim Thompson and David Goodis, and welcoming new ones, such as James Ellroy (a hit in France before he was a hit in the USA) and Derek Raymond/Robin Cook (a cult figure in France but still regarded as marginal in his native Britain). The rest of the world has been less generous in recognizing the contribution of French writers. In recent years the most exciting development came from Jean-Patrick Manchette, whose *O dingoes, O châteaux!* (1972; later called *Folle à tuer*) announced the arrival of the *néo-polar*, or *polar d'intervention sociale*: anarchist in spirit, dealing with social fragmentation but only accidentally with social realism, and free of the desire to write Literature with a capital L which has too often afflicted the crime and mystery novel in Britain and the USA. Outstanding among those who have explored the *néo-polar* is Didier Daeninckx, in *Meurtres pour mémoire* (1985; translated as *Murder in Memoriam*) and *Un Château en Bohème* (1994). An older tradition is represented by Sébastien Japrisot who, since his bravura performance in *La Dame dans l'auto avec les lunettes et un fusil* (1967; translated as *The Lady in the Car with Glasses and a Gun*), has step by step abandoned the classic puzzle for the less answerable conundrums of the *nouveau roman*.

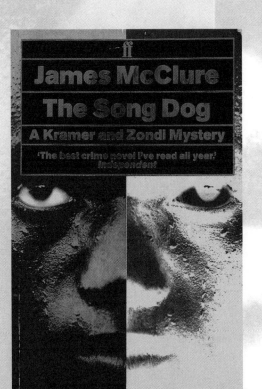

The tensions of apartheid South Africa provide the setting for James McClure's novels about Lieutenant Tromp Kramer and his Zulu assistant Sergeant Zondi.

The most exciting new writer in Germany is probably Jakob Arjouni, creator of the Turkish immigrant private eye Kemal Kayankaya, introduced in *Happy Birthday, Türke!* (1985; translated as *Happy Birthday, Turk!*), *Mehr Biere* (1987; translated as *More Beer*) and *Ein Mann, Ein Mord* (1991; translated as *One Man, One Murder*). Akif Pirinçci's *Felidae* (1989), a crime novel from a cat's point of view, enjoyed some international success. Pieke Biermann's prize-winning *Violetta* (1990; translated into English in 1996) is about Berlin and its divisions.

The best-known Spanish crime writer, inside and outside his country, is Manuel Vázquez Montalbán. His Barcelona private eye Pepe Carvalho first appeared in *Los Mares del Sur* (1979; translated as *Southern Seas*); the series continues. Other noteworthy books are Arturo Pérez-Reverte's *La Tabla de Flandes* (1990; translated as *The Flanders Panel*), a postmodernist variant on the conventional art mystery, and *El Club Dumas* (1993; translated as *The Dumas Club*); and *El Hombre Solo* (1994; translated as *The Lone Man*) by the Basque novelist Bernardo Atxaga.

The most highly regarded modern achievements in Italian crime writing are undoubtedly Leonardo Sciascia's novels of the Mafia; his first international success was *Il giorno della civetta* (1961), translated as *Mafia Vendetta* (1964) and later called *The Day of the Owl*. The Czech writer Josef Skvorecký's stories about his Prague detective – full of witty allusion to classic detective fiction – began with *Smutek poručika Borůvky* (1966), translated into English as *The Mournful Demeanour of Lieutenant Boruvka* (1973), and have continued since the author emigrated to Canada in 1968.

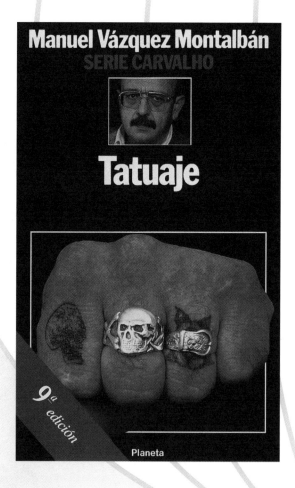

PIEKE BIERMANN
HERZRASEN

DEUTSCHER
KRIMIPREIS 1994

Australian crime writing has had an international influence ever since the publication of Fergus Hume's *Mystery of a Hansom Cab* in 1886 (see the feature 'A Surprise Bestseller', p. 36). Arthur Upfield's series about the half-Aboriginal detective, Inspector Napoleon Bonaparte – introduced as long ago as 1928 in *The Barrakee Mystery* (called *The Lure of the Bush* in USA) – has provided delayed and indirect inspiration for the US writer Tony Hillerman's current series about Lieutenant Joe Leaphorn, Sergeant Jim Chee and Navajo tribal customs. Today the most interesting Australian writer is probably Peter Corris, whose series about the Sydney private eye Cliff Hardy started with *The Dying Trade* (1980).

The emergence of distinctively Canadian crime writing from the shadow of Britain and the USA is represented by three well-established series: Howard Engel's novels about the private eye Benny Cooperman, starting with *The Suicide Murders* (1980); Ted Wood's novels about Reid Bennett, police chief in Murphy's Harbour, still continuing with, for example, *A Clean Kill* (1995); and Eric Wright's novels about Inspector Charlie Salter of the Metropolitan Toronto Police, started with *The Night the Gods Smiled* (1983).

The potential of the crime novel or thriller in cultures suffering dictatorship or post-colonial crisis remains curiously unexplored. A modest start was made by two well-known series preoccupied by the tensions of apartheid South Africa: Wessel Ebersohn's novels about the white prison psychiatrist Yudel Gordon, starting with *A Lonely Place to Die* (1979), and James McClure's novels about Lieutenant Tromp Kramer and his Zulu assistant Sergeant Zondi of Pietermaritzburg, starting with *The Steam Pig* (1971).

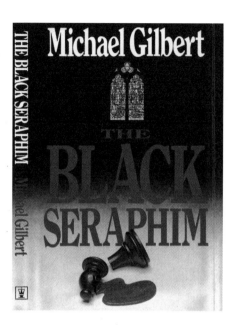

More recently the debate has been joined by those academic critics who go further in challenging the distinction between genre literature or paraliterature and literature proper, as they throw into question all our inherited assumptions about low culture, high culture and the superiority of the established canon. Though their jargon may be so resolutely fashionable as to render it mysterious to outsiders, the issues they raise are as old as detective fiction itself. Indeed, some of the issues were already being aired before detective fiction had acquired the name. But writers and readers have probably never asked such questions as often and as urgently as they are asking them today.

COSY BRITAIN?

Some would still say that questions about the form and future of crime and mystery writing are not being asked often or urgently enough in Britain, where writers have by and large taken a modest definition of their task and a familiar approach to their subject. Commercially,

this has proved to be no bad thing. British crime and mystery writing has enlarged its international reputation well beyond America and the rest of the English-speaking world to hold considerable sway throughout Europe and in Japan. But the reputation it now enjoys is for upholding the solid, old-fashioned virtues, and not for experimenting with the new or exploring the dangerous edge of things.

If one is looking for a representative figure – representative, at least, of the best in what British crime and mystery writing has reliably offered its audience – one could not do better than choose Michael Gilbert. His career has covered the entire period since the Second World War and has earned him his fair share of recognition on the international scene as well as at home. It began in 1947 with *Close Quarters*, a novel in fact written before the war and so still quite literally breathing a pre-war spirit. The setting, a cathedral close, is at once 'closed' in formal terms and genteel in social terms – a familiar combination from the Golden Age and precisely, one would have expected, the sort of device that would soon become extinct. Yet Gilbert returned to Melchester (as he followed Thomas Hardy in calling his cathedral city) again in 1983 with *The Black Seraphim*. And rather than looking simply archaic, the book confirmed that more of the very British past of the British mystery story remained usable than sceptics had supposed. The old conventions could still be made to work.

They still can. Even the ecclesiastical setting itself is enjoying something of a vogue at the moment in the work of writers like D.M. Greenwood and Kate Charles. Gilbert himself, meanwhile, has covered a good deal of ground elsewhere in the search for satisfying or ingenious variants on the closed setting: a solicitor's office in *Smallbone Deceased* (1950) and a prisoner-of-war camp in *Death in Captivity* (1952; called *The Danger Within* in USA), for example. Nor did he stay completely inside the narrow definition of crime and mystery as a puzzle. Not even the writers of the Golden Age themselves had done that: Margery Allingham, Michael Innes and Ngaio Marsh all made gestures towards the adventure story and the thriller once the early, purist stage of their careers had passed. The quest for variety made their successors more eclectic. In Gilbert's case, both *The Final Throw* (1982; called *End-Game* in USA) and *The Long Journey Home* (1985), for example, are chase novels whose relaxed tone allies them with Innes' work of the 1940s and Buchan's Richard Hannay novels rather than the hi-tech violence of Hollywood action thrillers.

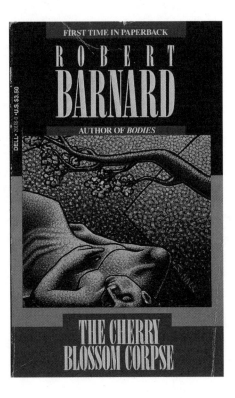

FIRST TIME IN PAPERBACK

ROBERT
BARNARD

AUTHOR OF *BODIES*

THE CHERRY
BLOSSOM CORPSE

The old conventions can still be made to work, but the novelist has to work rather harder at them. If he propounds a puzzle, it has to tease without being laboriously technical. If he roots the puzzle in a distinctive milieu, the milieu has to be realized with a conviction that novelists of the Golden Age regarded as unnecessary or even a distraction from their central purpose. And these things in turn mean that the novel has to be written – not just planned and plotted – with a respect for the craft of writing in which Chandler had magnificently shown the way. In Gilbert's work the result is an ironic wit as dry as sherry served by an old-school family solicitor and, equally reminiscent of the solicitor's office, a steady refusal to be shocked by any depth of folly or viciousness to which people are capable of sinking. In *Death of a Favourite Girl* (1980; called *The Killing of Katie Steelstock* in USA) he can look unblinkingly at the amorality which efficient police work may call for; in *The Night of the Twelfth* (1976) he can approach (without quite confronting) a peculiarly contemporary horror.

Most writers carrying on the tradition Gilbert upheld in the post-war years settle for a lighter tone. His brand of wit without his occasional bleakness sustains the work of a writer like Robert Barnard, who has a claim to be Gilbert's truest contemporary heir in his ingenious choice of locales giving scope for humorous observation. Comedy is the most characteristic way British crime and mystery writers have added zest to the essentially conservative ingredients of their recipes. Setting their novels in the past or setting them abroad, usually somewhere in continental Europe, has proved increasingly popular for much the same reasons.

Having the Last Laugh

In 1988 the Crime Writers' Association added a new category to its annual awards when it inaugurated the Last Laugh Dagger (as it is now called, though it was originally known as the *Punch* Award, after its first sponsor). In doing so, the CWA formally acknowledged the part humour has played since the days when Conan Doyle made Holmes and Watson's friendship into an engaging clash of personalities. Writers of the Golden Age produced 'don's delights' and hard-boiled writers honed their wise-cracks. In fact virtually all schools of crime writing have found humour a useful way of leavening the doughier aspects of the plot. Indeed, the humour has often been at the expense of the plot, since it so naturally slips into burlesquing the conventions of the form itself. And, purists have complained, humour always carries the risk of swamping the plot and diluting the mystery. Certainly, few writers have managed to strike an ideal balance between comedy and mystery, and virtually none has managed to sustain the balance over the course of a prolonged series.

One for the Money

'I loved it. A raunchy, funny book – Stephanie tumbles through the plot like M Magoo on speed. I couldn't stop turning the pages' – Liza Co

JANET EVANOVICH

Janet Evanovich and Mike Ripley are both past recipients of the 'Last Laugh Dagger' awarded by the Crime Writers' Association.

Yet the effort has always proved attractive, and never more so than in current British crime writing, which includes (for example) Nancy Livingston's series about Mr Pringle, introduced in *Trouble in Aquitaine* (1985), and Mike Ripley's Angel series, started by *Just Another Angel* (1988). Comedy blends easily with the British theatrical mystery, as Simon Brett's novels about Charles Paris and Simon Shaw's novels about Philip Fletcher have shown. And it goes well with mysteries involving foreign holidays, like Sarah Caudwell's series about Professor Hilary Tamar and her circle, or Delano Ames' series about Jane and Dagobert Brown of the 1950s.

Ames' novels belong on the list of half-forgotten comic mysteries which some readers still remember and treasure. It also includes Richard Hull's savage *Murder of My Aunt* (1934), Pamela Branch's zany *The Wooden Overcoat* (1951), Joyce Porter's Inspector Dover series starting with *Dover One* (1964) and Lawrence Payne's series about Chief Inspector Sam Birkett, starting with *The Nose on My Face* (1962; called *The First Body* in USA). Many readers would make particular claims for Nancy Spain's novels, above all perhaps *Poison in Play* (1946), set at Wimbledon, and *Not Wanted on Voyage* (1951), a superb comic version of the cruise-ship mystery. And most readers would assign a special place to Colin Watson's Inspector Purbright series – started with *Coffin, Scarcely Used* (1958) – with its portrait of goings-on in the East Anglian town of Flaxborough, 'a high-spirited place ... like Gomorrah'.

For all its refreshing vulgarity, Colin Watson's work still just about belongs in the British genteel tradition. Its witty, ironic voice has been echoed on the other side of the Atlantic in Emma Lathen's long-running series, started by *Banking on Death* (1961), about her Wall Street banker, John Putnam Thatcher. More characteristic of American writing is the 'screwball' comedy, used in the 1930s and 1940s to parody the attributes of Golden Age fiction by Elliot Paul in his Homer Evans series, but also combined with hard-boiled writing by Jonathan Latimer in his Bill Crane novels and by Craig Rice in her series about John J. Malone, introduced in *8 Faces at 3* (1939; called *Death at Three* in UK). Screwball comedy has resurfaced in Carl Hiaasen's Florida mysteries, which started with *Tourist Season* (1986) and have since gathered a cult following. Here it mingles with exuberant tastelessness and, unfortunately, an increasingly messianic environmentalism.

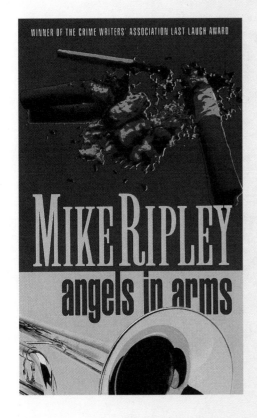

WINNER OF THE CRIME WRITERS' ASSOCIATION LAST LAUGH AWARD

MIKE RIPLEY
angels in arms

Writers like Gilbert and Barnard are united in their acceptance that what they produce may be only, in Thomas Narcejac's phrase, *une machine à lire* – a machine for reading – but that producing efficient machines for reading requires its own professionalism. This makes them typical, though where American professionalism is likely to announce itself in mastery of some branch of technical expertise, British professionalism prefers instead to capture the distinctive atmosphere of a particular place and to observe its characteristic inhabitants with wry detachment. Gilbert and Barnard, however, are untypical in their refusal to commit themselves to a series character. Gilbert has written more than once about the policemen Hazelrigg and Petrella, and since the early 1980s Barnard has produced novels featuring Perry Trethowan of Scotland Yard. But neither

TV cops: Roy Marsden as P.D. James' Commander Adam Dalgliesh.

has relied on a detective who runs through all their work. And that, probably, is why neither is among the handful of British names likely to turn up on best-seller lists and TV screens throughout the world.

The names which do turn up most often on the best-seller lists and TV screens are those of P.D. James, Ruth Rendell and Colin Dexter: the creators of, respectively, Commander Adam Dalgliesh, Chief Inspector Reginald Wexford and Chief Inspector Morse, to give these heroes their current ranks. It is by the names of their heroes rather than their own that these writers are familiar to much of their public, who often think of themselves as reading 'A Chief Inspector Wexford Novel' or 'The New Chief Inspector Morse' rather than works by Ruth Rendell or Colin Dexter. Crime and mystery writing can attract restless

TV cops: George
Baker (to the right)
as Ruth Rendell's
Chief Inspector
Wexford.

talents like Gilbert or Barnard (or Julian Symons, another contemporary instance) who refuse to settle down with a series character. It certainly offers notorious cases, from Conan Doyle to Nicolas Freeling, of authors who have wearied of their creations and killed them off, or tried to. But the authors whom the public has usually taken most enduringly to its heart are those who succeeded in creating, as Chandler did with Marlowe and Simenon with Maigret, a character who would serve their requirements through all the changing seasons. For both writer and audience such a character grows to be like a pair of old shoes, taken up again and again in comfortable and familiar expectation.

The series character, then, may well be the most persistent convention of crime and mystery writing: not just one that writers scorn at their peril but also the one that most stubbornly links them to the repetitive, formulaic realm of

'genre literature'. But at the same time, it is through the series character that crime and mystery writing can be most responsive to the climate of the age, the mood and fashion of the moment. Writers and readers may still admire Marlowe or Maigret and fervently wish to see their like again, but that is without supposing for a moment that Marlowe or Maigret themselves would carry any conviction in a contemporary context. They simply would not do. The setting in which they move and even the type of criminal puzzle they tackle might hold good, but they themselves would not. Their attitudes, their styles of life, even their most superficial mannerisms would betray them.

And, of course, nothing about the fiction of the Golden Age has dated more dramatically or more cruelly than the personality of the detective it usually favoured. His private income, his connoisseurship about wine and first editions, his breezy chatter and his air of negligent superiority make him the least usable part of the past. Some of those novelists from the Golden Age who continued into the post-war period – like Margery Allingham and Ngaio Marsh – toned down their heroes in a rather shamefaced way. The writers who succeeded them needed to make a more radical break. Dalgliesh, Wexford and Morse stand in witness of the fact that the consensus has now swung in favour of policemen. The gifted amateur still makes regular appearances, but usually in the more broadly comic novels, where he has an unfeasibly happy knack of stumbling repeatedly on corpses and obligingly confiding witnesses. In America, thanks to Chandler's continuing influence, the private eye is still almost mandatory, but in Britain policemen have become a standard part of the furniture.

RUTH RENDELL
A SLEEPING LIFE

'The best woman crime writer we have had since Sayers, Christie, Allingham and Marsh.'
Edmund Crispin, Sunday Times

Exactly what sort of change, and how big a change, does this involve? It does not signify a conversion to the 'police procedural'. But it does owe something to the same consideration which influenced earlier novelists who, without being interested in the technical rigours of the 'police procedural', had still adopted policemen as heroes and taken on board a certain amount of police business. Simenon was the supreme case of a direct, unfussy writer whose surety of instinct in getting rid of unnecessary mannerism and ornament let in a great deal of fresh air. Maigret's profession gave him, ready-made and without the need for special explanation, reason for being at the scene of the crime, authority for investigating it and, besides, an organization at his back to handle those mundane aspects of detection in which Simenon was not expert and, as he was shrewd enough to realize, his readers were not greatly interested anyway. Besides, Maigret's profession freed Simenon

from the need to over-determine his personality: he could plausibly seem ordinary while still displaying intelligence and sensitivity.

In other words, Maigret simplified matters. Later generations of writers in Britain, looking for ways of shedding baggage from the Golden Age, took heart from his example. Dalgliesh, Wexford and Morse are all heroes in the Maigret mould in that their advantages for their creators lay in what they were not as much as what they were. But, of course, no fictional character – much less a hero designed to sustain a series – can ever be a completely neutral, value-free presence. Even Simenon, who prized radical simplicity, did not set himself that goal. Maigret had to be allowed his fondness for beer and cognac, his favourite bars, his quiet dinners at home with Madame Maigret. And it is hardly surprising that in seeking to endow their policemen with personality, British writers should have shown a lingering reluctance to break entirely with the genteel and intellectual heroes of the Golden Age.

That reluctance is particularly apparent in the case of P.D. James. Adam Dalgliesh was the earliest of these heroes and, when he first appeared in *Cover Her Face* (1962), he was not just a policeman but a gentleman and a spare-time poet too. This combination is not impossible, nor even inherently implausible, but it announced the writer's determination to make her hero as little the policeman as she could get away with – in fact, scarcely more the policeman than Marsh's Roderick Alleyn, whom James might well have had more in mind than Maigret. When the series made the transition to TV, she was left wryly noting that Dalgliesh's manners had lost some of their immaculacy.

In their original conceptions, both

Rendell's and Dexter's heroes were potentially more radical. *From Doon with Death* (1964) and the other early Wexford novels made him boorish, as well as middle-aged and overweight. *Last Bus to Woodstock* (1975) made much of Morse's beer-drinking and his immersion in the town rather than the university life of Oxford. They were deliberately unromantic, where Dalgliesh had something of the older-generation matinée idol about him from the start. That did not make them typical policemen any more than it necessarily made them convincing or 'realistic' characters, but it did at least suggest the writers' desire to adjust the stereotypes to fit a new milieu. The passing years have softened them. Wexford has grown (in his creator's word) 'nicer', and has acquired a taste for literary quotation – a long-standing habit which surprisingly few fictional detectives, however new or modern or different they are meant to be,

can manage to break. Morse, too, has been slowly nudged up-market: not exactly away from the beer, but certainly towards opera and the university. His uneasy transformation was dramatically accentuated when he appeared in the TV adaptations as alternately dyspeptic and urbane.

These changes suggest several intriguing by-ways of inquiry: into the temptation for writers to put themselves in their series characters, for example, and into the differences of taste between book readers and television viewers. More centrally, both the way Dalgliesh, Wexford and Morse were first portrayed and the way their portrayals have changed over the years demonstrate how strong the pull of the past remains. It is almost as if the attributes of Golden Age fiction still possess their own involuntary life, a magnetism for writers otherwise bent on resisting them. Or, to put the matter more positively, these attributes turn out

TV cops: John Thaw as Colin Dexter's Chief Inspector Morse, with Kevin Whately as Sergeant Lewis.

to be serviceable at all sorts of unexpected turns. Take, for instance, the device of giving the detective a subordinate companion, explored by Conan Doyle in his use of Watson as a foil to Holmes and developed by Golden Age writers into a variety of relationships embodying the hierarchies of the time: master helped by faithful servant, husband helped by admiring wife, gentleman amateur helped by plodding professional, and so forth. So dated do these relationships look that one might have thought British writers would have dropped the device altogether – as American novelists have by and large done in obedience to Chandler's example. Yet, in fact, it can easily be adapted to create the investigating team of senior and junior policeman which has become a staple of recent fiction.

The older generation of writers has made the least use of it. P.D. James' Dalgliesh is supported by a team and has on occasion been called in to support

James' women detectives, Cordelia Gray in *An Unsuitable Job for a Woman* (1972) and *The Skull Beneath the Skin* (1982) and Inspector Kate Miskin in *A Taste for Death* (1986). Yet for all the suavity of his manners, he still strikes the reader as the most solitary of detectives, the most aloof in his meditation. Morse's companion, Sergeant Lewis, is one of the least satisfactory features of Dexter's novels; the TV adaptations were wise to revamp his character. Rendell has given added weight to Wexford's priggish assistant Burden (who, she says, 'generally expresses what I abhor') as the series has developed, but without realizing the full possibilities of the investigating team as an alliance or misalliance of opposites – temperamentally, politically, even ideologically.

Among contemporary British novelists, Reginald Hill has taken up the task most fruitfully. Ever since *A Clubbable Woman* (1970) he has steadily explored the unlikely partnership between Dalziel and Pascoe, the one not just reactionary but unquenchably coarse, the other not just liberal but conscientiously progressive. The result has proved as satisfying as anything current British writing has to offer in showing how a fundamentally conservative form can be made to serve as a vehicle for alert social comedy and even sharp contemporary observation. Yet in his recent additions to the series Hill has also thought it necessary to add to his original pair of detectives by expanding the role of Pascoe's wife, the feminist Ellie, and introducing Sergeant Wield, the closet homosexual. The implication is obvious: because male and married, Pascoe could no longer be relied on as the voice of modernity. He could no longer give the books the wryly contemporary note at which Hill aims.

Successful mystery writers can still be eager to avoid typecasting. Ruth Rendell, known for Chief Inspector Wexford, publishes more disquieting thrillers as Barbara Vine. Reginald Hill (opposite), known for Dalziel and Pascoe, also publishes as Patrick Ruell.

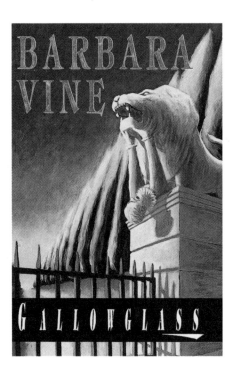

TV cops: Helen Mirren as Detective Chief Inspector Jane Tenison in Lynda La Plante's *Prime Suspect*.

Other police series have been predictably eager to follow suit in breaking the traditional mould – in fact rather more eager than the police force itself has been in real life. The pairing of senior policeman and junior policewoman has become the new convention, looking not just familiar but already rather shop-worn in a novel like Christopher Lee's *The Bath Detective* (1995), though still capable of promise in, for example, the series Barry Maitland has begun with *The Marx Sisters* (1994) and *The Malcontenta* (1995). Here, at least, the formal hierarchy of male boss and female subordinate realizes some of its potential as a paradigm of contemporary male-female tensions. The same tensions can be approached more directly when the hierarchy is inverted, as in Lynda La

Plante's *Prime Suspect* TV dramas (first screened in 1991) in which the woman is the boss and the man her resentful subordinate.

This situation, though without the resentment, had already been anticipated in the series of novels Trevor Barnes embarked on with *A Midsummer Killing* (1989). Here Detective Superintendent Blanche Hampton is intermittently harried in her private life by a wimpish husband, whom she is in the process of discarding, and assisted in her detective investigations by a sergeant who is gay, black and stylish. Whether one applauds or derides this virtuoso display of political correctness is beside the point. What is not in dispute is that Trevor Barnes' series and the *Prime Suspect* dramas aspire to the same virtues of solid entertainment professionally delivered that most crime writing in England has aimed at since the Second World War. The changes which

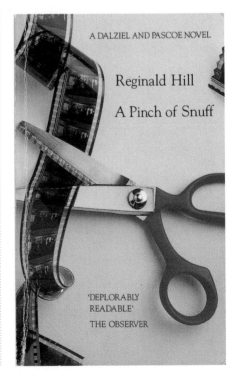

A DALZIEL AND PASCOE NOVEL

Reginald Hill

A Pinch of Snuff

'DEPLORABLY READABLE'
THE OBSERVER

reviewers are quick to label controversial or innovative are merely cosmetic. That does not mean they are necessarily to be despised, but it does mean that one day they will look as dated – as quaintly or hopelessly of their period – as Lord Peter Wimsey's monocle.

The closest approach to a distinctive new school is found in the police novels associated most of all with the names of Bill James, who began his series about Assistant Chief Constable Iles and Detective Chief Superintendent Colin Harpur with *You'd Better Believe It* (1985), and John Harvey, who began his series about Detective Inspector Charlie Resnick with *Lonely Hearts* (1989). It finds a milder expression in the work of several other writers: Bill Knox, whose series about Colin Thane began with *Deadline for a Dream* (called *In at the Kill* in USA) as long ago as 1957 but changed tempo with novels like *The Hanging Tree* (1983); Frank Palmer, who began his series about 'Jacko' Jackson with *Testimony* and *Unfit to Plead* (both 1992); and Ian Rankin, who has begun a promising series about Inspector Rebus with *Knots and Crosses* (1987). To one degree or another all these series have a precedent in *Laidlaw* (1977) and *The Papers of Tony Veitch* (1983) by William McIlvanney, a novelist whose ventures into crime fiction have been as sparing as they have proved influential.

It is significant that several of these writers should have a background in newspaper crime reporting. Their work – particularly that of McIlvanney, James and Harvey – is thoroughly immersed in the contemporary actualities of police work and professional crime. Abandoning puzzles solved with leaps of individual brilliance, it deals instead with police teams hunting Post-Office raiders or video pirates. The setting is urban. James leaves the scene of his novels deliberately unnamed, though it is apparently in easy reach of London. Harvey's territory (and Palmer's too) is Nottingham. Rankin sets his Rebus novels in Edinburgh. McIlvanney and Knox write about Glasgow, a city with a fair claim to be the crime writers' capital of Britain, whose landscape of high-rise council flats, betting shops and queues outside the local DSS offices epitomizes the atmosphere of these novels. Approving reviewers usually like to call the result 'tough' or 'gritty'.

In fact, its characteristic weakness is a slickness apparent in the narrative cross-cutting and the habit of tailoring the subsidiary characters down to fit the short attention span such narrative encourages. But that is putting the case against them at its harshest; these novels also often possess some of the strengths associated with the British tradition of regional realism. And they hold another, related, promise in the way they adapt and extend the 'police procedural'. This by definition concentrated on investigative procedure, often with such intensity that it left no room for the investigators themselves to be anything more than ciphers. The new police novels, John Harvey's Resnick series in particular, do not make this mistake. They take a certain care to get the technicalities of police work right, as one would expect, but that is not where the emphasis really falls.

It falls instead on the police force as an organization controlling the lives of policemen even more thoroughly than it manages to control the lives of criminals. At their best – in McIlvanney's *Laidlaw* or Harvey's *Wasted Years* (1993) or James' *Roses, Roses* (1993) – the novels portray a bureaucracy which forges personal rivalries or friendships, satisfies

Ian RANKIN

Let It Bleed

An Inspector Rebus Novel

'Tough and authentic-sounding thriller...'
LITERARY REVIEW

Policemen old and new: P.D. James' Dalgliesh, in the genteel tradition, and Ian Rankin's Rebus, from a tougher school.

A homage by the French crime and mystery magazine *Polar* to Robin Cook, whose bleak and bloody 'Factory' novels were far more successful in France (where he lived) than in Britain (where they appeared under the pseudonym of Derek Raymond).

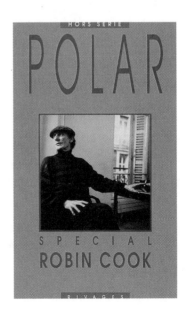

**Bringing the tough
guy up to date?
Joseph Hansen's
series is set in the
familiar Southern
California landscape
but features a gay
detective.**

rest for their deliberately limited goals,
their resolutely lightweight tone, their
innate conservatism. At last, so the
familiar rhetoric goes, Britain has started
to produce crime novelists as 'tough'
and as 'gritty' as those the USA
produces. In Britain, and in continental
Europe as well, making crime fiction
tough and gritty – in other words
contemporary, adult and serious – has
for a long time now been taken to
mean the same thing as catching up with
the USA.

At the moment Elmore Leonard and
James Ellroy are the writers most often
taken to typify what is most American in
American crime writing, and hence what
is most to be admired and emulated by
foreigners. To their names some would
add, more controversially, that of Andrew
Vachss. And yet, apart from having little
in common with British police novelists
of whatever tendency, these three hardly
constitute a natural group. They have
common ground in their preoccupation
with urban sleaze and their ability to
excite some readers (and repel others) by
the intensity of that preoccupation, but
much the same could be said of many
mainstream US novelists. It may give
their publishers a common marketing
angle and their detractors a common
charge against them, but it hardly creates
a literary school.

Leonard, the best established and
most amiable of the three, has rooted his
work in a street wisdom capable of
sounding good-humoured as well as
brutal. Brutality, however, was certainly
more to the fore in books like *City
Primeval* (1980) and *Split Images* (1981),
which traced the unfolding conflict
between cops and psycho killers – psycho
killers being as common as cops in crime
fiction these days. But the stories were
actually more like urban Westerns than

or frustrates personal ambitions and,
above all, shapes the private lives of those
who serve it. These are precisely the
themes which mainstream fiction of the
last forty years or so has neglected in its
readiness to ignore the world of work as
somehow unworthy of serious scrutiny,
concentrating instead, almost in isolation,
on the lives people lead in their leisure
time. It is no small achievement of crime
writing to have put them back on the
literary agenda.

TOUGH AMERICA?

Critics in Britain who loudly welcome
(and, as often as not, end up overpraising)
the new type of police novel are letting
readers know where they stand among
the ideological differences and polemical
divisions of the present scene. To those
discontent with the general trend of
crime writing since the war, novelists
like Bill James or John Harvey make
convenient sticks with which to beat the

anything else. The resemblance was deliberate: Leonard has also produced cowboy novels in the course of his writing career. Mercifully, however, he did not treat the Western as the Great American Myth – the solemn way it is usually treated in American art – but wryly, as one of the more dangerous games American boys love to play.

Wryness has sounded an increasingly dominant note in his work as it has gravitated from the harshness of inner-city Detroit to more benign climates, and as Leonard has developed his fascination with working criminals, albeit fairly spaced-out working criminals. He obviously prizes them most for the mixture of gaudiness and banality with which he everywhere stamps their speech and, indeed, his own narrative voice. And he reserves a particular fondness for small-timers – characters such as Stick in the 1983 novel which bore his name – who nevertheless manage to roll with the punches and sometimes even enjoy a small triumph. That has taken him dangerously close to the self-indulgent territory of the 'caper novel'. But at its best – *Freaky Deaky* (1988), for instance – his later work offers a comedy of modern American manners all the more satisfying for being acted by the unlikeliest of casts.

To characterize Leonard in this way is to point the contrast with Ellroy in the sharpest possible terms. In *Blood on the Moon* (1984) – the first of a trio about LA cop Lloyd Hopkins, and another novel which pits lawman against psycho – Ellroy invokes the Western every bit as deliberately as Leonard, though less wryly and less detachedly. Wryness and detachment have little room in his temperament. And he is less interested in finding echoes of the Western than in asserting that the cop's hunt for the psycho is also the cop's hunt for himself and his own past. That assertion reappears yet more contentiously in Andrew Vachss' novels about Burke, the criminal-turned-enforcer who first appears in *Flood* (1985). Burke at once shares in the psychic life of those he hunts and blows them away with the greatest moral rectitude, an ambivalence so sharply pointed as to suggest that Vachss is deliberately reviving the clichés of pulp fiction in order to ironize them. In Ellroy's case a determination to expose what lies behind official rectitude has

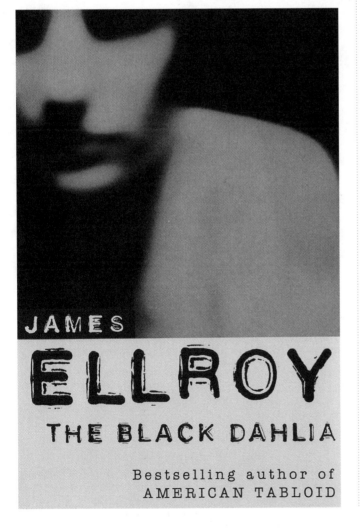

Urban sleaze becomes urban nightmare in the novels of James Ellroy's 'LA Quartet'.

JAMES

ELLROY

THE BLACK DAHLIA

Bestselling author of
AMERICAN TABLOID

taken him to the 'LA Quartet', composed of *The Black Dahlia* (1987), *The Big Nowhere* (1989), *LA Confidential* (1990) and *White Jazz* (1992). Literally it is a saga of corrupt police in the 1950s; implicitly it studies the underside of both the American public psyche and the writer's own psyche. Ellroy's work dramatizes an era which is both his own traumatic childhood and the heyday of a society headed – quite explicitly by the end of *American Tabloid* (1995) – towards the Kennedy assassination.

At which point it reaches out to join recent American mainstream writing, albeit American mainstream writing in some of its most clichéd and self-regarding preoccupations. Rather than following it on to that ground, it is worth looking again but more precisely at what writers like Ellroy, Vachss and Leonard do or do not have in common. They are not a school in the sense critics usually attach to the term, and temperamentally there is no obvious affinity between Leonard's essential geniality, Vachss' pulp earnestness and Ellroy's shrill ambition. Yet they all begin with big cities and mean streets. The most obvious thing they all find there is a street talk which can both be put in the mouths of their characters and wrought into a literary language for the novels themselves to speak. And the theme of their utterance is the nature and limits of male strength: at once a celebration and a questioning of the capacities brought into play when men who are detectives and men who are criminals fall into conflict with themselves and each other.

This is perhaps no more than a wordy way of saying that the work of all three writers lies, however remotely, in the long shadow Chandler still casts. British crime writing since the 1950s has devoted a great deal of its energy to preserving what it could from its Golden Age past, while from time to time heeding the call from critics to catch up with America. But in America itself crime writing has also been preoccupied with the past, albeit a different past and in a different spirit. It has been wrestling with the challenge, eventually the problem, of what to do in Chandler's wake. Of course, there is no obvious lack of other precedents, other models for writers to turn to: Hammett in the original hard-boiled generation itself, for example, and Ross Macdonald in the immediate post-war generation. Apart from private-eye novels, there were James M. Cain's and Patricia Highsmith's bleakly subversive crime novels and Ed McBain's 87th Precinct novels. However, Chandler's example dominated the rest, dwarfing the work not just of contemporaries but of several generations of successors as well. At first it was simply too commanding and too exciting to be ignored. But even today, it remains stubbornly present as something new writers routinely have to reckon with.

Psychos and serial killers, who appeared in the 'crime novel' from Graham Greene's *Brighton Rock* onwards, have also been doing well at the cinema box office ever since Alfred Hitchcock.

Most fundamentally, Chandler's example confirmed the private-eye novel as the dominant mode of American crime writing and it defined the general contours which the story would take. A solitary investigator sets out on a quest – typically, though not invariably, the search for a missing person – and completes it despite the indifference or hostility from the rich and the powerful encountered along the way. This description, which could serve as a summary of the Marlowe novels, also summarizes at least half of the crime novels being written in America at the moment. It is also, of course, generalized in the extreme. One of the great strengths and attractions of myths is the room they leave for individual variation, apparently endless variation, on a simple theme. And so it has proved with Chandler's legacy, which admirers have been quick to grant the status of myth.

As well as being distinctively American, Chandler's novels were also convincingly local. The Southern California they portrayed was not just a representative moral ethos but a convincingly realized place as well: a specific map of cheap hotels, all-night diners and mansions with limousines outside the door and swimming pools in the grounds. Other writers from Ross Macdonald onwards have been content to stay literally on the same terrain. Southern California remains in a special sense the home of the private-eye novel, just as the private-eye novel is the most enduring literary form Southern California has produced. It has, after all, precisely the required combination of glamour and sleaze, of entrenched power and rootlessness. Yet even the original hard-boiled generation of the 1930s and 1940s wrote about private eyes in San Francisco and New York.

ROBERT B. PARKER

· A SPENSER NOVEL ·

THE WIDENING GYRE

DELL·19535·U.S. $2.95
CAN. $3.75

SPENSER IS "A BREAKTHROUGH
FIGURE IN DETECTIVE FICTION."
—THE WASHINGTON POST

Their successors have taken the obvious cue in adapting the form to other regions and other cities. Robert B. Parker's Spenser novels, one of the longest running as well as most highly praised of current series, take place in Boston. Detroit is the setting for Loren D. Estleman's Amos Walker novels, Seattle for Earl W. Emerson's Thomas Black novels, and Cleveland for Les Roberts' Milan Jacovich novels. Virtually the entire map of the USA is now dotted with private eyes.

It takes no greater feat of imagination to shift the private-eye novel from Los Angeles to Boston or Detroit than it does, in British terms, to shift the puzzle from the country house to a prisoner-of-war camp or a health-and-fitness clinic. Nor does it involve any bigger jump to alter the characters who embody the corrupt established interests ranged against the private investigator. Chandler himself liked to draw them from the fringes of the movie business – in revenge, perhaps, for his own time in Hollywood – and he had something of a vendetta against quack doctors. Quack doctors often still appear in the private-eye novel: like cops on the take, apparently, they never change. And they have been joined by a whole host of characters who wear the contemporary face of moneyed corruption: drug barons, condominium developers, environmental polluters and experts in financial fraud involving computers. The commercial interests controlling professional sport have become a special favourite, and investigations into the underside of American pro-football a recognizable sub-genre since William Campbell Gault's *Day of the Ram* (1956), about Brock Callahan, ex-guard for the Los Angeles Rams.

By such continuing acts of renovation do popular art forms keep themselves looking reasonably fresh without losing touch with their roots. Keeping itself fresh is particularly important in the case of the private-eye novel, whose appeal has always depended in part on offering an up-to-the-minute diagnosis, or indictment, of what ails America. Yet keeping in touch with its roots is equally important to a form which still owes much of its authority to Chandler's achievement. And Chandler's influence has not been limited to the formulae which dictate the general outlines of the story. It has also been linguistic. More than anything else Chandler gave the private-eye novel a style and an attitude. He gave it the wisecrack, the one-line quip which proclaims the hero's independence of the people who threaten and harass him. And he gave it the simile, sometimes wittily authoritative in judging his enemies, sometimes openly nostalgic in mourning a lost poetry.

The ghosts of Chandler's wisecracks and similes still stalk the pages of private-eye novels, though looking increasingly pallid these days. They kept some of their original energy at, say, the time in the late 1960s and early 1970s when Ross Thomas, using the pseudonym of Oliver Bleeck, wrote his series about Philip St Ives, the go-between who negotiates the return of stolen property to its owners. The books are essentially amiable variants on the private-eye formula and make a good fist of imitating that side of the Marlowe novels which is simply engaging comedy. Yet they are also a warning of how easily the private-eye novel could sink into glibness and how quickly its hero could land up looking a smartass. Nobody could doubt that has happened in a sentence such as this one from a recent novel: 'My present bank account would fit in a midget's navel with room left over the for the lint'.

Robert B. Parker's Spenser novels pay tribute to the tradition of Hammett, Chandler and Ross Macdonald while trying to reach an accommodation with contemporary sensibilities.

Where the Private Eyes Are

All the characters listed on the map are licensed private investigators, except for a few amateurs from the older generation and some later detectives who are not technically PI's but regularly do a PI's work. California has been the favourite setting from the days of *Black Mask* up to the present generation of women PIs, though nowadays detectives of either sex are as likely to walk the shopping malls of the suburbs as the mean streets of the inner city. Outside the golden triangle of Los Angeles–San Francisco–New York, a few puzzles remain: why, for instance, so many detectives in Boston (and Cambridge, its neighbour across the Charles river) but so thin a showing in Philadelphia?

Seattle
Thomas Black (Earl W. Emerson)
John Denson (Richard Hoyt)
Pam Nilsen, member of collective (Barbara Wilson)

Just over the border:
Vancouver, BC
Meg Lacey (Elisabeth Bowers)

WASHINGTON

MONTANA

OREGON

IDAHO

WYOMING

San Francisco
Dan Banion, journalist (Robert Finnegan)
Carver Bascombe (Kenn Davis)
The Continental Op and Sam Spade (Dashiell Hammett)
Mike Haller (Max Byrd)
Dan Kearney Associates, auto repossessors (Joe Gores)
Sharon McCone (Marcia Muller)
The Nameless Detective (Bill Pronzini)
Rebecca Schwartz, lawyer, and Paul McDonald, mystery writer (in separate series by Julie Smith)
Sam Train (Ernest Savage)

Sacramento
Kat Colorado (Karen Kijewski)

NEVADA

Salt Lake City
Moroni Traveler (Robert Irvine)

UTAH

Denver
Jacob Lomax

Oakland
Jeri Howard (Janet Dawson)

CALIFORNIA

COLORADO

Las Vegas
Bill Lennox (Willis Todhunter Ballard) See also Hollywood
Red Diamond (Mark Schorr)

Santa Barbara
Kinsey Millhone (Sue Grafton, who calls it 'Santa Teresa')

San Fernando Valley
V. Daniel (David M. Pierce)

ARIZONA

NEW MEXICO

Los Angeles
Lew Archer (Ross Macdonald)
Jacob Asch (Arthur Lyons)
Otis Beagle (Frank Gruber, under his own name and as Charles K. Boston)
Dave Brandstetter, insurance investigator (Joseph Hansen)
Brock, the Rock, Callahan and Joe Puma (heroes of separate series by William Campbell Gault)
Bertha Cool and Donald Lam (Erle Stanley Gardner, writing as A.A. Fair)
Alex Delaware, clinical psychologist (Jonathan Kellerman)
Mike Faraday (Basil Copper, a British writer)
Aaron Gunner (Gar Anthony Harwood)
Sam Hunter (L.A. Morse)
Simon Lash (Frank Gruber)
Rex McBride (Cleve F. Adams)
Philip Marlowe (Raymond Chandler)
Perry Mason, lawyer (Erle Stanley Gardner)
Fergus O'Breen (Anthony Boucher)
Easy Rawlins (Walter Mosley)
Regan Reilly (Carol Higgins Clark)
Saxon (Les Roberts)
Vince Slader (Ovid Demaris)
Delilah West (Maxine O'Callaghan)

La Jolla
Kiernan O'Shaughnessy (Susan Dunlap)

San Diego
Max Thursday (Wade Miller)

(Hollywood, Los Angeles)
Joe Copp (Don Pendleton)
Rick Holman (Carter Brown, an Australian writer)
Thomas Kyd (Timothy Harris)
Bill Lennox, trouble-shooter for film company (Willis Todhunter Ballard)
Toby Peters (Stuart M. Kaminsky)
Shell Scott (Richard S. Prather)
Dan Turner (Robert Leslie Bellem)
Whistler (Robert Campbell)

Chicago
Barr Breed (Bill S. Ballinger)
Bill Crane (Jonathan Latimer)
Jimmy Flannery, city official (Robert Campbell)
Ed and Ambrose Hunter (Fredric Brown)
Cooper MacLeish, taxi-driver (Sam Reaves)
John J. Malone, lawyer (Craig Rice)
Mac (Thomas B. Dewey)
Paul Pine (Howard Browne)
Peter Shane, criminologist (Francis Bonnamy)
V.I. Warshawski (Sara Paretsky)

Just over the border:
St Catherines, Ontario
Benny Cooperman (Howard Engel, who calls it 'Grantham')

Cleveland
Milan Jacovich (Les Roberts)

Detroit
Amos Walker (Loren D. Estleman)

Cincinnati
Patricia Delaney (Sharon Gwyn Short)
Harry Stoner (Jonathan Valin)

Concord
Homer Kelly, lawyer (Jane Langton)

Cambridge
Tom Bethany, security consultant (Jerome Doolittle)
Harvey Blissberg (Richard Rosen)

Saratoga
Charlie Bradshaw (Stephen Dobyns)

Rochester
Jessica James, reporter (Meg O'Brien)

Boston
Carlotta Carlyle and Michael Spraggue, actor (in separate series by Linda Barnes)
Brady Coyne, lawyer (William G. Tapply)
J.F. Cuddy (Jeremiah Healy)
Stoner McTavish, travel agent (Sarah Dreher)
Kent Murdock and Flashgun Casey, press photographers (in separate series by George Harmon Coxe)
Spenser (Robert B. Parker)

Philadelphia
Carney Wilde (Bart Spicer)

Washington DC
Ben Safford, congressman (R.B. Dominic, the other pseudonym used by Emma Lathen)

Charlottesville
Loren Swift (Doug Hornig)

Cedar Rapids
Jack Dwyer and Walsh (in separate series by Ed Gorman)

Indianapolis
Albert Samson (Michael Z. Lewin)

St Louis
Arlo Nudger (John Latz)

Atlanta
Callahan Garrity (Kathy Hogan Trocheck)

New Orleans
Lew Griffin (James Sallis)

New Iberia
Dave Robicheaux, former New Orleans policeman (James Lee Burke)

Tampa
Matthew Hope, lawyer (Ed McBain, who calls it 'Calusa')

Fort Lauderdale
Travis McGee, 'salvage consultant' (John D. MacDonald)

Miami
Michael/Mike Shayne (Brett Halliday)

New York
R.J. Brooks (Stephen Humphrey Bogart)
Burke (Andrew Vachss)
Peter Chambers (Henry Kane)
Timothy Dane (William Ard)
Kate Fansler, university teacher (Amanda Cross)
Johnny Fletcher and Sam Cragg (Frank Gruber)
Dan Fortune (Michael Collins)
Kinky Friedman (Kinky Friedman)
Mike Hammer (Mickey Spillane)
Jim Hanvey (Octavus Roy Cohen)
Bart Hardin, columnist (David Alexander)
Henry Hyer (Kurt Steel)
Miles Jacoby (Robert J. Randisi)
Scott Jordan, lawyer (Harold Q. Masur)
Lauren Laurano (Sandra Scoppettone)
Johnny Liddell (Frank Kane)
Captain Duncan Maclain (Baynard Kendrick)
Ed Noon (Thomas Avallone)
Pam and Jerry North, amateurs (Frances and Richard Lockridge)
Ellery Queen, gentleman amateur (Ellery Queen)
Philip St Ives, professional go-between (Ross Thomas, writing as Oliver Bleeck)
John Shaft (Ernest Tidyman)
Matt Scudder (Lawrence Block)
Desmond Shannon (M.V. Heberden)
John Putnam Thatcher, banker (Emma Lathen)
Mitch Tobin (Donald E. Westlake, writing as Tucker Coe)
Philo Vance, gentleman amateur (S.S. Van Dine)
Nero Wolfe and Archie Goodwin (Rex Stout)

Or this, from another recent novel: 'He was the kind of man who'd use vanity plates on a getaway car'. Nor, to judge from this passage, is the poetic simile faring any better than the wisecrack: 'As I drove up Capillo Hill, the very air seemed gray, sueded with twilight. Streetlights flicked on like a series of paper lanterns strung festively from pole to pole.'

It would be easy to fill the rest of this chapter with similar quotations, equally strained, equally artificial, equally ineffective. Such a display would do more than confirm the fact that wisecracks and similes are hard to write and harder still to make the basis of a literary language: Chandler himself knew that, and by no means all of his own wisecracks and

similes work. It would also confirm that a great deal of recent writing sounds as if it is about to collapse beneath the weight of its own mannerisms. Given that private-eye fiction has always placed a particular emphasis on style, it is not surprising that its current problems should so obviously betray themselves in a failure of style.

But no literary problems are ever just in the style. It has been obvious for some time that the private eye as Chandler conceived him has become a problem, even a burden. To start with, writers could imitate Chandler in the same happy way that British writers imitated Conan Doyle in the immediate aftermath of the Sherlock Holmes stories. But once that phase of innocence was past, the need to vary the original model set in. A popular device was simply to invert one of the hero's chief characteristics and so to play with the reader's disappointed expectation on encountering a private eye who is, say, physically inept or nervous in manner. Several series – Michael Z. Lewin's novels about Albert Samson, Stephen Dobyns' novels about Charlie Bradshaw and Howard Engel's novels about Benny Cooperman, for example – still manage to sustain themselves quite amiably in this fashion, as minor, comic variants on the great theme whose name is Marlowe.

Meanwhile, the simple passage of time was enforcing the need for change, if only in the private eye's personal habits. They soon dated and now can look every bit as antiquated as the habits of the genteel amateur from the Golden Age. Take Marlowe's smoking and drinking, for instance. These were not just incidental details or mannerisms of the age, but touches which served on more or less every page to assert his persona, much as they did for Humphrey Bogart's image on the screen. Nowadays smoking is reserved

James Lee Burke's series about Louisiana detective Dave Robicheaux combines the tradition of the private-eye novel with the conventions of Southern Gothic.

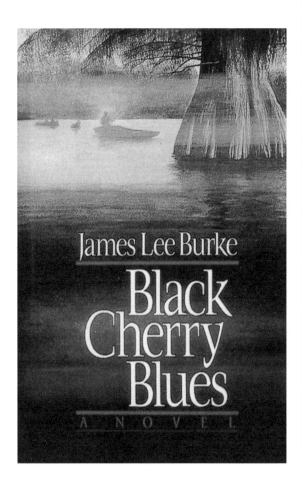

James Lee Burke

Black Cherry Blues

A NOVEL

making his heirs over, so that now private eyes usually have either a failed marriage to brood over in the evenings or a live-in partner to discuss their problems with. Some are gay, though in the long-running series about the insurance investigator Dave Brandstetter which Joseph Hansen began with *Fadeout* in 1970, the result hardly presents the new vantage point on the form and its hero one might have hoped for.

All these changes to Chandler's portrait of the private eye raise obvious questions. At what point are writers forced to take something essential away from the character and so make a decisive break with the tradition? When they do make the break, what new hero will emerge? And what new form will he inhabit? If no comprehensive answer is yet possible, that is because male private-eye novelists have so far proved every bit as reluctant to abandon their legacy as British writers have been to shake the remaining dust of Golden Age traditions out of their writing. Robert B. Parker's novels illustrate that reluctance and all the problems it creates as clearly as any work the contemporary scene can offer. Parker began writing about Spenser in *The Godwulf Manuscript* as long ago as 1973, with a hero deliberately named after a Renaissance poet just as Marlowe had been named after a Renaissance dramatist. Such knowing little nods of homage to Chandler have come to seem almost obligatory.

The fact that Parker has a much crisper line in wisecracks than most of his contemporaries has not made the process of homage any easier or more fertile in the long run. Spenser has continued to work out in the gym, carry a gun and muscle in on situations to provoke a violent response, because that is what private eyes have to do to keep the plot moving along. He has even been given a

for the villains, and private eyes, rather than being hard-drinkers, are more likely to be recovering alcoholics – as Lawrence Block's Matt Scudder, James Lee Burke's Dave Robicheaux and Meg O'Brien's Jessica James all are.

The transformation of the old private eye whose continual swigging from the bottle in the desk drawer never stopped him handling the case into the new private eye whose failure with alcohol still threatens him: that is more than a new literary convention born lazily of the new political correctness. By replacing invulnerability with vulnerability, it follows Ross Macdonald in challenging the old myths of male strength which the private eye embodied. So it is hardly surprising that his sex life should have needed revising too. Even in its time Marlowe's alternation between puritan disdain and predatory flirtatiousness toward women was plainly the least satisfactory aspect of Chandler's novels. Again, Ross Macdonald set the trend in

Too cool to be true? Robert Ulrich as Robert B. Parker's private eye Spenser, with Avery Brooks as Hawk, in the US TV series.

triumphant embodiment of the character's ability to adapt and grow. Or that is what he is meant to be. In fact, *Double Deuce* and all the recent Spenser novels merely underline the glaring inconsistencies in the old tough guy with the bulge of a shoulder-holster under the armpit of his jacket, who is also a new man brimming with tender self-awareness and health food.

By no means all contemporary writers languish in this blind alley. Walter Mosley, for example, does not. On the surface the series about Easy Rawlins that he began with *Devil in a Blue Dress* (1990), set in Los Angeles in the 1950s, looks like just another example of the current fashion for historicism which in America has manifested itself in Chandler pastiche and Ellroy's 'LA Quartet'. But by portraying Chandler's territory and period from the vantage point of a black detective, Mosley is not so much offering homage as attempting genuine revision. *Devil in a Blue Dress* discovers new meaning in the private eye's lack of official power and his conflict with established authority. And, instead of celebrating the heroic isolation in which Marlowe lived, it locates him in a community, expert in how the underprivileged and excluded manage to survive.

Genuine revision of another sort has come from the female private-eye novels which began to appear in the late 1970s. Marcia Muller's *Edwin of the Iron Shoes* (1977) is usually identified as the first. Initially they were issued by small, often feminist presses, but mainstream publishing has since enthusiastically adopted them, discovering the mass marketability of Sara Paretsky and Sue Grafton. Paretsky's V.I. Warshawski novels and Sue Grafton's Kinsey Millhone novels are now among the best-known

black friend, the impossibly cool Hawk, with whom he can refine the clipped language of the macho code into almost Zen-like utterance. Yet he has also been given a partner, the psychotherapist Susan, with whom he can demonstrate a liberated male sensibility which belongs thoroughly to the 1980s and 1990s. These days the novels alternate rhythmically between Spenser's conversations with Hawk and his conversations with Susan, an uneasy device which leaves little space for the plot to move forward except in violent leaps and bounds.

Parker's intention is made clear when, in *Double Deuce* (1992), he has Spenser explain himself to another character:

'I used to be a fighter. I used to be a cop. Now I am a private detective,' I said. 'I read a lot. I love Susan.'

I paused for a moment thinking about it.

'The list,' I said, 'is probably in reverse order.'

'A romantic,' she said. 'You don't look it.'

Spenser, in other words, is a walking history of the fictional private eye, a

American private-eye series. There are signs in Britain that Liza Cody's Anna Lee novels are on their way to achieving the same status, and perhaps also Val McDermid's Kate Brannigan novels. The mere fact that female private-eye novels should flourish in Britain as well as America is remarkable, since until their advent one would have said that the private-eye novel was quintessentially American – and therefore, like many quintessentially American artifacts, capable of being successfully translated to continental Europe but never to Britain.

The other thing one might have said about the private-eye novel was that it was quintessentially male: male code,

The film version of the first of Walter Mosley's Easy Rawlins novels, which revisit the world of Chandler but from the perspective of the black ghetto.

male strength, male hero, male fantasy. Other attributes of Marlowe could be dropped or changed, but never his gender. But that was exactly what made a new generation of women, largely feminist, writers attack the form – since what they have done has amounted to an attack, though of a particularly creative and refreshing sort. Freshness may have grown less and less apparent in Paretsky's work, where the careful contrivance of plots to provide both conventional mystery and the maximum number of confrontations between her heroine and macho authority soon began to look depressingly slick. But freshness can still be found in the work of Sue Grafton or Karen Kijewski or Meg O'Brien.

You're a Damned Good Man, Sister:

'You're a damned good man, sister.'

Sam Spade to Effie Perine, in Hammett's *The Maltese Falcon*

Just in time I remembered I was a competent professional and not a dipshit lovesick bimbo.

Kat Colorado in Karen Kijewski's *Katwalk*

Predecessors

Scholars have variously claimed Mrs Henry Wood's *East Lynne* (1861), Mary Elizabeth Braddon's *Lady Audley's Secret* (1865) or Seeley Register's *The Dead Letter* (1866) as the first female crime novel. The earliest books with women detectives are *The Female Detective* (1864), represented on the title page as being edited by Andrew Forrester, Junior, and an anonymous and elusive 'yellowback' which bibliographers used to think first appeared as *The Experiences of a Lady Detective* in 1861 but now believe saw the light of day as *The Revelations of a Lady Detective* in 1864.

Michele Slung published a useful collection of early work, *Crime On Her Mind*, in 1975. Its appearance was timely, since the Miss Marple generation of women crime novelists and detectives had by then given way to a new generation which struck a different note. The significant texts include P.D. James' *An Unsuitable Job for a Woman* (1972), which introduced Cordelia Gray, and Amanda Cross' series about Kate Fansler, which began with *In the Last Analysis* (1964) but did not really hit its stride until books such as *Death in a Tenured Position* (1981; called *A Death in the Faculty* in UK) and *No Word from Winifred* (1986). Critics still debate the proportions of conservatism and feminism they express. What is not disputed is that writers like James and Cross have now been supplanted in their turn by more emphatically feminist writers, chiefly but not exclusively in America. By and large their writing has focused on women private eyes.

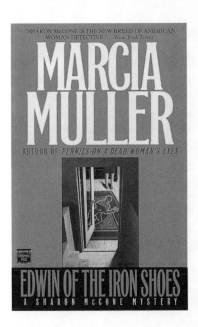

"SHARON McCONE IS THE NEW BREED OF AMERICAN WOMAN DETECTIVE." —*New York Times*

MARCIA MULLER

AUTHOR OF *PENNIES ON A DEAD WOMAN'S EYES*

EDWIN OF THE IRON SHOES

A SHARON McCONE MYSTERY

The Pioneer

Marcia Muller (US)

Edwin of the Iron Shoes (1977) launched a continuing series about Sharon McCone. Muller has also written about two amateur detectives: Elena Oliverez, introduced in *Tree of Death* (1983), and Joanna Stark, introduced in *The Cavalier in White* (1986).

Radical feminist/lesbian agendas

M.F. Beal (US)

Angel Dance (1977), about Chicano detective Kat Guerrara, has been claimed by one critic as 'the first and best lesbian crime novel'

Sarah Dreher (US)

Her lesbian detective gives her name to the first novel in the series, *Stoner McTavish* (1985).

Maria-Antònia Oliver (Spain)

Estudi en lila (1985; translated from the Catalan as *Study in Lilac*, 1987) features Barcelona detective Lònia

Guiu and a fleeting appearance from Spain's best-known male detective, Manuel Vázquez Montalbán's Pepe Carvalho.

Barbara Wilson (US)

Her series character Pam Nilsen, introduced in *Murder in the Collective* (1984), tackles a predictable list of feminist issues. *Gaudi Afternoon* (1990) is a comic crime novel set in Barcelona.

Helen Zahavi (UK)

A Dirty Weekend (1991) is the serial-killer novel to end all serial-killer novels.

Eve Zaremba (Canada)

Helen Keremos features in a series of hard-boiled lesbian pulp, started in *A Reason to Kill* (1978).

Bestsellers

Liza Cody (UK)

Her series character is Anna Lee, introduced in *Dupe* (1980).

Sue Grafton (US)

Her series character is Kinsey Millhone, introduced in *'A' is for Alibi* (1982).

Sara Paretsky (US)

Her series character is V.I. Warshawski, introduced in *Indemnity Only* (1982).

Most promising

Linda Barnes (US)

Her series character is Carlotta Carlyle, introduced in *A Trouble of Fools* (1987). She earlier wrote a series about a male amateur detective, Michael Spraggue, starting with *Blood Will Have Blood* (1982).

Karen Kijewski (US)

Her series character is Kat Colorado, introduced in *Katwalk* (1989).

Val McDermid (UK)

She is best known for Kate Brannigan, her series character introduced in

Dead Beat (1992), but started with Lindsay Gordon, a socialist feminist lesbian journalist, introduced in *Report for Murder* (1987).

Meg O'Brien (USA)

Her series character is Jessica ('Jesse') James, an investigative reporter introduced in *A Salmon in the Soup* (1990) but at her free-wheeling best in *Hare Today, Gone Tomorrow* (1991).

Also...

Sarah Dunant (UK)

Her series character is Hannah Wolfe, introduced in *Birth Marks* (1991). Only for those who can take wisecracking cleverness at its most strained.

Gillian Slovo (UK)

Her series character is Kate Baeier, an investigative journalist in the first book, *Morbid Symptoms* (1984), but a private eye by the third, *Death Comes Staccato* (1987). Only for those with a high threshold for political solemnity.

Linda *Barnes*

Coyote

A Carlotta Carlyle Mystery

'Linda Barnes is once again brilliant' *Robert B. Parker*

When their private eyes rescue men from burning buildings or ignore their boyfriends' plea not to visit the sinister warehouse without first telling the cops, the slam-bang innocence of the pulps is revived and a new dimension of knowing modernity added.

This can make the sophistication of most male private-eye novels look tired and hollow, but it is still the sort of simple fun which quickly palls with familiarity. A more profound change has been wrought by the way the female private-eye novels handle the first-person narrative that has been an almost universal convention since Chandler. For all his bravura with wisecrack and simile, the language in which Marlowe used to tell the story was always reticent at its core. Spenser may profess himself ready to let his emotions hang out in the modern way but, when it comes to it, clipped utterance punctuated by ellipsis and silence is central to his strength in the story. Revelation would destroy it. Female private eyes, by contrast, pack their narrative with all the private clutter of their lives. They catalogue the contents of their handbags, complain about the problems they have with tights, vent their dislike of doing the housework and confide their exasperation with men. Their refusal to be aloof from the reader over such things – even the sort of mundane detail male narrators tend to edit out as beneath their and the story's dignity – makes them more familiar, more genuinely vulnerable. And that radically alters their status as detectives.

Not just private-eye novels but most crime stories have depended on the detective's in-built detachment from the mystery he investigates: the detachment of the scientist from the phenomena he studies or of the judge from the case he hears. He might form purely human likes or dislikes but the solution to the mystery usually reproves him for doing so: the private eye falling in love with the woman client who turns out to be deceiving him and so has to be rejected or punished at the end is a cliché. The story is there to be affected by the detective, not the detective by the story. 'I like to move into people's lives and then move out again', explains Lew Archer. 'I never saw any of them again – except the cops', says Marlowe, asking the reader both to admire and pity the unchanged solitude to which the conclusion of *The Long Good-Bye* once more returns him.

Female private eyes do not have this knack. They are implicated much more deeply in their stories. Their cases come

The Feminist Bookshelf

Patricia Craig and Mary Cadogan
The Lady Investigates: Women Detectives and Spies in Fiction. 1986.

Suzanne Dutruch
Les Techniques et les thèmes du roman policier anglais (Auteurs feminins) 1920–1950. 1985.

Kathleen Gregory Klein
The Woman Detective: Gender and Genre. 1988.

Sally R. Munt
Murder by the Book? Feminism and the Crime Novel. 1994.

Maureen T. Reddy
Sisters in Crime: Feminism and the Crime Novel. 1988.

novels use the same device but not nearly so often and usually just as a device. In the female private-eye novels personal involvement is not just a convenience to get the story going but a signal that its theme will be the detective's own self-discovery and self-definition. She is not just there to solve a mystery but to learn about herself by understanding women from her family past better, or to see herself more clearly by comparing her life with the fate of women friends. That, perhaps, is to state the matter in terms of what these novels promise rather than what they always manage to deliver. But the promise is palpably there, and the often rough-and-ready performance still carries its own excitement. And who would have thought, even a few years ago, that the private-eye novel could be nudged into becoming a form of spiritual autobiography?

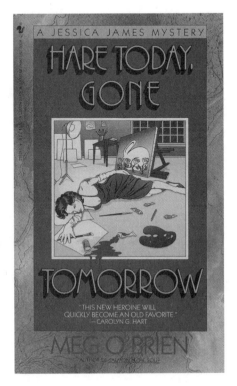

Not all of the new female private eyes are private eyes: Sara Paretsky's V.I. Warshawski is a professional, but Meg O'Brien's Jesse James is a journalist who stumbles across mysteries by chance.

from their private lives in the first place, often from hearing that someone they know has got into trouble. Typical plots hinge on the problems of relatives or old friends: aunts in Paretsky's *Killing Orders* (1985) and *Burn Marks* (1990), a mother in O'Brien's *Hare Today, Gone Tomorrow* (1991), old friends in Kijewski's *Katwalk* (1989) and Sandra Scoppetone's *I'll Be Leaving You Always* (1993), and an accident-prone boyfriend in McDermid's *Crack Down* (1994). Male private-eye

The Fig Tree Murder

'STILL AS FERTILE AS YOUR FAVOURITE OASIS' *Literary Review*

A Slight Case of Historicism

Conscientious surveys always used to make a point of remembering the American writer Melville Davisson Post's *Uncle Abner, Master of Mysteries*, published in 1918 but set in Virginia before the Civil War, and Robert van Gulik's stories about Judge Dee in China during the Tang dynasty. But they mentioned them only in passing and only as oddities. For most of its short life crime and mystery fiction has worn a resolutely contemporary face. However much it may now depend on nostalgia, the appeal of nineteenth-century pioneers like Poe or Wilkie Collins or Conan Doyle originally lay in their being up-to-the-minute in their settings and state-of-the-art in their plots.

Mysteries which dipped into history were rare, an exercise to be indulged in only by an author as safely established as Agatha Christie, who took the cue from the archaeological excavations of her second husband, Max Mallowan, and set *Death Comes as the End* (1944) in ancient Egypt. When Josephine Tey wanted to reopen the murder of the Princes in the Tower and the question of Richard III's guilt in *The Daughter of Time* (1951) she still could not abandon Inspector Grant, the modern detective she had used in previous novels, even though she had to make him bedridden and bored enough to pass his time thinking about history.

Michael Pearce's Mamur Zapt, Head of the Secret Police, investigates in Edwardian Cairo.

We do things differently these days. Each new season brings its crop of mysteries set in the past, and often in remote places too: the latest addition to Lindsey Davis' series about the Roman secret agent Marcus Didius Falco, for example, or Michael Pearce's series about the Mamur Zapt in Cairo, or Gillian Linscott's series about suffragette Monica Minter at the time of the First World War, or J. Robert Janes' series about a Gestapo man and a French *flic* working together in Occupied France. The list could easily be lengthened by adding, still more or less at random, the names of Anton Gill (ancient Egypt), Ian Morson and P.C. Doherty (medieval England), P.F. Chisholm (Elizabethan England), Jeremy Sturrock (Regency Bow Street Runners), Richard Grayson (Paris in La Belle Epoque) and Philip Kerr (Berlin under the Third Reich). Most of these books lie somewhere in the shadow of the recent success of Ellis Peters' novels about Brother Cadfael, a twelfth-century monk of Shrewsbury Abbey. And Cadfael's popularity – which came a little late in a sequence originally started in the late 1970s – surely owes a good deal to the international reputation achieved by Umberto Eco's medieval mystery, *The Name of the Rose*, in the 1980s. Mystery and historical fiction have joined together, it seems, to create their own hybrid.

The Name of the Rose is a historical novel and, for that matter, a mystery novel only in passing and almost incidentally. History and mystery are just two of the cards in the postmodernist pack that Eco shuffles with gleeful skill. But under their cowls and togas the other writers just mentioned are a conventional crowd, and they are at their most conventional in sticking to the rules laid down in the 1920s and 1930s. No deconstruction for them: they take the body from the country-house library and drop it in the sewers of Elizabethan London or the tomb of the pharaohs instead. But they are doing something more than demonstrate the innate conservatism of the genre. In turning to the past, mystery writers are also observing a coming-of-age rite. The mystery story may have had only a short life, but by now that life does extend to something like a century and a half. Mysteries have their own traditions to celebrate and to treat with respect. They can look history in the face with confidence. And that perhaps is why so many writers now turn in particular to the Victorian age, the very period which saw the development of the form they are still practising.

The fashion for Victorian murder mysteries got off to a distinguished start with help from: Nicholas Blake, who abandoned his amateur detective Nigel Strangeways for the story of an actual crime to produce a minor classic in *A Tangled Web* (1956, later called *Death and Daisy Bland* in USA); the historian R.J. White, who also used Victorian cases in two unjustly neglected books, *The Smartest Grave* (1961) and *The Women of Peasenhall* (1969); H.R.F. Keating, who freed himself

from his best-known creation, Inspector Ghote, in *The Underside* (1974) and *A Remarkable Case of Burglary* (1975); and Julian Symons in *The Blackheath Poisonings* (1978), *Sweet Adelaide* (1980), based on the Adelaide Bartlett poisoning case, and *The Detling Murders* (1982; called *The Detling Secret* in USA). Peter Lovesey's *Wobble to Death* (1970) started a series about Sergeant Cribb and Constable Thackeray. Other Victorian series include: Francis Selwyn's Sergeant Verity novels, starting with *Cracksman on Velvet* (1974; later called *Sergeant Verity and the Cracksman*); John Buxton Hilton's Inspector Thomas Brunt novels, starting with *Rescue from the Rose* (1976); Anne Perry's Inspector Thomas Pitt novels, starting with *The Cater Street Hangman* (1979); Elizabeth Peters' novels about archaeologist Amelia Peabody and her husband Radcliffe Emerson, starting with *The Curse of the Pharaohs* (1981); and Ray Harrison's Sergeant Bragg and Constable Morton novels, starting with *French Ordinary Murder* (1983).

Except for Elizabeth Peters, all of these writers are British. Americans have yet to get excited about their own nineteenth-century past, unless Caleb Carr's *The Alienist* (1994), set in the New York of the 1890s, announces a new trend. For them the time and the place to revisit are Los Angeles in the 1940s or 1950s, the heyday both of the tough private eye and of Hollywood. James Ellroy in his 'LA Quartet' and Walter Mosley in his Easy Rawlins series are revisionists, boldly rereading and rewriting America's past. Most of their colleagues are working in a

Ellis Peters pioneered the medieval mystery novel.

THE
SUMMER
OF THE
DANES

·A· MEDIAEVAL·
·WHODUNNIT·

ELLIS·PETERS

The eighteenth Chronicle of Brother Cadfael

simple spirit of homage to Chandler: Andrew Bergman, for example, in *The Big Kiss-Off of 1944* (1974) and *Hollywood and LeVine* (1975); and Stuart M. Kaminsky, whose *Bullet for a Star* (1977) started a long-running series about Hollywood private eye Toby Peters. *Bullet for a Star* works Errol Flynn, Sydney Greenstreet and Peter Lorre into the story; the Marx Brothers, Gary Cooper, Bette Davis and Judy Garland make guest appearances in later books. Robert B. Parker, creator of a contemporary private eye in his Spenser novels, has unwisely completed the fragment of the Marlowe novel that Chandler left behind at his death in *Poodle Springs* (1989), and continued the story of *The Big Sleep* in *Perchance to Dream* (1991). Crime and mystery fiction is no more capable than any of the other popular arts of resisting the fact that we live in a time of revival – the age of the sequel.

Past Celebrities as Detectives

From combining history with mystery, it is only a short step to ransacking the past for well-known figures to press into the service of detection. The stories in Lilian de la Torre's *Dr Sam: Johnson, Detector* (1946) deserve a niche among the minor classics, not just for the happy perception that Dr Johnson's relations with Boswell prefigure those between Holmes and Watson, but also for a knack of literary ventriloquism which puts most pastiches of the Holmes stories well in the shade. A short list of later books would have to include:

George Baxt's *The Dorothy Parker Murder Case* (1984), with Dorothy Parker and her colleague Alexander Woolcott as detectives.

John Dickson Carr's *The Hungry Goblin* (1972), which makes Wilkie Collins the detective. Jonathan Whicher, one of the police detectives Dickens had written about, appears in Carr's previous Victorian mystery, *Scandal at High Chimneys* (1956). The

protagonist of an earlier short story, 'The Gentleman from Paris', is plainly meant to be Edgar Allan Poe.

Michael Dibdin's *A Rich Full Death* (1986), with Robert Browning investigating a murder among the Anglo-American colony of expatriates in nineteenth-century Florence.

Margaret Doody's *Aristotle Detective* (1978), with the philosopher applying the principles of his logical system to detection.

Joe Gores' *Hammett* (1975), in homage to the writer's credentials as a Pinkerton's detective; the film version by Wim Wenders (1982) pays tribute to the *film noir*.

Peter Lovesey's *Bertie and the Tin Man* (1988) and other books with 'Bertie' in the title, with the future Edward VII playing detective.

Theodore Mathieson's *The Devil and Ben Franklin* (1961), with Benjamin Franklin as the detective – a device which recurs in Donald Zochert's *Murder in the Hellfire Club* (1978).

Elliott Roosevelt's *The Hyde Park Murder* (1935) and *Murder and the First Lady* (1940), in which the son of Franklin D. and Eleanor Roosevelt turns his mother into a detective and arranges for guest appearances by such figures as Joseph Kennedy and J. Edgar Hoover.

William Rushton's *W.G. Grace's Last Case* (1984), combining the British passions for Victoriana and cricket.

Eric Zencey's *Panama* (1995), with Henry Adams – writer as well as grandson and great-grandson of US Presidents – drawn into mysteries in 1890s Paris surrounding the Panama Canal project.

It's Different Abroad: so the title of a thriller by Henry Calvin reminded readers in 1963. It's a pity that the novel should have been virtually forgotten, not least because of the deft way Calvin presents the viewpoint of a resilient and resourceful heroine in a time when thriller heroines still tended to be anything but resilient and resourceful. Helen MacLeish, self-described 'spinster', needs these qualities to survive the adventures that come her way when she sets off on a holiday in Normandy. There, it turns out, the dangers are as likely to come from untrustworthy Brits as from sinister foreigners. In its amiable fashion, the novel lives up to a title which breathes all the excitement that the British stubbornly insisted on feeling when they began their post-war rediscovery of Europe, despite the chilly climate of currency restrictions and adverse exchange rates.

This rediscovery, which has permeated British life from cooking to constitutional politics, has left its mark on British crime and mystery novels as well. Holidays abroad had always made a tempting subject. That is hardly surprising, since crime and mystery novels are often not only read by people lying on foreign beaches but written by people who like to make their time lying on foreign beaches a profitable as well as pleasant way of using up their royalty cheques. But in the years after the Second World War novels satisfying this appetite took on both a new energy and a new atmosphere. A form which had previously pandered to hostile stereotypes of foreigners – not from any deep-seated xenophobia so much as an inveterate habit of casually absorbing the clichés of its time – became increasingly Europhiliac. The phrase 'it's different abroad' carried more allurement than warning.

The new spirit first made itself felt in the series by Delano Ames (an American who spent many years in Britain) about Jane and Dagobert Brown, one of the few husband-and-wife detective teams whose jokiness is not immediately tiresome. *Corpse Diplomatique* (1950) took them to a very English *pension* in Nice, *Murder, Maestro Please* (1952) to a music festival in the French Pyrenees loosely inspired by the one the cellist Pablo Casals used to run at Prades, and *Lucky Jane* (1959; called *For Old Crime's Sake* in USA) on a newspaper prizewinners' trip to the imaginary Mediterranean island of Tabarca. The witty dialogue and generally sunny atmosphere, both winning by a long chalk over the actual business of detection, helped to set the tone for the flurry of holiday novels which followed. The tourist coach joined the express train and the cruise liner as a favourite setting for mysteries on the move.

Soon it became *de rigueur* for series detectives – from Ngaio Marsh's Roderick Alleyn and Christianna Brand's Inspector Cockrill to Patricia Moyes' Henry Tibbett – to take busmen's holidays abroad from time to time. Even John Putnam Thatcher, Emma Lathen's American banker-detective, could be found far away from the bustle of Wall Street in *When in Greece* (1969). Novelists who liked to avoid writing to a recurrent formula could turn their hand to studying the British (or Anglo-American) expatriate communities in Europe, as Michael Gilbert did in *The Etruscan Net* (1969; called *The Family Tomb* in USA), about Florence, and Paula Gosling did in *The Woman in Red* (1983), about Spain. Even the original holiday novel that Delano Ames had refined could be inventively adapted in Sarah Caudwell's current series about Professor Hilary Tamar and her circle of legal *protégés*, at their best when they made their debut in *Thus Was Adonis Murdered* (1981), about Venice. *The Shortest Way to Hades* (1984) and *The Sirens Sang of Murder* (1989) visit the Greek islands, an increasingly popular destination which also turns up in Joan Aiken's *Last Movement* (1977), Nancy Livingston's *Incident at Parga* (1987) in her series about Mr Pringle, and T.J. Binyon's *Greek Gifts* (1988).

For all their kindliness towards Europe, these novels remain as essentially British as any country-house murder mystery from the 1920s or 1930s, and as essentially innocent in their fun. They celebrate the British at play. The way to a deeper immersion in Europe was suggested by the example of Simenon, taken up by Nicolas Freeling in two series: his books about Inspector Van der Valk of the Amsterdam police, begun with *Love in Amsterdam* (1962; called *Death in Amsterdam* in USA) and abruptly curtailed when Van der Valk is killed in *A Long Silence* (1972; called *Auprès de Ma Blonde* in USA); and his books about Henri Castang, the Frenchman introduced in *A Dressing of Diamond* (1974), who has since gravitated from one EC centre, Strasbourg, to another, Brussels.

An expatriate Englishman who has declared himself a European, Freeling has proved ideally equipped to show his fellow-countrymen how to write of continental Europe from the inside. Both Van der Valk and Castang are essentially heirs to Maigret: reflective, in but not of the bureaucracies which pay their salaries, eventually loyal to private values rather than public duty. Indeed, some readers at first found Van der Valk a character conceived too thoroughly in Maigret's shadow, though few felt inclined to maintain the criticism when the series reached its maturity in *Gun Before Butter* (1963; called *Question of Loyalty* in USA), *Double-Barrel* (1964), *Criminal Conversation* (1965) and *The King of the Rainy Country* (1966). Now it is Freeling himself who casts the long shadow. Since he began writing, British (and occasionally American) series about European police detectives have prolif-erated so widely that they form one of the liveliest sub-genres of crime and mystery fiction at the moment. ▼···

NICOLAS FREELING

A HENRI CASTANG MYSTERY NOVEL

YOU WHO KNOW

After killing off his popular Dutch detective, Van der Valk, Nicolas Freeling turned to a French policeman, Henri Castang.

France

Pierre Audemars (a British writer of Swiss Huguenot descent) anticipated Freeling's Castang novels with a neglected but long-running series about Inspector Pinaud of the Sûreté, starting with *The Two Impostors* (1958) and ending with *A Small Slain Body* (1985). Its most memorable feature is its freedom with the facts of French geography, which at times almost makes the country as mythical a place as the 'Poictesme' of the American novelist James Branch Cabell. Otherwise, the attractions of France as a setting (food, wine and mysteries rooted in the history of the Occupation) are also its dangers, and more likely to be taken up in holiday novels than Euro-police series. *Blood is Thicker Than Beaujolais* (1995), by the Canadian wine critic Tony Aspler, brings a reminder of some of the pitfalls. Mark Hebden's series about the Burgundian Inspector Pel, begun with *Death Set to Music* (1979) and thereafter bearing Pel's name in the title, is repetitive but engaging. It made a pleasantly relaxed end to the career of a writer who had previously been known, under his real name of John Harris, for action and adventure novels; since his death the series has been continued by his daughter, writing as Juliet Hebden. Marvin Albert, an American expatriate in France, uses a Franco-American private eye, Pete (or Pierre-Ange) Sawyer, in a series beginning with *The Stone Angel* (1986).

Spain

As well as his Jane and Dagobert Brown series, Delano Ames wrote four novels – beginning with *The Man in the Tricorn Hat* (1960) – about Juan Llorca, a policeman in the days of Franco's dictatorship. Memories of Franco, and hence the tensions between past and present, form a recurrent theme of Julian Rathbone's Spanish novels – *Bloody Marvellous* (1975), *Carnival* (1976), *A Raving Monarchist* (1978) and, best of all, *Lying in State* (1985) – as well as David Serafin's series about Superintendent Luis Bernal of Madrid, introduced in *Saturday of Glory* (1979). As befits a writer whose pseudonym masks the Alphonso XIII Professor of Spanish at Oxford, the Bernal books are meticulously detailed (sometimes too meticulously detailed) in their handling of Spanish history and social customs, as also of police procedures. Roderic Jeffries' books about the Mallorcan Inspector Enrique Alvarez, introduced in *Mistakenly in Mallorca* (1974), are encumbered with overly clever plots which sometimes fail to deceive but are sensitive to the tension between islanders and tourists and between islanders and *forasteros* (or mainland Spanish). Sensitivity to local nuance cannot be found in John and Emery Bonett's earlier series about Inspector Salvador Borges, introduced in *Better Dead* (1964; called *Better Off Dead* in USA).

Italy

Italy's recent history of political corruption and instability has made it an obvious setting for police series with a particular edge of disquiet, in which the heroes are often Maigrets with the ghost of Aldo Moro and the threat of official cover-up on their minds. The acknowledged contemporary master is Michael Dibdin in the Aurelio Zen series, which began with *Ratking* (1988). Its success has proved unfortunate only in deflecting some of the praise which should also go to: Magdalen Nabb's more modest series about Marshal Guarnaccia of Florence, started in *Death of an Englishman* (1981); Timothy Williams' series about Commissario Trotti of an unnamed north Italian city, started in *Converging Parallels* (1982); and Donna Leon's series about Commissario Brunetti of Venice, started in *Death at La Fenice* (1992). Timothy Holme's novels about Commissario Peroni, introduced in *The Neapolitan Streak* (1980), feel lightweight by comparison.

Holland, Germany and Beyond

Janwillem van de Wetering (writing in both Dutch and English) bravely followed Freeling in making the Amsterdam police his subject, in *Outsider in Amsterdam* (1975), though the mixture of street wisdom and Zen wisdom displayed by Adjutant Grijpstra and Sergeant de Gier trailed off into inconsequence as the books themselves sometimes deserted Amsterdam in favour of, for example, Japan in *The Japanese Corpse* (1977) and the USA in *The Maine Massacre* (1979). Much more rewarding than van de Wetering's later novels is Julian Rathbone's mini-series about Commissioner Jan Argand, composed of *The Euro-Killers* (1979), *Base Case* (1981) and *Watching the Detectives* (1983). Set in 'Brabt', an imaginary country between Belgium and Holland, it provides a microcosm of current European political ills: big business, the American military presence and resurgent fascism. Rathbone, who has also written about Spain (see above) and Turkey, bid fair to write the definitive contemporary Euro-mystery with *Accidents Will Happen* (1995), not least for the ironic savagery with which it treats the politics of nuclear-waste disposal, a topic that preoccupies many current thriller writers. No longer the heirs to Maigret's nicety of conscience and subtlety of imagination, Rathbone's policemen and women are slovenly or ambitious bureaucrats confronted by sleaze on a truly European scale. The setting of *Accidents Will Happen*, which Rathbone calls 'Burg', lies roughly where Bremen does on the map of Germany without actually being Bremen: the story could happen anywhere.

Edgars, Daggers and Other Prizes

USA

The Mystery Writers of America, founded in 1945, presents America's leading annual prizes, the **Edgar Allan Poe Awards**. The Edgars, as they are affectionately known, include categories for the **Best First Novel** (first awarded in 1946), the **Best Novel** (first awarded in 1954), **Best Paperback Original** (first awarded in 1971) and **Grand Master**, a title bestowed since 1955 on writers of outstanding achievement. A steadily expanding range of Raven awards, special awards and scrolls also covers short stories, novels for children and young adults, criticism, biography, non-fictional accounts of crime, films, TV dramas and plays.

Other prizes, awarded by publishers and organizations of fans, include: the Agatha Awards (from members of Malice Domestic), the American Mystery Awards (from subscribers to *Mystery Scene*), the Anthony Awards (from members of Bouchercon), the Macavity Awards (from members of Mystery Readers International), the Malice Domestic Contest for the Best First Traditional Novel (sponsored by St Martin's Press and Macmillan London), the Nero Awards (from the Wolfe Pack, the international organization of Rex Stout's admirers), the Best First Private Eye Novel (sponsored by St Martin's Press, Macmillan London and the Private Eye Writers of America) and the Shamus Award (from the Private Eye Writers of America).

1946
Best First Novel: Julius Fast, *Watchful at Night*

1947
Best First Novel: Helen Eustis, *The Horizontal Man*

1948
Best First Novel: Fredric Brown, *The Fabulous Clipjoint*

1949
Best First Novel: Mildred Davis, *The Room Upstairs*

1950
Best First Novel: Alan Green, *What a Body*

1951
Best First Novel: Thomas Walsh, *Nightmare in Manhattan*

1952
Best First Novel: Mary McMullen, *Strangle Hold*

1953
Best First Novel: William Campbell Gault, *Don't Cry For Me*

1954
Best Novel: Charlotte Jay, *Beat Not the Bones*
Best First Novel: Ira Levin, *A Kiss Before Dying*

1955
Grand Master: Agatha Christie
Best Novel: Raymond Chandler, *The Long Good-Bye*
Best First Novel: Jean Potts, *Go, Lovely Rose*

1956
Best Novel: Margaret Millar, *Beast in View*
Best First Novel: Lane Kauffman, *The Perfectionist*

1957
Best Novel: Charlotte Armstrong, *A Dram of Poison*
Best First Novel: Donald McNutt Douglas, *Rebecca's Pride*

1958
Grand Master: Vincent Starrett
Best Novel: Ed Lacy, *Room to Swing*
Best First Novel: William Rawle
Weeks, *Knock and Wait Awhile*

1959
Grand Master: Rex Stout
Best Novel: Stanley Ellin,
The Eighth Circle
Best First Novel: Richard Martin
Stern, *The Bright Road to Fear*

1960
Best Novel: Celia Fremlin,
The Hours Before Dawn
Best First Novel: Henry Slesar,
The Grey Flannel Shroud

1961
Grand Master: Ellery Queen
Best Novel: Julian Symons,
The Progress of a Crime
Best First Novel: John Holbrooke
Vance, *The Man in the Cage*

1962
Grand Master: Erle Stanley Gardner
Best Novel: J.J. Marric (John
Creasey), *Gideon's Fire*
Best First Novel: Suzanne Blanc,
The Green Stone

1963
Grand Master: John Dickson Carr
Best Novel: Ellis Peters,
Death and the Joyful Woman
Best First Novel: Robert L. Fish,
The Fugitive

1964
Grand Master: George Harmon Coxe
Best Novel: Eric Ambler,
The Light of Day
Best First Novel: Cornelius
Hirschberg, *The Florentine Finish*

1965
Best Novel: John le Carré,
The Spy Who Came in From the Cold
Best First Novel: Harry Kemelman,
Friday the Rabbi Slept Late

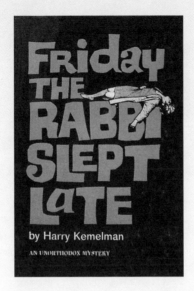

1966
Grand Master: Georges Simenon
Best Novel: Adam Hall,
The Quiller Memorandum
Best First Novel: John Ball,
In the Heat of the Night

1967
Grand Master: Baynard Kendrick
Best Novel: Nicolas Freeling,
The King of the Rainy Country
Best First Novel: Ross Thomas,
The Cold War Swap

1968
Best Novel: Donald E. Westlake,
God Save the Mark
Best First Novel: Michael Collins,
Act of Fear

1969
Grand Master: John Creasey
Best Novel: Jeffrey Hudson,
A Case of Need
Best First Novels: E. Richard
Johnson, *Silver Street*; Dorothy
Uhnak, *The Bait*

1970
Grand Master: James M. Cain
Best Novel: Dick Francis, *Forfeit*
Best First Novel: Joe Gores,
A Time for Predators

1971
Grand Master: Mignon G. Eberhart
Best Novel: Maj Sjöwall and Per
Wahlöö, *The Laughing Policeman*
Best First Novel: Lawrence Sanders,
The Anderson Tapes
Best Paperback Original: Dan J.
Marlowe, *Flashpoint*

1972
Grand Master: John D. MacDonald
Best Novel: Frederick Forsyth,
The Day of the Jackal
Best First Novel: A.H.Z. Carr,
Finding Maubee
Best Paperback Original: Frank
McAuliffe, *For Murder I Charge More*

1973
Grand Master: Judson Philips
Best Novel: Warren Kiefer,
The Lingala Code
Best First Novel: R.H. Shimer,
Squaw Point
Best Paperback Original: Richard
Wormser, *The Invader*

1974
Grand Master: Ross Macdonald
Best Novel: Tony Hillerman,
Dance Hall of the Dead
Best First Novel: Paul E. Erdman,
The Billion Dollar Sure Thing
Best Paperback Original: Will Perry,
Death of an Informer

1975
Best Novel: Jon Cleary,
Peter's Pence
Best First Novel: Gregory Mcdonald,
Fletch
Best Paperback Original: Roy
Winsor, *The Corpse That Walked*

1976
Grand Master: Eric Ambler
Best Novel: Brian Garfield,
Hopscotch
Best First Novel: Rex Burns,
The Alvarez Journal
Best Paperback Original: John R.
Feegal, *Autopsy*

EDGAR AWARD WINNER
DANCE HALL OF THE DEAD
TONY HILLERMAN
PLUTO CRIME

1977
Grand Master: Graham Greene
Best Novel: Robert B. Parker, *Promised Land*
Best First Novel: James Patterson, *The Thomas Berryman Number*
Best Paperback Original: Gregory Mcdonald, *Confess, Fletch*

1978
Grand Masters: Daphne du Maurier, Dorothy B. Hughes, Ngaio Marsh
Best Novel: William H. Hallahan, *Catch Me, Kill Me*
Best First Novel: Robert Ross, *A French Finish*
Best Paperback Original: Mike Jahn, *The Quark Maneuver*

1979
Grand Master: Aaron Marc Stein
Best Novel: Ken Follett, *The Eye of the Needle*
Best First Novel: William L. DeAndrea, *Killed in the Ratings*
Best Paperback Original: Frank Bandy, *Deceit and Deadly Lies*

1980
Grand Master: W.R. Burnett
Best Novel: Arthur Maling, *The Rheingold Route*
Best First Novel: Richard North Patterson, *The Lasko Tangent*
Best Paperback Original: William L. DeAndrea, *The Hog Murders*

1981
Grand Master: Stanley Ellin
Best Novel: Dick Francis, *Whip Hand*
Best First Novel: Kay Nolte, *The Watcher*
Best Paperback Original: Bill Granger, *Public Murders*

1982
Grand Master: Julian Symons
Best Novel: William Bayer, *Peregrine*
Best First Novel: Stuart Woods, *Chiefs*
Best Paperback Original: L.A. Morse, *The Old Dick*

1983
Grand Master: Margaret Millar
Best Novel: Rick Boyer, *Billingsgate Shoal*
Best First Novel: Thomas Perry, *The Butcher's Boy*
Best Paperback Original: Teri White, *Triangle*

1984
Grand Master: John le Carré
Best Novel: Elmore Leonard, *La Brava*
Best First Novel: Will Harriss, *The Bay Psalm Book Murder*
Best Paperback Original: Margaret Tracy, *Mrs White*

1985
Grand Master: Dorothy Salisbury Davis
Best Novel: Ross Thomas, *The Briarpatch*
Best First Novel: Richard Rosen, *Strike Three, You're Dead*
Best Paperback Original: Warren Murphy and Molly Cochran, *Grand Master*

1986
Grand Master: Ed McBain
Best Novel: L.R. Wright, *The Suspect*
Best First Novel: Jonathan Kellerman, *When the Bough Breaks*
Best Paperback Original: Warren Murphy, *Pigs Get Fat*

1987
Grand Master: Michael Gilbert
Best Novel: Barbara Vine (Ruth Rendell), *A Dark-Adapted Eye*
Best First Novel: Larry Beinhart, *No One Rides for Free*
Best Paperback Original: Robert Campbell, *The Junkyard Dog*

1988
Grand Master: Phyllis A. Whitney
Best Novel: Aaron Elkins, *Old Bones*
Best First Novel: Deidre S. Laiken, *Death Among Strangers*
Best Paperback Original: Sharyn McCrumb, *Bimbos of the Death Sun*

1989
Grand Master: Hillary Waugh
Best Novel: Stuart M. Kaminsky, *A Cold Red Sunrise*
Best First Novel: David Stout, *Carolina Skeletons*
Best Paperback Original: Timothy Findley, *The Telling of Lies*

1990
Grand Master: Helen McCloy
Best Novel: James Lee Burke, *Black Cherry Blues*
Best First Novel: Susan Wolfe, *The Last Billable Hour*
Best Paperback Original: Keith Peterson, *The Rain*

1991
Grand Master: Tony Hillerman
Best Novel: Julie Smith, *New Orleans Mourning*
Best First Novel: Patricia Daniels, *Post Mortem*
Best Paperback Original: David Handler, *The Man Who Would Be F. Scott Fitzgerald*

1992

Grand Master: Elmore Leonard
Best Novel: Lawrence Block,
A Dance at the Slaughterhouse
Best First Novel: Peter Blauner,
Slow Motion Riot
Best Paperback Original: Thomas
Adcock, *Dark Maze*

1993

Grand Master: Donald E. Westlake
Best Novel: Margaret Maron,
Bootlegger's Daughter
Best First Novel: Michael Connelly,
The Black Echo
Best Paperback Original: Dana
Stabenow, *A Cold Day for Murder*

1994

Grand Master: Lawrence Block
Best Novel: Minette Walters,
The Sculptress
Best First Novel: Laurie King,
A Grave Talent
Best Paperback Original: Steven
Womack, *Dead Folks' Blues*

1995

Grand Master: Mickey Spillane
Best Novel: Mary Willis Walker,
The Red Scream
Best First Novel: George Dawes
Green, *The Caveman's Valentine*
Best Paperback Original: Lisa
Scottoline, *Final Appeal*

1996

Grand Master: Dick Francis
Best Novel: Dick Francis,
Come To Grief
Best First Novel: David Housewright,
Penance
Best Paperback Original: William
Heffernan, *Tarnished Blue*

UK

The Crime Writers' Association, founded in 1953 with John Creasey as its first Chairman, presents the most prestigious annual awards. The **CWA Diamond Dagger** goes to an author for making an outstanding contribution to crime fiction; sponsored by Cartier, it was established in 1986. The **CWA Gold Dagger** is awarded to the best crime novel; it began as the Crossed Herrings Award in 1955. Since 1969 the runners-up award has been known as the **CWA Silver Dagger**. Both Gold and Silver Daggers are now sponsored by The Macallan. The **CWA John Creasey Memorial Dagger** (which began as the John Creasey Memorial Award in 1973) goes to the best crime novel by an author who has not previously published a novel, and the **CWA Last Laugh Dagger** (which began as the *Punch* Award in 1988) to the most amusing crime novel. The **CWA Dagger in the Library** (which began as the Golden Handcuffs Award in 1992) is presented to an author popular with library readers. The **CWA '92 Award** was presented between 1990 and 1992 to the best crime novel with a Continental setting. The **CWA Rumpole Award**, introduced in 1990 and named after the character created by John Mortimer, is an occasional prize for a crime novel with a legal setting.

1955

Winston Graham, *The Little Walls*
Runners-up: Leigh Howard, *Blind Date*; Ngaio Marsh, *Scales of Justice*; Margot Bennett, *The Man Who Didn't Fly*

1956

Edward Grierson, *The Second Man*
Runners-up: Sarah Gainham, *Time Right Deadly*; Arthur Upfield, *Man of Two Tribes*; J.J. Marric (John Creasey), *Gideon's Week*

1957

Julian Symons, *The Colour of Murder*
Runners-up: Ngaio Marsh, *Off With His Head*; George Milner, *Your Money or Your Life*; Douglas Rutherford, *The Long Echo*

1958

Margot Bennett, *Someone from the Past*
Runners-up: Margery Allingham, *Hide My Eyes*; James Byrom, *Or Be He Dead*; John Sherwood, *Undiplomatic Exit*

1959

Eric Ambler, *Passage of Arms*
Runners-up: James Mitchell, *A Way Back*; Menna Gallie, *Strike for a Kingdom*

1960

Gold Dagger: Lionel Davidson, *The Night of Wenceslas*
Runners-up: Mary Stewart, *My Brother Michael*; Julian Symons, *Progress of a Crime*

1961

Gold Dagger: Mary Kelly, *The Spoilt Kill*
Runners-up: John le Carré, *Call for the Dead*; Allan Prior, *One Way*

1962
Gold Dagger: Joan Fleming,
When I Grow Rich
Runners-up: Eric Ambler, *The Light of
Day*; Colin Watson, *Hopjoy Was Here*

1963
Gold Dagger: John le Carré,
The Spy Who Came in from the Cold
Runners-up: Nicolas Freeling, *Gun
Before Butter*; William Haggard, *The
High Wire*

1964
Gold Dagger: H.R.F. Keating,
The Perfect Murder
Best Foreign: Patricia Highsmith,
The Two Faces of January
Runners-up: Gavin Lyall, *The Most
Dangerous Game*; Ross Macdonald,
The Chill

1965
Gold Dagger: Ross Macdonald,
The Far Side of the Dollar
Best British: Gavin Lyall,
Midnight Plus One
Runners-up: Dick Francis, *For Kicks*;
Emma Lathen, *Accounting for Murder*

1966
Gold Dagger: Lionel Davidson,
A Long Way to Shiloh
Best Foreign: John Ball,
In the Heat of the Night
Runner-up: John Bingham,
The Secret Agent

1967
Gold Dagger: Emma Lathen,
Murder Against the Grain
Best British: Eric Ambler, *Dirty Story*
Runner-up: Colin Watson,
Lonelyheart 4122

1968
Gold Dagger: Peter Dickinson,
Skin Deep
Best Foreign: Sébastien Japrisot,
*The Lady in the Car with Glasses
and a Gun*
Runner-up: Nicholas Blake,
The Private Wound

1969
Gold Dagger: Peter Dickinson,
A Pride of Heroes
Silver Dagger: Francis Clifford,
Another Way of Dying
Best Foreign: Rex Stout,
The Father Hunt

1970
Gold Dagger: Joan Fleming,
Young Man I Think You're Dying
Silver Dagger: Anthony Price,
The Labyrinth Makers

1971
Gold Dagger: James McClure,
The Steam Pig
Silver Dagger: P.D. James,
Shroud for a Nightingale

1972
Gold Dagger: Eric Ambler,
The Levanter
Silver Dagger: Victor Canning,
The Rainbird Pattern

1973
Gold Dagger: Robert Littell,
The Defection of A.J. Lewinter
Silver Dagger: Gwendoline Butler,
A Coffin for Pandora
John Creasey Memorial Award:
Kyril Bonfiglioli, *Don't Point That
Thing at Me*

1974
Gold Dagger: Anthony Price,
Other Paths to Glory
Silver Dagger: Francis Clifford,
The Grosvenor Square Goodbye
John Creasey Memorial Award:
Roger L. Simon, *The Big Fix*

1975
Gold Dagger: Nicholas Meyer,
The Seven-Per-Cent Solution
Silver Dagger: P.D. James,
The Black Tower
John Creasey Memorial Award:
Sara George, *Acid Drop*

1976
Gold Dagger: Ruth Rendell,
A Demon in My View
Silver Dagger: James McClure,
Rogue Eagle
John Creasey Memorial Award:
Patrick Alexander, *Death of a
Thin-skinned Animal*

1977
Gold Dagger: John le Carré,
The Honourable Schoolboy
Silver Dagger: William McIlvanney,
Laidlaw
John Creasey Memorial Award:
Jonathan Gash, *The Judas Pair*

1978
Gold Dagger: Lionel Davidson,
The Chelsea Murders
Silver Dagger: Peter Lovesey,
Waxwork
John Creasey Memorial Award:
Paula Gosling, *A Running Duck*

1979
Gold Dagger: Dick Francis,
Whip Hand
Silver Dagger: Colin Dexter,
Service of All the Dead
John Creasey Memorial Award:
David Serafín, *Saturday of Glory*

1980
Gold Dagger: H.R.F. Keating,
The Murder of the Maharajah
Silver Dagger: Ellis Peters,
Monk's Hood
John Creasey Memorial Award:
Liza Cody, *Dupe*

1981

Gold Dagger: Martin Cruz Smith,
Gorky Park
Silver Dagger: Colin Dexter,
The Dead of Jericho
John Creasey Memorial Award:
James Leigh, *The Ludi Victor*

1982

Gold Dagger: Peter Lovesey,
The False Inspector Dew
Silver Dagger: S.T. Haymon,
Ritual Murder
John Creasey Memorial Award:
Andrew Taylor, *Caroline Minuscule*

1983

Gold Dagger: John Hutton,
Accidental Crimes
Silver Dagger: William McIlvanney,
The Papers of Tony Veitch
John Creasey Memorial Award:
Carol Clemeau, *The Ariadne Papers*,
and Eric Wright, *The Days the Gods
Smiled*

1984

Gold Dagger: B.M. Gill,
The Twelfth Juror
Silver Dagger: Ruth Rendell,
The Tree of Hands
John Creasey Memorial Award:
Elizabeth Ironside, *A Very Private
Enterprise*

1985

Gold Dagger: Paula Gosling,
Monkey Puzzle
Silver Dagger: Dorothy Simpson,
Last Seen Alive
John Creasey Memorial Award:
Robert Richardson, *The Latimer
Mercy*

1986

Diamond Dagger: Eric Ambler
Gold Dagger: Ruth Rendell,
Live Flesh
Silver Dagger: P.D. James,
A Taste for Death
John Creasey Memorial Award:
Neville Steed, *Tinplate*

COLIN DEXTER
THE NEW INSPECTOR MORSE

WINNER OF
THE GOLD DAGGER
AWARD FOR THE CRIME
NOVEL OF THE YEAR

THE
WENCH
IS
DEAD

1987

Diamond Dagger: P.D. James
Gold Dagger: Barbara Vine (Ruth
Rendell), *A Fatal Inversion*
Silver Dagger: Scott Turow,
Presumed Innocent
John Creasey Memorial Award:
Denis Kilcommons, *Dark Apostle*

1988

Diamond Dagger: John le Carré
Gold Dagger: Michael Dibdin,
Ratking
Silver Dagger: Sara Paretsky,
Toxic Shock
John Creasey Memorial Award:
Janet Neel, *Death's Bright Angel*
Punch Award: Nancy Livingston,
Death in a Distant Land

1989

Diamond Dagger: Dick Francis
Gold Dagger: Colin Dexter,
The Wench is Dead
Silver Dagger: Desmond Lowden,
The Shadow Run
John Creasey Memorial Award:
Annette Roome, *A Real Shot in the
Arm*
Last Laugh Dagger: Mike Ripley,
Angel Touch

1990

Diamond Dagger: Julian Symons
Gold Dagger: Reginald Hill,
Bones and Silence
Silver Dagger: Mike Phillips,
The Late Candidate
John Creasey Memorial Award:
Patricia Cornwell, *Postmortem*
Last Laugh Dagger: Simon Shaw,
Killer Cinderella
CWA '92 Award: Michael Dibdin,
Vendetta
Rumpole Award: Frances Fyfield,
Trial by Fire

1991

Diamond Dagger: Ruth Rendell
Gold Dagger: Barbara Vine (Ruth
Rendell), *King Solomon's Carpet*
Silver Dagger: Frances Fyfield,
Deep Sleep
John Creasey Memorial Award:
Walter Mosley, *Devil in a Blue Dress*
Last Laugh Dagger: Mike Ripley,
Angels in Arms
CWA '92 Award: Barbara Wilson,
Gaudi Collective

1992

Diamond Dagger: Leslie Charteris
Gold Dagger: Colin Dexter,
The Way Through the Woods
Silver Dagger: Liza Cody, *Bucket Nut*
John Creasey Memorial Award:
Minette Walters, *The Ice House*
Last Laugh Dagger: Carl Hiaasen,
Native Tongue
CWA '92 Award: Timothy Williams,
Black August
Golden Handcuffs: Catherine Aird

1993

Diamond Dagger: Ellis Peters
Gold Dagger: Patricia Cornwell,
Cruel and Unusual
Silver Dagger: Sarah Dunant,
Fatlands
John Creasey Memorial Award:
not awarded
Last Laugh Dagger: Michael Pearce,
Mamur Zapt and the Spoils of Egypt
Golden Handcuffs: Margaret Yorke

1994

Diamond Dagger: Michael Gilbert
Gold Dagger: Minette Walters,
The Scold's Bridle
Silver Dagger: Peter Høeg,
Miss Smilla's Feeling for Snow
John Creasey Memorial Award:
Doug J. Swanson, *Big Town*
Last Laugh Dagger: Simon Shaw,
The Villain of the Earth
Golden Handcuffs: Robert Barnard

1995

Diamond Dagger: Reginald Hill
Gold Dagger: Val McDermid,
The Mermaids Singing
Silver Dagger: Peter Lovesey,
The Summons
John Creasey Memorial Award:
Janet Evanovich, *One for the Money*
Last Laugh Dagger: Laurence
Shames, *Sunburn*
Dagger in the Library: Lindsey Davis

1996

Diamond Dagger: H.R.F. Keating
Gold Dagger: Ben Elton, *Popcorn*
Silver Dagger: Peter Lovesey,
Bloodhounds
John Creasey Memorial Award:
not awarded
Last Laugh Dagger: Janet Evanovich,
Two for the Dough
Dagger in the Library:
Marian Babson

FRANCE

Maurice Endrèbe founded the
Grand Prix de Littérature Policière
in 1948 and still administers it.
Purely honorific but carrying great
prestige, it has separate categories
for French novels and for foreign
novels translated into French (which
has usually, though not invariably,
meant novels from the UK and the
USA). Non-French titles are given in
their original language.

1948

French: Léo Malet,
Le Cinquième Procédé (translated
as *Mission to Marseilles*)
Foreign: Frances Noyes Hart,
The Bellamy Trial

1949

French: Odette Sorensen,
La Parole est au mort
Foreign: Patrick Quentin,
Puzzle for Pilgrims

1950

French: Géo-Charles Veran,
Jeux pour mourir
Foreign: Marta Albrand,
After Midnight

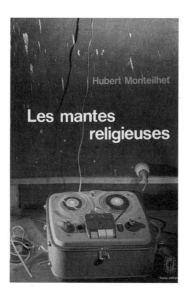

Les mantes religieuses — Hubert Monteilhet

1951

French: Jacques et Germaine
Decrest, *Fumées sans feu*
Foreign: Joel Townsley Rogers,
The Red Right Hand

1952

French: André Piljean,
Passons la monnaie
Foreign: Patricia MacGerr,
Follow As the Night

1953

French: Jean-Pierre Conty,
Opération odyssée
Foreign: Geoffrey Holiday Hall,
The End is Known; Louis Malley,
Horns for the Devils

1954

French: François Brigneau,
La Beauté qui meurt
Foreign: William Irish (Cornell
Woolrich), *The Body in Grant's Tomb*

1955

French: Gilles Morris-Dumoulin,
Assassin mon frère
Foreign: Michael Gilbert,
Death in Captivity

1956

French: Guy Venayre,
Les Petites Mains de la justice
Foreign: Joseph Hayes,
The Desperate Hours

1957

French: Michel Lebrun,
Pleins feux sur Sylvie
Foreign: Charles Williams,
Nothing in Her Way

1958

French: Frédéric Dard,
Le Bourreau pleure
Foreign: Patricia Highsmith,
The Talented Mr Ripley

1959

French: Fred Kassak,
On n'enterre pas le dimanche
Foreign: Chester Himes, *La Reine
des pommes* (translated into English
as *For Love of Imabelle* and, later,
A Rage in Harlem)

1960
French: Paul Gerrard, *Deuil en rouge*
Foreign: Donald Downes,
Orders to Kill

1961
French: Hubert Monteilhet,
Les Mantes religieuses (translated
as *Praying Mantis* in UK and *The
Praying Mantises* in USA)
Foreign: Thomas Sterling,
The Evil of the Day (also called
Murder in Venice)

1962
French: Pierre Forquin,
Le Procès du diable
Foreign: Suzanne Blanc,
The Green Stone

1963
French: Sébastien Japrisot,
Piège pour Cendrillon (translated
into English as *Trap for Cinderella*)
Foreign: Shelley Smith,
The Ballad of the Running Man

1964
French: Michel Carnal,
La Jeune morte
Foreign: John D. MacDonald,
A Key to the Suite

1965
French: Marc Delory,
Bateau en Espagne
Foreign: Nicolas Freeling,
Gun Before Butter

1966
French: Laurence Oriol,
L'Interne de service (translated
into English as *Short Circuit*)
Foreign: Adam Hall,
Berlin Memorandum

1967
French: Jean-Pierre Alem,
Le Crocodile dans l'escalier
Foreign: Audrey Erskine Lindop,
I Start Counting

1968
French: Dominique Fabre,
Un Beau Monstre
Foreign: Giorgio Scerbanenco,
Traditori di tutti (Italy; *A tous les
rateliers* in French, *Duca and the
Milan Murders* in English)

1969
French: Francis Ryck,
Drôle de pistolet (translated
into English as *Loaded Gun*)
Foreign: John Dickson Carr,
Fire, Burn; Josephine Tey, *The
Daughter of Time*

1970
French: Paul Andreota, *Zigzags*
Foreign: Antonis Samarkis,
To Lathos

1971
French: René Reouven,
L'Assassin maladroit
Foreign: Dorothy Uhnak, *The Ledger*;
Anders Bodelsen, *Hændeligt Uheld*
(Denmark; *Crime sans châtiment* in
French, *One Down* in English in USA
and *Hit and Run, Run, Run* in UK)

1972
French: Gilbert Tanugi,
Le Canal rouge
Foreign: Laird Koenig and Peter L.
Dixon, *The Children Are Watching*

1973
French: Jean-Patrick Manchette,
O dingos, O châteaux (later called
Folle à tuer)
Foreign: E.V. Cunningham (Howard
Fast), *Millie*

1974
French: André-Paul Duchâteau,
De 5 à 7 avec la mort
Foreign: Stanley Ellin,
Mirror, Mirror on the Wall

Jean-François Coatmeur, winner of
the 1976 Grand Prix de Littérature
Policière, with the film director
Claude Chabrol (to the left) and
Maurice Endrèbe, the founder of
the award.

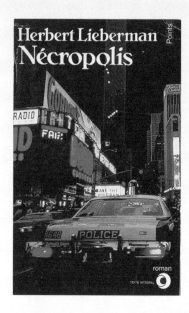

1975
French: Yvon Toussaint, *Un Incident indépendant de notre volonté*
Foreign: Edward Boyd and Roger Parkes, *The Dark Number*

1976
French: Jean-François Coatmeur, *Les Sirènes de minuit*
Foreign: Eric Ambler, *Doctor Frigo*

1977
French: Christopher Diable, *La plus longue course d'Abraham Coles, chauffeur de taxi*
Foreign: Herbert Lieberman, *City of the Dead*

1978
French: Madeleine Coudray, *Dénouement devant l'aube*
Foreign: Ellery Queen, *And on the Eighth Day...*

1979
French: Joseph Bialot, *Le Salon du prêt à saigner*
Foreign: Stanislaw Lem, *Katar* (Poland; *La Rhume* in French, *The Chain of Chance* in English)

1980
French: Dominique Roulet, *Le Crime d'Antoine*
Foreign: Mary Higgins Clark, *A Stranger is Watching*

1981
French: Pierre Siniac, *Aime le maudit*, *L'Unijambiste de la côte* and *Reflets changeants sur mare de sang*
Foreign: Manuel Vázquez Montalbán, *Los Mares del Sur* (Spain; *Marquises, si vos rivages ...* in French, *Southern Seas* in English)

1982
French: Jean-Pierre Cabannes, *L'Audience solonnelle*
Foreign: John Crosby, *Party of the Year*

1983
French: Jean Mazarin, *Collabo song*
Foreign: Frederick Forsyth, *No Comebacks*

1984
French: René Belletto, *Sur la terre comme au ciel*
Foreign: Janwillem van de Wetering, *The Maine Massacre*

1985
French: Didier Daeninckx, *Meurtres pour mémoire*
Foreign: Peter Lovesey, *Swing, Swing Together*

1986
French: Gérard Delteil, *N'oubliez pas l'artiste*; Christian Gernigon, *La Queue de scorpion*
Foreign: Elmore Leonard, *City Primeval*

1987
French: Jacques Sadoul, *Trois morts au soleil*
Foreign: Tony Hillerman, *Dance Hall of the Dead*

1988
French: Jean-Paul Demure, *Aix Abrupto*
Foreign: P.D. James, *A Taste for Death*; Andrew Vachss, *Strega*

1989
French: Tito Topin, *Un gros besoin d'amour*
Foreign: Bill Pronzini, *Hidden Valley*

1990
French: Michel Quint, *Billard à l'étage*
Foreign: Elizabeth George, *A Great Deliverance*

1991
French: Hervé Jaouen, *Hôpital souterrain*
Foreign: Thomas Harris, *The Silence of the Lambs*

1992
French: Tonino Benacquista, *La Commedia des rates*
Foreign: James Lee Burke, *Black Cherry Blues*

1993
French: Paul Couturiau, *Boulevard des Ombres*
Foreign: Arturo Pérez-Reverte, *La Tabla de Flandes* (Spain; *Le Tableau du maître flamand* in French, *The Flanders Panel* in English)

1994
French: Jean-Jacques Fiechter, *Tire à part*
Foreign: Michael Dibdin, *Cabal*

1995
French: Philippe Huet, *La Main morte*
Foreign: Richard North Patterson, *Degree of Guilt*

1996
French: Jean-Jacques Oppel, *Ambernave*
Foreign: Caleb Carr, *The Alienist*

The Crime and Mystery Bookshelf

This section is devoted to general books about crime and mystery. For books on particular writers, periods and schools see: 'The Sherlock Holmes Bookshelf' (p. 55), 'The Golden Age Bookshelf' (p. 85), 'The Hard-Boiled Bookshelf' (p. 119), 'The Simenon Bookshelf' (p. 130) and 'The Feminist Bookshelf' (p. 186).

Of reference books, Lesley Henderson's *Twentieth-Century Crime and Mystery Writers* (third edition, 1991) is indispensable but too expensive for most private shelves. Though dated, Jacques Barzun and Wendell Hertig Taylor's *A Catalogue of Crime* (1971) and Chris Steinbrunner and Otto Penzler's *Encyclopedia of Mystery and Detection* (1976) are still worth consulting. Allen J. Hubin's *Crime Fiction 1749–1980: A Comprehensive Bibliography* (1984) and its 1988 supplement (bringing the list up to 1985) are exhaustive.

The studies listed below are just a brief selection from the huge bibliography of works about crime and mystery fiction. Nevertheless, they cover a wide range. The approaches vary from the coffee-table to the academic, and the critics from old buffers to postmodernists and feminists. Critical standards are not generally high: Symons' *Bloody Murder* remains the most wide-ranging history, and the essays by Auden, Chandler and Wilson the best stimulants to thought about the genre.

Auden W.H. 'The Guilty Vicarage', in *The Dyer's Hand*. 1963.

Binyon T.J. *'Murder Will Out': The Detective in Fiction*. 1989.

Cawelti John G. *Adventure, Mystery and Romance*. 1976.

Champigny Robert. *What Will Have Happened: A Philosophical and Technical Essay on Mystery Stories*. 1977.

Chandler Raymond. 'The Simple Art of Murder' (1944), in *The Simple Art of Murder*. 1950.

Grossvogel David I. *Mystery and Its Fictions: From Oedipus to Agatha Christie*. 1979.

Haycraft Howard. *Murder for Pleasure: The Life and Times of the Detective Story*. Revised edition, 1951.

Knight Stephen. *Form and Ideology in Crime Fiction*. 1980.

Messac Régis. *Le 'Detective Novel' et l'influence de la pensée scientifique*. 1929.

Murch Alma E. *The Development of the Detective Novel*. Revised edition, 1968.

Ousby Ian. *Bloodhounds of Heaven: The Detective in English Fiction from Godwin to Doyle*. 1976.

Palmer Jerry. *Thrillers: Genesis and Structure of a Popular Genre*. 1978.

Routley Erik. *The Puritan Pleasures of the Detective Story: A Personal Monograph*. 1972.

Stewart R.F. *... And Always a Detective: Chapters in the History of Detective Fiction*. 1980.

Symons Julian. *Bloody Murder* (originally called *Mortal Consequences* in USA). 1972; revised edition, 1992.

Watson Colin. *Snobbery with Violence*. 1971.

Wilson Edmund. 'Who Cares Who Killed Roger Ackroyd?', in *Classics and Commercials*. 1951.

Winks Robin W. (editor). *Detective Fiction: A Collection of Critical Essays*. 1980.

Winn Dilys (editor). *Murder Ink: The Mystery Reader's Companion*. 1977.

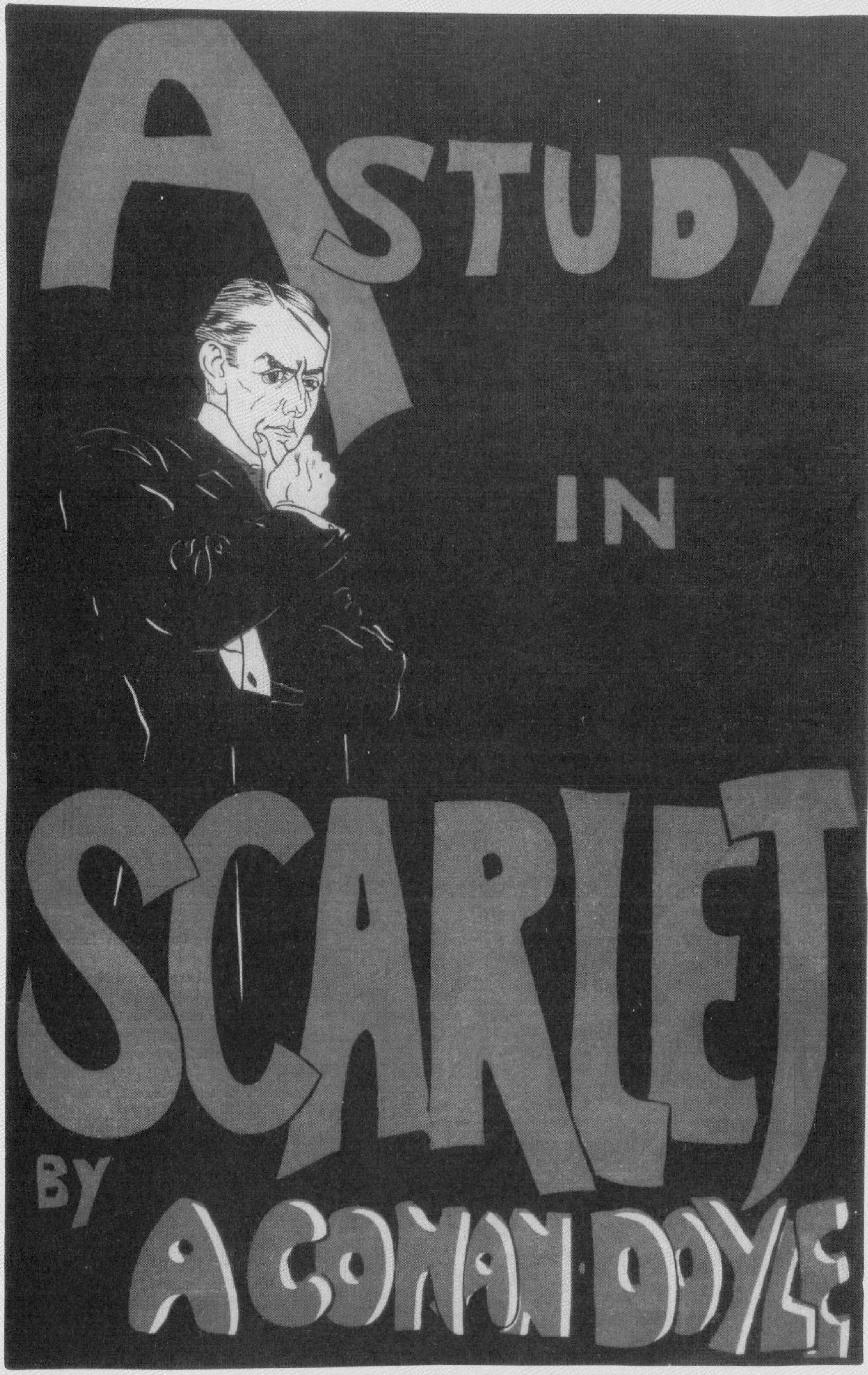
A STUDY
IN
SCARLET
BY
A. CONAN DOYLE

Chronology

1725
Execution of Jonathan Wild, thief and self-styled Thief-Taker General of Great Britain and Ireland

1753
Bow Street Runners, or Officers, founded in London by Henry Fielding, magistrate at Bow Street in 1748–54

1774
First of many editions of *The Newgate Calendar*

1794
William Godwin's *Caleb Williams*

1812
Eugène-François Vidocq becomes first chief of the Sûreté in Paris; retires in 1827

1827
Richmond: or, Scenes in the Life of a Bow Street Runner, written anonymously but probably by Thomas Gaspey

1828–29
Ghost-written and unauthorized *Mémoires de Vidocq*, immediately translated into English

1829
London's Metropolitan Police founded

Adolf Müllner's *Der Kaliber*, claimed as the first German detective story

1832
Edward Bulwer Lytton's *Eugene Aram*

1835
First appearance of Honoré de Balzac's Vautrin, in *Le Père Goriot*

1839
William Harrison Ainsworth's *Jack Sheppard*; Bow Street Runners disbanded

1841
Edgar Allan Poe's first Dupin story, 'The Murders in the Rue Morgue', published in *Graham's Magazine* (revised for inclusion in *Tales*, 1845)

1842
Detective Department, or Office, of the Metropolitan Police founded in London

1842–43
Poe's second Dupin story, 'The Mystery of Marie Rogêt', serialized in *Snowden's Ladies' Companion* (revised for inclusion in *Tales*, 1845)

1845
Poe's third and last Dupin story, 'The Purloined Letter', published in *The Gift* and then in *Tales*

1850
Charles Dickens' articles, 'A Detective Police Party' and 'Three Detective Anecdotes', published in *Household Words* in June and September

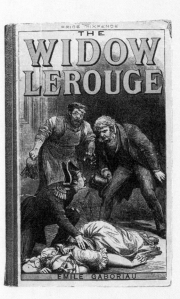

Allan Pinkerton founds the Pinkerton National Detective Agency in Chicago

1851
Dickens' article 'On Duty with Inspector Field' published in *Household Words* in June

1852–53
Dickens' *Bleak House* published in monthly parts (and in book form in 1853)

1856
Recollections of a Detective Police-Officer by 'Waters' (William Russell) published as a 'yellowback' (previously serialized in *Chambers's Edinburgh Journal*, 1849–53)

1859–60
Wilkie Collins' *The Woman in White* serialized in England in *All the Year Round* and in America in *Harper's Magazine* (published in book form in 1860)

1861
Mrs Henry Wood's *East Lynne*

1862
Mary Elizabeth Braddon's *Lady Audley's Secret*

Victor Hugo's *Les Misérables*

1863
Tom Taylor's play, *The Ticket-of-Leave Man*

1865
First appearance of Emile Gaboriau's Inspecteur Lecoq and Père Tabaret, in the newspaper serialization of *L'Affaire Lerouge* (published in book form in 1866; translated as *The Widow Lerouge*)

1868
Collins' *The Moonstone* serialized in *All the Year Round* and published in book form

1870

The first six parts of Dickens' *The Mystery of Edwin Drood* published; novel incomplete at his death in June

1874

Allan Pinkerton's *The Expressman and the Detective*

1876

Publication in Italy of Cesare Lombroso's pamphlet *L'Uomo delinquente*, later enlarged, identifying the 'criminal type'

1878

Detective Department of London's Metropolitan Police expanded to Criminal Investigation Department ('Scotland Yard')

First appearance of Anna Katharine Green's Ebenezer Gryce, in *The Leavenworth Case: A Lawyer's Story*

1882

Robert Louis Stevenson's *The New Arabian Nights*

1885

The French Sûreté adopts anthropometry, Alphonse Bertillon's system of criminal identification

1886

Robert Louis Stevenson's *Kidnapped*

First appearance of Nick Carter, in a story written by John Russell Coryell in *The New York Weekly*

Fergus Hume's *The Mystery of a Hansom Cab* published in Australia; bestseller when reissued in UK in 1887 by The Hansom Cab Publishing Company

1887

First appearance of Sir Arthur Conan Doyle's Sherlock Holmes, in *A Study in Scarlet*, published in *Beeton's Christmas Annual* (published in book form in 1888)

1890

Conan Doyle's *The Sign of Four*, the second Sherlock Holmes novel, published in the February edition of *Lippincott's Magazine* in the USA

1891

Conan Doyle's 'A Scandal in Bohemia', first of the series of stories collected in *The Adventures of Sherlock Holmes* (1892), appears in July issue of *The Strand Magazine*

Francis Galton's *Fingerprints* revives interest in Britain in fingerprinting for criminal identification

1892

The 'death' of Sherlock Holmes, in 'The Final Problem', published in December issue of *The Strand Magazine* and collected in *The Memoirs of Sherlock Holmes* (1894)

Israel Zangwill's *The Big Bow Mystery*

1893

First appearance of Sexton Blake, in a story by Hal Meredith in a boys' weekly magazine

....

The unidentified actor who played Sherlock Holmes in the first screen adaptation, a silent film made in 1900.

1894

First appearance of Holmes on stage, in *Sherlock Holmes, Private Detective*, by Charles Rodgers

Arthur Morrison's collection, *Martin Hewitt, Investigator*

Police in Britain adopt a modified version of Bertillon's anthropometry for criminal identification

1895

M.P. Shiel's collection, *Prince Zaleski*

First appearance of Guy Boothby's Dr Nikola, in *A Bid for Fortune, or Dr Nikola's Vendetta*

1897

Bram Stoker, *Dracula*

Police in Germany adopt Bertillon's anthropometry

1899

First appearance of E.W. Hornung's Raffles, in *The Amateur Cracksman*

First stage appearance of William Gillette as Holmes, in his own *Sherlock Holmes* (USA)

1900

First appearance of Holmes on film, in *Sherlock Holmes Baffled* (USA)

1901

Police in Britain change from anthropometry to fingerprinting

1901–02

The Hound of the Baskervilles, the third Sherlock Holmes novel, serialized in *The Strand Magazine* (separately published in 1902)

1903

Sherlock Holmes returns to life in 'The Adventure of the Empty House', published in *The Strand Magazine* and collected in *The Return of Sherlock Holmes* (1905)

Erskine Childers' *The Riddle of the Sands*

1906

Edgar Wallace's first novel, *The Four Just Men*

Robert Barr's *The Triumphs of Eugène Valmont*

1907

First appearance of R. Austin Freeman's Dr Thorndyke, in *The Red Thumb Mark*

First appearance of Jacques Futrelle's Professor S.F.X. Van Dusen, in *The Thinking Machine* (also called *The Problem of Cell 13*)

First appearance of Gaston Leroux's Joseph Rouletabille, in *Le Mystère de la chambre jaune* (translated as *The Mystery of the Yellow Room*, 1908)

Maurice Leblanc's collection, *Arsène Lupin, Gentleman-Cambrioleur*

1908

FBI (Federal Bureau of Investigation) founded, as part of the US Department of Justice

1909

Baroness Orczy's *The Old Man in the Corner*

Mary Roberts Rinehart's first crime novel, *The Circular Staircase*

First appearance of Carolyn Wells' Fleming Stone, in *The Clue*

First screen appearance of Nick Carter, in France

1910

First appearance of A.E.W. Mason's Inspector Hanaud, in *At the Villa Rose*

Baroness Orczy's *Lady Molly of Scotland Yard*

Gaston Leroux's *Le Fântome de l'Opéra* (translated as *The Phantom of the Opera*, 1911)

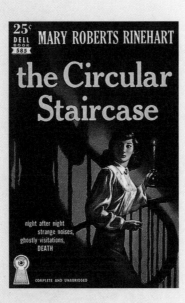

25¢ DELL BOOK 585

MARY ROBERTS RINEHART

the Circular Staircase

night after night strange noises, ghostly visitations, DEATH

COMPLETE AND UNABRIDGED

1911

First appearance between hard covers of G.K. Chesterton's Father Brown, in *The Innocence of Father Brown*

1913

E.C. Bentley's *Trent's Last Case* (UK; called *The Woman in Black* in USA)

William Hope Hodgson's collection *Carnacki, The Ghost-Finder*

Marie Belloc Lowndes' novel about Jack the Ripper, *The Lodger*

First appearance of Sax Rohmer's Dr Fu-Manchu, in *The Mystery of Dr Fu-Manchu* (UK; called *The Insidious Dr Fu-Manchu* in USA)

1914

Ernest Bramah's first collection of stories about his blind detective, Max Carrados

1914–15

The Valley of Fear, the fourth and last Sherlock Holmes novel, serialized in *The Strand Magazine* (separately published in 1915)

1915

First appearance of John Buchan's Richard Hannay, in *The Thirty-Nine Steps* (filmed by Alfred Hitchcock in 1935)

1916

William Gillette plays Holmes on screen, in an adaptation of his own *Sherlock Holmes* (USA)

1917

His Last Bow, fourth collection of Sherlock Holmes stories, first published in *The Strand Magazine* from 1893 onwards

1918

Melville Davisson Post's *Uncle Abner, Master of Mysteries*

1920

First appearance of Sapper's Bull-Dog Drummond, in *Bull-Dog Drummond*

First appearance of H.C. Bailey's Reggie Fortune, in *Call Mr Fortune*, a collection of short stories

First appearance of Agatha Christie's Hercule Poirot, in *The Mysterious Affair at Styles*

Freeman Wills Crofts' first novel, *The Cask*

Black Mask founded by H.L. Mencken and George Jean Nathan

1922

A.A. Milne's *The Red House Mystery*

First appearance of Agatha Christie's Tommy and Tuppence Beresford, in *The Secret Adversary*

John Barrymore plays Holmes on screen, in an adaptation of Gillette's *Sherlock Holmes* (USA)

1923

First appearance of Dorothy L. Sayers' Lord Peter Wimsey, in *Whose Body?*

'My guest was lying with a knife
through his heart!' Illustration to *The
Thirty-Nine Steps* by William Nickless.

1923 cont...

Black Mask publishes Carroll John
Daly's 'Knights of the Open Palm',
marking the first appearance of Race
Williams, and Dashiell Hammett's
'Arson Plus', marking the first
appearance of the Continental Op

First appearance of Octavus Roy
Cohen's Jim Hanvey, in a collection
of stories, *Jim Hanvey, Detective*

1924

First appearance of Edgar Wallace's
Mr J.G. Reeder, in *Room 13*

First appearance of Freeman Wills
Crofts' Inspector French, in *Inspector
French's Greatest Case*

First appearance of Philip
MacDonald's Colonel Anthony
Gethryn, in *The Rasp*

FBI reorganized by J. Edgar Hoover,
its director until his death in 1972

First appearance of Earl Dell Biggers'
Charlie Chan, in *The House Without
a Key*

1925

First appearance of John Rhode's Dr
Lancelot Priestley, in *The Paddington
Mystery*

First appearance of Roger
Sheringham, in *The Layton Court
Mystery* by Anthony Berkeley
(Anthony Berkeley Cox, who also
wrote as Francis Iles)

Ronald Knox's first detective novel,
The Viaduct Murder

1926

Agatha Christie's *The Murder of
Roger Ackroyd*

First appearance of Christopher
Bush's Ludovic Travers, in *The
Plumley Inheritance*

First appearance of G.D.H. and
M. Cole's Honourable Everard
Blatchington, in *The Blatchington
Tangle*

Ritual murder
among the
bright-
young-things

PENGUIN
BOOKS

The Crime at Black Dudley

Margery Allingham

COMPLETE & UNABRIDGED

2/6

First appearance of S.S. Van Dine's Philo Vance, in *The Benson Murder Case*

Joseph T. Shaw becomes editor of *Black Mask*

1927

Last appearance of Sherlock Holmes, in *The Case-Book of Sherlock Holmes*, stories published 1921–27 in *The Strand Magazine*

First appearance of J.J. Connington's Sir Clinton Driffield, in *Murder in the Maze*

Frances Noyes Hart's *The Bellamy Trial*

1928

The Detection Club founded in Britain by Anthony Berkeley, with G.K. Chesterton as its first 'Ruler'

Spoof Holmesian scholarship launched with an essay by Ronald Knox included in *Essays in Satire*

W. Somerset Maugham's collection of spy stories, *Ashenden*

First appearance of Patricia Wentworth's Miss Maud Silver, in *Grey Mask*

First appearance of Leslie Charteris' Simon Templar (The Saint), in *Meet the Tiger*

First appearance of Arthur W. Upfield's Inspector Napoleon Bonaparte, in *The Barrakee Mystery* (Australia; called *The Lure of the Bush* in USA)

1929

Ronald Knox first codifies his 'Ten Commandments' for detective fiction

First appearance of Margery Allingham's Albert Campion, in *The Crime at Black Dudley* (UK; called *The Black Dudley Mystery* in USA)

First appearance of Josephine Tey's Inspector Grant, in *The Man in the Queue* (UK; later called *Killer in the Crowd* in USA)

First appearance of Gladys Mitchell's Mrs (later Dame) Beatrice Lestrange Bradley, in *Speedy Death*

First appearance of Henry Wade's Chief Inspector Poole, in *The Duke of York's Steps*

First appearance of C.H.B. Kitchin's Malcolm Warren, in *Death of My Aunt*

First appearance of Ellery Queen's detective, also called Ellery Queen, in *The Roman Hat Mystery*

First appearance of Hammett's Continental Op in a novel, *Red Harvest*

W.R. Burnett's *Little Caesar*

First appearance of Rufus King's Lieutenant Valcour, in *Murder by the Clock*

First screen appearance of Clive Brook as Holmes, in *The Return of Sherlock Holmes*, the first talkie with Holmes, based on 'The Dying Detective' and 'His Last Bow'

Erich Kästner's children's novel, *Emil und die Detektive* (*Emil and the Detectives*)

1930

Death of Conan Doyle

First appearance of Agatha Christie's Miss Marple, in *Murder at the Vicarage*

First appearance of John Dickson Carr's Henri Bencolin, in *It Walks by Night*

First appearance of H.C. Bailey's Joshua Clunk, in *Garstons* (UK; called *The Garston Murder Case* in USA)

First screen appearance of Arthur Wontner as Holmes, in *The Sleeping Cardinal* (UK; called *Sherlock Holmes' Fatal Hour* in USA)

Dashiell Hammett's *The Maltese Falcon*

First appearance of Anthony Abbott's Thatcher Colt, in *About the Murder of Geraldine Foster* (USA; called *The Murder of Geraldine Foster* in UK)

First appearance of Helen Reilly's Inspector McKee, in *The Diamond Feather*

First appearance of Holmes on radio, played by William Gillette (USA)

1931

Malice Aforethought by Francis Iles (Anthony Berkeley Cox, who also wrote as Anthony Berkeley)

The Floating Admiral, first collaborative novel by members of the Detection Club, with G.K. Chesterton, Canon Victor L. Whitechurch, G.D.H. and M. Cole, Henry Wade, Agatha Christie, John Rhode, Milward Kennedy, Dorothy L. Sayers, Ronald Knox, Freeman Wills Crofts, Edgar Jepson, Clemence Dane and Anthony Berkeley each contributing a chapter

First appearance of E.C.R. Lorac's Inspector MacDonald, in *The Murder on the Burrows*

1931 cont...

Raymond Massey plays Holmes in the film *The Speckled Band*

Dashiell Hammett's *The Glass Key*

First appearance of Chester Gould's Dick Tracy, first comic-strip detective

First appearance of Georges Simenon's Maigret, in *M. Gallet, décédé* (translated as *The Death of Monsieur Gallet*, 1932 in USA, 1933 in UK, and later called *Maigret Stonewalled*), the first of 10 Maigret novels published by Fayard in the course of the year

1932

Before the Fact by Francis Iles (who had previously written as Anthony Berkeley)

First appearance of C. Daly King's Michael Lord, in *Obelists en Route*

Rudolph Fisher's *The Conjure Man Dies: A Mystery Tale of Dark Harlem*, the first crime novel by a black American

First appearance of Maigret on film, played by Pierre Renoir in *La Nuit du carrefour*, directed by his brother Jean Renoir, and by Abel Tarride in *Le Chien jaune*

1933

First appearance of John Dickson Carr's Gideon Fell, in *Hag's Nook*

J.C. Masterman's *An Oxford Tragedy*

First appearance of E.R. Punshon's Bobby Owen, in *Information Received*

Christopher St John Sprigg's first novel, *Crime in Kensington* (UK; called *Pass the Body* in USA)

First appearance of Erle Stanley Gardner's Perry Mason, in *The Case of the Velvet Claws*

Raymond Chandler publishes his first mystery story, 'Blackmailers Don't Shoot', in *Black Mask*

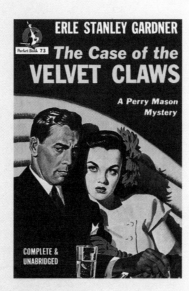

ERLE STANLEY GARDNER
Pocket Book 73
The Case of the
VELVET CLAWS
A Perry Mason Mystery
COMPLETE & UNABRIDGED

1934

First appearance of Ngaio Marsh's Roderick Alleyn, in *A Man Lay Dead*

First appearance of Carter Dickson's (i.e. John Dickson Carr's) Sir Henry Merrivale, in *The Plague Court Murders*

F. Tennyson Jesse's *A Pin to See the Peepshow*

First appearance of Rex Stout's Nero Wolfe, in *Fer-de-Lance*

Dashiell Hammett's last completed novel, *The Thin Man*, inspiration for a series of films about Nick and Nora Charles (played by William Powell and Myrna Loy)

James M. Cain's *The Postman Always Rings Twice* (first filmed in 1946)

1935

Dorothy L. Sayers' *Gaudy Night*

First appearance of Nicholas Blake's Nigel Strangeways, in *A Question of Proof*

First appearance of Jonathan Latimer's Bill Crane, in *Murder in the Madhouse*

First appearance of John P. Marquand's Mr Moto, in *No Hero* (USA; called *Mr Moto Takes a Hand* in UK)

1936

Eric Ambler's first novel, *The Dark Frontier*

First appearance of Michael Innes' John Appleby, in *Death at the President's Lodging* (UK; called *Seven Suspects* in USA)

First appearance of Leo Bruce's Sergeant Beef, in *Case for Three Detectives*

James M. Cain's *Double Indemnity* (filmed by Billy Wilder, with a script by Wilder and Raymond Chandler, in 1944)

First appearance of Patrick Quentin's Peter Duluth and his future wife Iris, in *A Puzzle for Fools*

The President's Mystery Story, an idea by President F.D. Roosevelt and developed by Rupert Hughes, Samuel Hopkins Adams, Anthony Abbott, Rita Weiman, S.S. Van Dine and John Erskine

Joseph T. Shaw resigns editorship of *Black Mask*

First appearance of Holmes on TV, played by Louis Hector (USA)

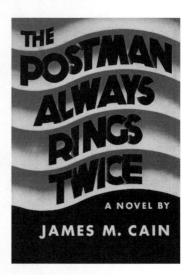

THE **POSTMAN ALWAYS RINGS TWICE**
A NOVEL BY
JAMES M. CAIN

1937

Last appearance of Dorothy L. Sayers' Lord Peter Wimsey, in *Busman's Honeymoon*

First appearance of Josephine Bell's Dr David Wintringham and Inspector Steven Mitchell, in *Murder in Hospital*

First appearance of Cyril Hare's Inspector Mallett, in *Tenant for Death*

1938

Graham Greene's *Brighton Rock*

First appearance of John Creasey's the Honourable Richard Rollison, 'The Toff', in *Introducing the Toff*

First appearance of Francis Durbridge's Paul Temple and his wife Steve in a BBC radio serial (last radio serial broadcast in 1968)

First appearance of Helen McCloy's Dr Basil Willing, in *Dance of Death*

1939

Eric Ambler's *The Mask of Dimitrios* (UK; called *A Coffin for Dimitrios* in USA), filmed by Jean Negulesco in 1944, with Peter Lorre

Geoffrey Household's *Rogue Male* (UK; called *Man Hunt* in USA, and filmed under this title by Fritz Lang in 1942)

First appearance of Raymond Chandler's Philip Marlowe in a novel, *The Big Sleep*

First appearance of Anthony Boucher's Fergus O'Breen, in *The Case of the Crumpled Knave*

First screen appearance of Basil Rathbone as Holmes, with Nigel Bruce as Watson, in *The Hound of the Baskervilles*; the partnership lasts for 14 films and a series on NBC radio, until 1946

1940

First appearance of Elizabeth (or E.X.) Ferrars' Toby Dyke, in *Give a Corpse a Bad Name*

Cornell Woolrich's *The Bride Wore Black* (filmed by François Truffaut as *La Mariée était en noir* in 1967)

Nine Times Nine by H.H. Holmes (Anthony Boucher)

First appearance of Frances and Richard Lockridge's Mr and Mrs North, in *The Norths Meet Murder*

First appearance of Elizabeth Daly's Henry Gamadge, in *Unexpected Night*

1941

First appearance of Christianna Brand's Inspector Charlesworth, in *Death in High Heels*, and Inspector Cockrill, in *Heads You Lose*

Ellery Queen's Mystery Magazine founded

John Huston's film of Hammett's *The Maltese Falcon*

Margaret Millar's first novel, *The Invisible Worm*

1942

First appearance of John Creasey's Inspector Roger West, in *Inspector West Takes Charge*

First appearance of Cyril Hare's Francis Pettigrew, joining Inspector Mallett, in *Tragedy at Law*

Jim Thompson's first novel, *Now and on Earth*

1943

First appearance of Holmes on BBC radio, played by Arthur Wontner

First appearance of Erle Stanley Gardner's Perry Mason on radio (USA)

First appearance of Léo Malet's Nestor Burma, in *120, rue de la gare*

1944

First appearance of Edmund Crispin's Gervase Fen, in *The Case of the Gilded Fly* (UK; called *Obsequies at Oxford* in USA)

Humphrey Bogart and the black bird in John Huston's film of *The Maltese Falcon* (1941)

1944 cont...

Ross Macdonald's first novel, *The Dark Tunnel*, published under his real name, Kenneth Millar

Chandler publishes 'The Simple Art of Murder' in *The Atlantic Monthly* (expanded and included in *The Simple Art of Murder*, 1950)

First appearance of Philip Marlowe on screen, in *Murder, My Sweet*, an adaptation of *Farewell My Lovely*, starring Dick Powell

1945

Julian Symons' first novel, *The Immaterial Murder Case*

First appearance of Lawrence Treat's Mitch Taylor and Jub Freeman (later joined by Bill Decker) in *V as in Victim*

Joel Townsley Rogers' *The Red Right Hand*

Mystery Writers of America founded

Marcel Duhamel begins publishing the Série Noire in France (French and American hard-boiled novels)

1946

Helen Eustis' first novel, *The Horizontal Man*

MWA presents first Edgar Allan Poe Award for Best First Novel to Julius Fast's *Watchful at Night*

Howard Hawks' film of Chandler's *The Big Sleep*, starring Humphrey Bogart

1947

First appearance of Roy Vickers' Department of Dead Ends, in a collection of stories, *The Department of Dead Ends* (enlarged edition, 1949)

Michael Gilbert's first novel, *Close Quarters*

First appearance of Mickey Spillane's Mike Hammer, in *I, The Jury*

1948

Josephine Tey's *The Franchise Affair*

Stanley Ellin's first short story, 'The Specialty of the House' (collected in *Mystery Stories*, 1956, called *The Speciality of the House and Other Stories* in UK and later called *Quiet Horror* in USA)

Maurice Endrèbe founds the Grand Prix de Littérature Policière, first awarded to Léo Malet's *Le Cinquième Procédé* and Frances Noyes Hart's *The Bellamy Trial*

1949

First appearance of Delano Ames' Jane and Dagobert Brown, in *She Shall Have Murder*

First appearance of Ross Macdonald's Lew Archer, in *The Moving Target*

Dragnet, US radio series starring Jack Webb as Sergeant Joe Friday, first broadcast; continues until 1956

First appearance of Judge Dee, in Robert van Gulik's *Dee Goong An* (Holland)

1950

Patricia Highsmith's first novel, *Strangers on a Train* (filmed by Alfred Hitchcock in 1951)

1951

Josephine Tey's *The Daughter of Time*

First appearance of Pierre Audemars' Inspector Pinaud, in *The Two Impostors*

First appearance of Holmes on British TV, played by Andrew Osborne and, later the same year, by Alan Wheatley

Black Mask absorbed by *Ellery Queen's Mystery Magazine*

1952

Holmes and Watson played on BBC radio by Carleton Hobbs and Norman Shelley in a series lasting until 1969

First stage production of Agatha Christie's *The Mousetrap*

Hillary Waugh's *Last Seen Wearing...*

Dragnet first screened on NBC TV (first screened in 1955 in UK); series continues until 1958 and is revived in 1967–69

First appearance of Friedrich Dürrenmatt's Bärlach, in *Der Richter und sein Henker* (Switzerland; translated as *The Judge and His Hangman*, 1954)

1953

Crime Writers' Association (CWA) founded in Britain, with John Creasey as its first Chairman

William P. McGivern's *The Big Heat*

Pierre Boileau and Thomas Narcejac's first joint novel, *Celle qui n'étais plus* (filmed by Henri-Georges Clouzot as *Les Diaboliques* in 1954; translated as *The Woman Who Was* in 1954, later called *The Woman Who Was No More* and *The Fiends*)

Auguste le Breton's *Du Rififi chez les hommes* (filmed by Jules Dassin in 1955)

Albert Simonin's *Touchez pas au grisbi!* (filmed by Jacques Becker in 1954)

Clouzot's film *Le Salaire de la peur* (*The Wages of Fear*)

Alain Robbe-Grillet's *Les Gommes* (translated as *The Erasers*, 1964)

1954

First appearance of Ian Fleming's James Bond, in *Casino Royale* (UK; called *You Asked For It* in USA)

Holmes and Watson played on BBC radio by John Gielgud and Ralph Richardson

MWA awards first Edgar for Best Novel, to Charlotte Jay, *Beat Not the Bones*

Alfred Hitchcock's film *Rear Window*, based on a story by William Irish (Cornell Woolrich)

Ronald Howard and H. Marion Crawford play Holmes and Watson in TV series in the USA (lasts until 1955)

Boileau and Narcejac's *D'entre les morts* (France; translated as *The Living and the Dead* in 1956 and filmed by Hitchcock as *Vertigo* in 1958)

1955

First appearance of J.J. Marric's (i.e. John Creasey's) Commander George Gideon, in *Gideon's Day* (UK; called *Gideon of Scotland Yard* in USA)

CWA establishes an annual award for the best crime novel (later called the Gold Dagger Award), this year presented to Winston Graham's *The Little Walls*; runners-up awards (later called the Silver Dagger Award) to Leigh Howard's *Blind Date*, Ngaio Marsh's *Scales of Justice*, Margot Bennett's *The Man Who Didn't Fly*

First appearance of Patricia Highsmith's Tom Ripley, in *The Talented Mr Ripley*

MWA awards the Grand Master title for the first time, to Agatha Christie

1956

Ed McBain's first 87th Precinct novel, *Cop Hater*

1957

First appearance of Bill Knox's Colin Thane, in *Deadline for a Dream*

First appearance of Erle Stanley Gardner's Perry Mason on US TV, played by Raymond Burr; series continues until 1966, with later attempts to revive it

....

Vera Clouzot and Simone Signoret in Henri-Georges Clouzot's *Les Diaboliques* (1954), adapted from Pierre Boileau and Thomas Narcejac's *Celle qui n'était plus* (1953).

1957 cont...

Seicho Matsumoto's first novel *Ten to Sen* (Japan; translated as *Points and Lines*, 1970)

1958

First appearance of Colin Watson's Inspector Purbright, in *Coffin, Scarcely Used*

Celia Fremlin's first novel, *The Hours Before Dawn*

Hammer film of *The Hound of the Baskervilles*, with Peter Cushing as Holmes and André Morrell as Watson

Last appearance of Raymond Chandler's Philip Marlowe in a completed novel, *Playback*

First appearance of Chester Himes' Coffin Ed Johnson and Grave Digger Jones, in *La Reine des pommes* (France; translated as *For Love of Imabelle*, 1959, and later as *A Rage in Harlem*)

First screen appearance of Jean Gabin as Maigret, in *Maigret tend un piège* (called *Maigret Sets a Trap* in UK and USA)

1959

First appearance of Hillary Waugh's Chief Fred Fellows, in *Sleep Long, My Love* (USA; called *Jigsaw* in UK)

1960

First appearance of Delano Ames' Juan Llorca, in *The Man in the Tricorn Hat*

Z-Cars, police drama series created by Troy Kennedy Martin, first screened by BBC TV; it continues for 667 episodes, until 1978

First appearance of Rupert Davies as Maigret on British TV, in a series eventually running to 52 episodes

First appearance of Dell Shannon's (i.e. Elizabeth Linington's) Inspector Luiz Mendoza and his LAPD team, in *Case Pending*

EMMA LATHEN
A JOHN PUTNAM THATCHER MYSTERY BY AMERICA'S AGATHA CHRISTIE
BANKING ON DEATH

1961

First appearance of John le Carré's George Smiley, in *Call for the Dead*

First appearance of Emma Lathen's John Putnam Thatcher, in *Banking on Death*

First appearance of Lesley Egan's (i.e. Elizabeth Linington's) Vic Varallo and his Glendale police team, in *A Case for Appeal*

Hubert Monteilhet's first novel, *Les Mantes religieuses* (translated as *Praying Mantis* in UK and *The Praying Mantises* in USA)

Leonardo Sciascia's first international success, *Il giorno della civetta* (Italy; translated as *Mafia Vendetta*, 1964, and later called *The Day of the Owl*)

1962

First appearance of Nicolas Freeling's Inspector van der Valk, in *Love in Amsterdam*

First appearance of P.D. James' Adam Dalgliesh, in *Cover Her Face*

Dick Francis' first novel, *Dead Cert*

Len Deighton's first spy novel, *The Ipcress File*

First appearance of Sara Woods' Anthony Maitland, in *Bloody Instructions*

First appearance of Richard Stark's Parker, in *The Hunter* (later retitled *Point Blank*)

1963

John le Carré's *The Spy Who Came in from the Cold*

1964

First appearance of Ruth Rendell's Chief Inspector Wexford, in *From Doon with Death*

First appearance of H.R.F. Keating's Inspector Ghote of Bombay, in *The Perfect Murder*

First appearance of John and Emery Bonett's Inspector Salvador Borges, in *Better Dead* (UK; called *Better Off Dead* in USA)

Holmes and Watson played in BBC TV series by Douglas Wilmer and Nigel Stock in series lasting until 1965

First appearance of John D. MacDonald's Travis McGee, in *The Deep Blue Good-By*

First appearance of Amanda Cross' Kate Fansler, in *In the Last Analysis*

First appearance of Elizabeth Linington's Sergeant Ivor Maddox and his Hollywood police team, in *Greenmask!* (author called Anne Blaisdell in UK)

1965

First appearance of John Ball's Virgil Tibbs, in *In the Heat of the Night*

First appearance of Maj Sjöwall and Per Wahlöö's Martin Beck, in *Roseanna* (Sweden; translated in 1967)

1966

First appearance of Catherine Aird's Inspector Sloan, in *The Religious Body*

First appearance of Julian Rathbone's Colonel Nur Bey, in *Diamonds Bid*

Sébastien Japrisot's *La Dame dans l'auto avec les lunettes et un fusil* (translated as *The Lady in the Car with Glasses and a Gun*, 1967)

First appearance of Josef Skvorecký's Lieutenant Boruvka, in *Smutek poručika Borůvky* (Czechoslovakia; translated as *The Mournful Demeanour of Lieutenant Boruvka*, 1973)

1968

Holmes and Watson played in BBC TV series by Peter Cushing and Nigel Stock

Anders Bodelsen's *Hændeligt Uheld* (Denmark; translated as *Hit and Run, Run, Run*, 1970)

1969

Elmore Leonard's first crime and mystery novel, *The Big Bounce*

Chabrol's film *Que la bête meure* (*This Man Must Die*), based on Nicholas Blake's *The Beast Must Die* (1938)

1970

First appearance of Reginald Hill's Dalziel and Pascoe, in *A Clubbable Woman*

First appearance of Peter Lovesey's Cribb and Thackeray, in *Wobble to Death*

Margaret Yorke's first novel, *Dead in the Morning*

First appearance of Tony Hillerman's Lieutenant Joe Leaphorn, in *The Blessing Way*

First appearance of Joseph Hansen's Dave Brandstetter, in *Fadeout*

Chabrol's film *Le Boucher* (*The Butcher*)

1971

Frederick Forsyth's *The Day of the Jackal*

First appearance of James McClure's South African detectives Kramer and Zondi, in *The Steam Pig*

Last appearance of Ellery Queen, in Ellery Queen's *A Fine and Private Place*

First appearance of Michael Z. Lewin's Albert Samson, in *Ask the Right Question* (1971)

MWA awards first Edgar for Best Paperback Original, to Dan J. Marlowe's *Flashpoint*

Columbo, TV series starring Peter Falk, first screened in the USA

Peter Falk as Columbo, California's least stylish detective, in the US TV series.

1972

First appearance of P.D. James' Cordelia Gray, in *An Unsuitable Job for a Woman*

First edition of Julian Symon's history, *Bloody Murder* (UK; called *Mortal Consequences* in USA)

George V. Higgins' first novel, *The Friends of Eddie Coyle*

First appearance of K.C. Constantine's Mario Balzic, in *The Rocksburg Railroad Murders*

Last appearance of Simenon's Maigret, in *Maigret et Monsieur Charles*

Jean-Patrick Manchette's *O dingoes, O châteaux!* (later called *Folle à tuer*)

1973

Publication of the last novel Agatha Christie wrote, *Postern of Fate*, featuring Tommy and Tuppence Beresford

First appearance of Nicolas Freeling's Henri Castang, in *A Dressing of Diamond*

CWA establishes the John Creasey Memorial Award (later called the John Creasey Memorial Dagger) for the best crime novel by an author who has not previously published a novel; first presented to Kyril Bonfiglioli's *Don't Point That Thing at Me*

Last appearance of Perry Mason, in Erle Stanley Gardner's posthumously published *The Case of the Postponed Murder*

First appearance of Robert B. Parker's Spenser, in *The Godwulf Manuscript*

1974

Robert Barnard's first novel, *Death of an Old Goat*

First appearance of Roderic Jeffries' Inspector Alvarez, in *Mistakenly in Mallorca*

1974 cont...

Nicholas Meyer's pastiche of the Sherlock Holmes stories, *The Seven-Per-Cent Solution*

1975

Last appearance of Hercule Poirot, in *Curtain* (written in the 1940s and originally intended for publication after Christie's death)

First appearance of Colin Dexter's Inspector Morse, in *Last Bus to Woodstock*

First appearance of Simon Brett's Charles Paris, in *Cast, in Order of Disappearance*

First appearance of Janwillem van de Wetering's Adjutant Grijpstra and Sergeant de Gier, in *Outsider in Amsterdam*

Starsky and Hutch, TV police series starring Paul Michael Glaser and David Soul, first screened in the USA; continues until 1979

1976

Death of Agatha Christie

Last appearance of Miss Marple, in *Sleeping Murder* (written in the 1940s)

Ross Macdonald
The Blue Hammer

A LEW ARCHER NOVEL

First appearance of David Williams' Mark Treasure in *Unholy Writ*

Last appearance of Ross Macdonald's Lew Archer, in *The Blue Hammer*

First appearance of Stephen Dobyns' Charlie Bradshaw, in *Saratoga Longshot*

1977

First appearance of Ellis Peters' Cadfael, in *A Morbid Taste for Bones*

First appearance of Antonia Fraser's Jemima Shore, in *Quiet as a Nun*

First appearance of Jonathan Gash's Lovejoy, in *The Judas Pair*

First appearance of William McIlvanney's Detective Inspector Jack Laidlaw, in *Laidlaw*

First appearance of an independent woman PI in American fiction, Marcia Muller's Sharon McCone, in *Edwin of the Iron Shoes*

M.F. Beal's *Angel Dance*

First appearance of Stuart M. Kaminsky's Toby Peters, in *Bullet for a Star*

1979

First appearance of Mark Hebden's Inspector Pel, in *Death Set to Music*

First appearance of James Melville's Superintendent Otani, in *The Wages of Zen*

First appearance of David Serafín's Superintendent Bernal, in *Saturday of Glory*

First appearance of Julian Rathbone's Commissioner Argand, in *The Euro-Killers*

First appearance of Manuel Vázquez Montalbán's Pepe Carvalho, in *Los Mares del Sur* (Spain; translated as *Southern Seas*, 1986)

First appearance of Wessel Ebersohn's South African detective Gordon Yudel in *A Lonely Place to Die*

Richard North Patterson's first novel, *The Lasko Tangent*

1980

First appearance of Liza Cody's Anna Lee, in *Dupe*

First appearance of Dan Kavanagh's Duffy, in *Duffy*

First appearance of Timothy Holme's Commissario Peroni, in *The Neapolitan Streak*

Hill Street Blues, TV police series, first screened in the USA; continues until 1987

First appearance of Howard Engel's Benny Cooperman, in *The Suicide Murders* (Canada)

First appearance of Peter Corris' Cliff Hardy, in *The Dying Trade* (Australia)

Umberto Eco's *Il nome della rosa* (Italy; translated as *The Name of the Rose*, 1983)

First appearance of Tony Hillerman's Sergeant Jim Chee, in *People of Darkness*

1981

First appearance of Magdalen Nabb's Marshal Guernaccia, in *Death of an Englishman*

First appearance of Sarah Caudwell's Professor Hilary Tamar and circle, in *Thus Was Adonis Murdered*

First appearance of Ruth Dudley Edwards' Robert Amiss, in *Corridors of Death*

James Ellroy's first novel, *Brown's Requiem*

First appearance of Martin Cruz Smith's Arkady Renko, in *Gorky Park*

First appearance of Stuart M. Kaminsky's Inspector Rostnikov, in *Death of a Dissident* (USA; called *Rostnikov's Corpse* in UK)

First appearance of Thomas Harris' Dr Hannibal Lecter, in *Red Dragon* (later titled *Manhunter*)

1982

First appearance of Timothy Williams' Commissario Trotti, in *Converging Parallels*

First appearance of Andrew Taylor's William Dougal, in *Caroline Minuscule*

First appearance of Sara Paretsky's V.I. Warshawski, in *Indemnity Only*

First appearance of Sue Grafton's Kinsey Millhone, in *'A' is for Alibi*

1983

Taggart, TV police drama series created by Glenn Chandler, first screened in Britain; continues until present

First appearance of Tony Hillerman's Sergeant Jim Chee, in *The Dark Wind*

First appearance of Loren D. Estleman's Amos Walker, in *Motor City Blue*

First appearance of Eric Sauter's Robert Lee Hunter, in *Hunter*

First appearance of Eric Wright's Inspector Charlie Salter, in *The Night the Gods Smiled* (Canada)

1984

Derek Raymond's first 'Factory' novel, *He Died With His Eyes Open*

First appearance of Gillian Slovo's Kate Baeier, in *Morbid Symptoms*

Holmes and Watson played on Granada TV in Britain by Jeremy Brett and David Burke in series lasting until 1985; second series (1986–88) has Edward Hardwicke as Watson

First appearance of Barbara Wilson's Pam Nilsen, in *Murder in the Collective*

Truffaut's film *Vivement dimanche!* (*Finally, Sunday!*), based on Charles Williams' *The Long Saturday Night* (1962)

FannyArdant Jean-LouisTrintignant

FINALLY, SUNDAY!
Vivement Dimanche!

A Film by François Truffaut

CHELSEA·CINEMA
202 KINGS ROAD SW3 TELEPHONE 351 3742

1985

First appearance of Bill James' Detective Chief Superintendent Harpur and Assistant Chief Constable Iles, in *You'd Better Believe It*

First appearance of Nancy Livingston's Mr Pringle, in *Trouble in Aquitaine*

First appearance of Andrew Vachss' Burke, in *Flood*

First appearance of Earl W. Emerson's Thomas Black, in *Rainy City*

First appearance of Sarah Dreher's Stoner McTavish, in *Stoner McTavish*

Didier Daeninckx's *Meurtres pour mémoire* (France; translated as *Murder in Memoriam*)

First appearance of Jakob Arjouni's Kemal Kayankaya, in *Happy birthday, Türke!* (Germany; translated as *Happy Birthday, Turk!*)

First appearance of Maria-Antònia Oliver's Lònia Guiu, in *Estudi en lila* (Spain; translated as *Study in Lilac*)

1986

CWA establishes the Diamond Dagger Award; first presented to Eric Ambler

Carl Hiaasen's first solo novel, *Tourist Season*

First appearance of Marvin Albert's Pete (Pierre-Ange) Sawyer, in *The Stone Angel*

1987

Ruth Rendell's first novel as Barbara Vine, *A Dark-Adapted Eye*

First appearance of Ian Rankin's Inspector Rebus, in *Knots and Crosses*

Inspector Morse, TV police drama series derived from Colin Dexter's novels, first screened in Britain

James Ellroy's *The Black Dahlia* begins his 'LA Quartet', continued in *The Big Nowhere* (1989), *LA Confidential* (1990) and *White Jazz* (1992)

First appearance of Linda Barnes' Carlotta Carlyle, in *A Trouble of Fools*

1988

CWA establishes the *Punch* Award (later called the Last Laugh Dagger); first presented to Nancy Livingston for *Death in a Distant Land*

First appearance of Michael Dibdin's Aurelio Zen, in *Ratking*

First appearance of Janet Neel's Francesca Wilson, in *Death's Bright Angel*

First appearance of Frances Fyfield's Helen West and Geoffrey Bailey, in *A Question of Guilt*

First appearance of Simon Shaw's Philip Fletcher, in *Murder Out of Tune*

First appearance of Mike Ripley's Angel, in *Just Another Angel*

First appearance of Michael Pearce's the Mamur Zapt, in *The Mamur Zapt and the Return of the Carpet*

First appearance of Elizabeth George's Detective Inspector Lynley, in *A Great Deliverance*

1989

First appearance of John Harvey's Detective Inspector Charlie Resnick, in *Lonely Hearts*

First appearance of Mike Phillips' Sam Dean, in *Blood Rights*

First appearance of Annette Roome's Chris Martin, in *A Real Shot in the Arm*

First appearance of Trevor Barnes' Detective Superintendent Blanche Hampton, in *A Midsummer Killing*

First appearance of Karen Kijewski's Kat Colorado, in *Katwalk*

Death of Simenon at Lausanne

1990

First appearance of Walter Mosley's Easy Rawlins, in *Devil in a Blue Dress*

First appearance of Meg O'Brien's *The Daphne Decisions* and *A Salmon in the Soup*

KAREN KIJEWSKI

WILD KAT

A Kat Colorado Mystery

In the bestselling tradition of Sue Grafton and Sara Paretsky

First appearance of Les Roberts' Milan Jacovich, in *Pepper Pike*

Arturo Pérez-Reverte's *La Tabla de Flandes* (Spain; translated as *The Flanders Panel*, 1994)

First appearance of Patricia Cornwell's Kay Scarpetta, in *Postmortem*

Pieke Biermann's *Violetta* (Germany; translated into English in 1996)

1991

Helen Zahavi's *A Dirty Weekend*

First appearance of Sarah Dunant's Hannah Wolfe, in *Birth Marks*

Lynda La Plante's TV police drama *Prime Suspect* first screened in Britain; followed by *Prime Suspect 2* in 1992, *Prime Suspect 3* in 1993 and a series in 1995

1992

CWA establishes the Golden Handcuffs Award (later called the Dagger in the Library) for an author popular with library readers; first presented to Catherine Aird

First appearance of Val McDermid's Kate Brannigan, in *Dead Beat*

Minette Walters' first novel, *The Ice House*

Victor Headley's *Yardie*

First appearance of Donna Leon's Commissario Brunetti, in *Death at La Fenice*

Donna Tartt's first novel *The Secret History*

Peter Høeg's *Frøken Smillas Fornemmelse for Sne* (Denmark; translated as *Miss Smilla's Feeling for Snow*, 1993)

1993

First appearance of Reginald Hill's Joe Sixsmith, in *Blood Sympathy*

Laurence Shames' first novel *Florida Straits*

1994

First appearance of Janet Evanovich's Stephanie Plum, in *One for the Money*

Caleb Carr's *The Alienist*

Bernardo Atxaga's *El Hombre Solo* (Spain; translated as *The Lone Man*, 1996)

1995

Eric Zencey's *Panama*

Jane Adams' *The Greenway*

First appearance of Laurie R. King's Kate Martinelli, in *A Grave Talent*

1996

Vicki Hendricks' *Miami Purity*

Michael Connelly's *The Poet*

Thomas A. Cook's *The Chatham School Affair*

John Morgan Wilson's *Simple Justice*

1997

Julian Rathbone's *Blame Hitler*

Grand Prix de Littérature Policière awarded to Brigitte Aubert's *La Mort des bois*

Acknowledgements

Jean-Pierre Deloux, Maurice B. Endrèbe, Lauric Guillaud, Alison Hennegan, Richard Reynolds, Priscilla Ridgway and Franziska Urban have all generously given me their time and expertise. I have been lucky, too, in the support and encouragement I have received from Andrew Lownie, my agent, and from the staff at Thames and Hudson. Anna Saunders knows what she has put into this book better than I do.

Ronald Knox's 'Ten Commandments' (p. 67) were included in his introduction to *The Best Detective Stories of 1928*, ed. R. Knox and H. Harrington (Faber and Gwire 1929). The extracts on p. 77 are quoted from *Literary Distractions* by Ronald Knox (Sheed and Ward 1958). Both by kind permission of A.P. Watt Ltd on behalf of The Earl of Oxford & Asquith.

Illustration Credits

Abbreviations: a *above*, c *centre*, b *below*, l *left*, r *right*.

By kind permission of Anglia Television Limited, Norwich 164; Courtesy Lord and Lady Attenborough 146; Courtesy Agencia Literaria Carmen Balcells, S.A., Barcelona 4c, 158b; Used by permission of Bantam Books, a division of Bantam Doubleday Dell Publishing Group, Inc., New York 80l, 116, 187b; Copyright ©.BBC, London 73, 76b, 131; Cartier, London 199; Steve Chibnall, The Pulp Archive 2, 7, 12, 92, 94, 95, 96, 97, 102br, 112, 117, 118; Central Broadcasting, Birmingham 167; All Rights Reserved. Columbia Pictures Corporation 150, 183; Courtesy Crime in Store, Covent Garden, London. Photo Kenneth Markham 1, 156; Jean Delannoy 132; Editions Denoël, Paris 202; First published by Diogenes Verlag Zürich 1987 158a; Used by permission of Dell Books, a division of Bantam Doubleday Dell Publishing Group, Inc., New York 77a, 77al, 99a, 161, 176, 209; Courtesy Maurice Endrèbe 203; Entertainment Film Distributors, London 174; Faber & Faber Ltd., London 157, 195; Editions Gallimard, Paris 171, 214; From DEATH AT PEMBERLEY by T.H. White, Victor Gollancz Ltd., London 73br, 74; Granada Television, Manchester 169a; Hamish Hamilton, London 162; HarperCollins Publishers Ltd, London 80ar, 163, 169b, 188; Wilhelm Heyne Verlag, Munich 13; From WILD KAT by Karen Kijewski, Headline Book Publishing Ltd., London. Photographers Mitchell Funk/The Image Bank and Tony Stone Images 184, 220, From CLOUDS OF WITNESS by Dorothy L. Sayers, Hodder & Stoughton Ltd., London 77br; Reproduced by permission of Hodder & Stoughton Ltd., London 160, 185b; Hulton Getty, London 125; Image Library, State Library of New South Wales, Sydney 36; ITC Entertainment, London 115l; © MGM/UA Communications Co. All Rights Reserved. 102ar, 11.; Arnoldo Mondadori Editore, Milan 5b; MTM International, London 165; Mysterious Press, New York 181, 185a, 193; Mystery Writers of America, New York 196; NBC Photo 141; Jacket design by Gunmar Säfström, photo by Lars Säfström, Courtesy Norstedts Verlag, Stockholm 138; Orion Books Ltd., London 171l; Orion Pictures International 145; Pan Books Ltd., London 76a, 148; Penguin Ltd., London 4a, 11, 60, 65, 187a, 200, 211; Presses de la Cité, Paris 4b, 122; By courtesy of Rank Film Distributors Limited, London 126; Peter Dyer/React. Photo Michele Turriani 173; Revcom International, Paris 215; Rotbuch Verlag, Hamburg 5a, 159; Editions du Seuil, Paris 204; Reprinted with the permission of Pocket Books, a division of Simon & Schuster, New York 5c, 80br, 90, 99b, 102al, 104, 142, 212; Theatre Museum, V & A, London 22–23, 81; © Turner Entertainment Co. 109, 111, 114, 115, 124, 212; Twentieth Century Fox Film Corporation. All Rights Reserved. 10, 128; Twickenham Film Studios 69; © 1997 by Universal City Studios, Inc. Courtesy of Universal Studios Publishing Rights. All Rights Reserved. 59, 144, 217; Viacom International 83; University Library, Cambridge 62; © Warner Bros. Pictures, Inc. 149; © Warner Bros. Television, Inc. 182; Warner Books Ltd. 190.

Index